This book is dedicated to those Plankholders of the Marine Special Operations Command—those first Marines who came to the new organization and laid the groundwork for what the Command has become today. They came from their Marine specialties—Force and Battalion Recon, the Foreign Military Training Unit, ANGLICO, and from the Corps at large. A few were veterans of Marine Detachment One. Many stayed on to contribute as civil servants following their uniformed service. These veteran Marines worked tirelessly to bring structure, pride, and professionalism to the new Command. It was through their dedication and vision that the Marine Special Operations Command was formed and shaped, and that Marine special operators now take their place alongside their Army, Navy, and Air Force special operators. Well done, gentlemen—well done indeed.

12683204

ALWAYS FAITHFUL, ALWAYS FORWARD

The Forging of a Special Operations Marine

DICK COUCH

BERKLEY CALIBER, NEW YORK

Published by the Berkley Publishing Group
An imprint of Penguin Random House LLC
375 Hudson Street, New York, New York 10014

Copyright © 2014 by Dick Couch.
Penguin supports copyright. Copyright fuels creativity, encourages diverse voices, promotes free speech, and creates a vibrant culture. Thank you for buying an authorized edition of this book and for complying with copyright laws by not reproducing, scanning, or distributing any part of it in any form without permission. You are supporting writers and allowing Penguin to continue to publish books for every reader.

BERKLEY CALIBER and its logo are registered trademarks of Penguin Random House LLC.

Berkley Caliber trade paperback ISBN: 978-0-425-26860-5

The Library of Congress has catalogued the Berkley Caliber hardcover edition as follows:

Couch, Dick, date.
Always faithful, always forward :
the forging of a Special Operations Marine / Dick Couch. — 1st edition.
p.   cm.
ISBN 978-0-425-26859-9
1. United States. Marine Special Operations Command—History—21st century.
2. United States. Marine Corps—Officers—Training of.   3. United States. Marine
Corps—Physical training.   4. Commando troops—Training of—United States.
5. Special operations (Military science)—United States—History—21st century.
I. Title.   II. Title: Forging of a Special Operations Marine.
VE23.C745 2014
359.9'6092—dc23
[B]
2014006176

PUBLISHING HISTORY
Berkley Caliber hardcover edition / June 2014
Berkley Caliber trade paperback edition / June 2015

PRINTED IN THE UNITED STATES OF AMERICA

10   9   8   7   6   5   4   3   2   1

Cover design by George Long.
Interior text design by Kristin del Rosario.

While the author has made every effort to provide accurate telephone numbers and Internet addresses at the time of publication, neither the author nor the publisher is responsible for errors, or for changes that occur after publication. Further, the publisher does not have any control over and does not assume any responsibility for author or third-party websites or their content.

ACKNOWLEDGMENTS

I would like to thank Major General Mark Clark, Commander, U.S. Marine Special Operations Command, and Colonel James Glynn, Commanding Officer, U.S. Marine Special Operations School, for so graciously permitting me to move freely about your Command and your training venues. And there are many others to whom I'm especially indebted—the class proctors, the phase officers-in-charge, the phase noncommissioned officers-in-charge, the tactical advisory cadres, and the training cadres at large. As serving special operators, you are in these pages in character and spirit, if not by your real names. Thank you all for your kindness, your courtesy, and for the honor of allowing me to walk the training lanes with The Few, The Proud, and in your case, The Very Special. And above all, thank you for your continuing service to our great nation.

MARSOC CSO CREED

My Title is Marine, but it is my choice and my choice alone to be a Special Operations Marine. I will never forget the tremendous sacrifices and reputation of those who came before me.

At all ranges my fires will be accurate. With surprise, speed, and violence of action, I will hunt enemies of my country and bring chaos to their doorstep. I will keep my body strong, my mind sharp, and my kit ready at all times.

Raider and Recon men forged the path I follow. With Determination, Dependability, and Teamwork I will uphold the honor and the legacy passed down to me. I will do the right thing always, and will let my actions speak for me. As a quiet professional, I will not bring shame upon myself or those with which I serve.

Spiritus Invictus, an Unconquerable Spirit, will be my goal. I will never quit, I will never surrender, I will never fail. I will adapt to the situation. I will gain and maintain the initiative. I will always go a little farther and carry more than my share.

On any battlefield, at any point of the compass I will excel. I will set the example for all others to emulate. At the tip of the spear, I will teach and prepare others to seek out, dismantle, and destroy our common enemies. I will fight side by side with my partners and will be the first in and last out of any mission.

Conquering all obstacles of mind, body, and spirit; the honor and pride of serving in special operations will be my driving force. I will remain always faithful to my brothers and always forward in my service.

CONTENTS

FOREWORD

Full disclosure: Dick Couch and I were classmates at the U.S. Naval Academy. I say "were" because Dick blazed through "The Boat School" in the four-year course and became a U.S. Navy SEAL. For reasons somewhat beyond my control, I took the five-year program and took my commission in the U.S. Marines. Beyond that, we are comrades-in-arms from a long-ago, faraway war called "Vietnam"; we both succeeded in writing about the privilege of keeping company with our nation's heroes; and we're friends.

Given that background, when Dick Couch asked me to do a foreword for this book, he was fairly certain I couldn't pass up the opportunity to sing the praises of U.S. Marines and brag about how tough they train and prepare for combat. Dick also knew that soldiers, sailors, airmen, Guardsmen, and Marines are my only "beat" for Fox News and that many of my fifty-plus overseas "embeds" since 9-11-01 have been with America's SOF—special operations forces. As usual, Dick was right on all counts.

But here's what Dick Couch didn't know when he asked me to write this "opening shot" for his latest work: When our Naval Academy "shipmate" Marine Commandant Mike Hagee announced the formation of Marine Corps Forces, Special Operations Command—known as MARSOC—I thought it was a lousy idea. To me—and many of our contemporaries—all Marines have always been "special." So when General Hagee was visiting the Marines with whom I was embedded in Ramadi, Iraq, I told him so.

The commandant acknowledged my sentiment that every Marine, regardless of military occupational specialty (MOS) or assigned responsibility is "special." But he also pointed out that "times have changed," and that "adapting to changed circumstances" has always been a hallmark of the Corps. I didn't agree then, but I must admit today, I was wrong. Given the nature of our self-declared enemies—radical Islamic jihadists and hyper-violent narco-terrorists—MARSOC is a great idea for the present—and likely for decades to come.

In *Always Faithful, Always Forward*, Dick Couch has documented the challenges of building MARSOC in the midst of a war. He rightly focuses on the process of selecting, training, equipping, and qualifying individual Marines as Critical Skills Operators ready for overseas deployment in harm's way. And, as could only be done by a special operator who has "been there—done that," Dick vividly describes the remarkable demands of the Individual Training Course and the exhaustive, comprehensive, step-by-step methods adopted by the Marines for preparing MARSOC operators for the perils of small-unit, independent operations in difficult and dangerous places.

Since 2008, I've had the privilege of accompanying MARSOC units in the shadows of the Hindu Kush, on the Horn of Africa, and in a handful of other "garden spots" around the globe. It's tough duty for tough men. Marines considering making the transition from a more "conventional" assignment to special operations ought to read this book before applying to MARSOC. As Dick Couch accurately points out in his descriptions of how the members of this organization are recruited, assessed, selected, and trained, MARSOC isn't a routine assignment or duty station.

Tactically, technically, physically, and professionally, every candidate is pushed to his limit—and then some. He will have to navigate a regimen of assessment, selection, training, and professional development the likes of which he never imagined. A Critical Skills Operator is first, foremost, and always a Marine, but he will also acquire a skill set that is unique to the Spec Ops world.

Always Faithful, Always Forward is not only the title of this book—and the motto of the Marine Corps Forces Special Operations Command—it's also the way MARSOC Marines live and fight. Though every team member retains the character and steadfastness that makes him a good Marine, independent operations, well away from conventional support, are incredibly demanding. Life in MARSOC means months away from home, numerous visits to remote training locations and ranges, and frequent, short-notice overseas deployments. "Always Faithful, Always Forward" isn't just a slogan—it's a way of life.

Dick's straightforward depiction of how these "double volunteers" are recruited, assessed, selected, and trained explains the kind of dedication and commitment I have seen in MARSOC Marines on the battlefield. Those qualities are amply evident in Captain Matt Lampert, a Marine Special Operations Officer I met last year on lonely outpost during his second combat deployment to Afghanistan.

Matt Lampert enlisted in the Marine Corps after high school in 1998. His outstanding enlisted service led to an appointment to the Naval Academy and his commissioning as a Marine Corps officer. Following initial training at The Basic School and the Infantry Officer's Course at Quantico, he served as a platoon and company commander in a Light Armored Reconnaissance unit. From there, he applied for MARSOC.

In 2010, after undergoing the rigorous screening and training process, Matt deployed to Afghanistan as team leader of Marine Special Operations Team Three, Charlie Company, 1st Marine Special Operations Battalion. Shortly into the deployment, he was on an operation with an Afghan commando unit near the town of Sangin in Helmand Province. He had just entered an insurgent compound when he was seriously wounded by an IED. In the deafening explosion, Matt Lampert lost both his legs above the knee. Yet even as his corpsman and teammates applied tourniquets to stanch the flow of blood, his concern was not for himself but for the Marines on his team. They would have to carry on without him—at least for this deployment.

For most warriors, injuries as severe at Matt's would mean the end of active service. But not for this Marine captain. Early in his recovery, he was visited by Major General Paul Lefebvre, then the Commanding General, Marine Corps Forces Special Operations Command. "Matt," he told his wounded Marine, "as soon as you get yourself up and around, I have a job for you, if you're interested." Matt was, and he took to his rehabilitation and new prosthetic legs with single-minded focus.

When I met him in Afghanistan—less than two years after losing his legs—and very nearly his life—Captain Matt Lampert was back with Charlie Company, 1st Marine Special Operations Battalion, as the company executive officer.

There have been other soldiers, sailors, airmen, Guardsmen, and Marines who have returned to the battlefield on one prosthetic leg. I have met several in Iraq and Afghanistan. But to my knowledge, no one else has ever returned to the fight missing both legs.

MARSOC Marines have a saying: *Vis Gregis Est Lupus*—"The Strength of the Pack Is the Wolf." I think they had this in mind when Marines like Captain Matt Lampert joined their ranks. I've always been grateful for being able to claim the title of being a U.S. Marine—and never more so than in the company of men like Matt Lampert.

Dick Couch, my old—yes, we *are* old—warrior-friend, you have performed yet another great service in writing *Always Faithful, Always Forward*. In the pages that follow, readers will see just what it takes to become a Marine Critical Skills Operator. Some who pick up this book will decide to test themselves and volunteer to serve as MARSOC Marines.

That's a good thing. Our country needs tough, smart, tenacious men like Matt Lampert and the Marines you so eloquently describe herein. My thanks too for supporting the MARSOC Foundation, a 501(c)(3) charity (www.marsocfoundation.org) dedicated to the welfare of wounded MARSOC warriors and their families. Bravo Zulu, brother.

SEMPER FIDELIS,
OLIVER NORTH, LIEUTENANT COLONEL USMC (RET.)
HOST OF *WAR STORIES* ON FOX NEWS
AUTHOR OF THE *AMERICAN HEROES* BOOK SERIES

INTRODUCTION

Let me say at the outset of this work that I consider myself among the most fortunate of authors. Not only am I fortunate, but I am doubly blessed. As a young man from a small town in southern Indiana, I was afforded the opportunity to attend the United States Naval Academy. That was in the summer of 1963. As my parents drove me to the city and put me on the train that would take me from Indianapolis to Annapolis, I was filled with dreams of travel, ships, service, and adventure. My time aboard a Navy destroyer following my graduation from Annapolis and my subsequent service in Navy Underwater Demolition and SEAL teams following my time at sea made those dreams a reality and then some. Following my active service, I joined the Central Intelligence Agency, and it was just as exciting and rewarding. Collectively, those experiences were my first blessing. However, special operations and field intelligence work are the province of young men. Along about my mid-forties, when I knew my operational glass was well past half-empty, I began my career as a writer.

I began by writing novels. The first was *SEAL Team One*, where the reader and I followed a young man through Basic Underwater Demolition/SEAL training and into combat in Vietnam. It very much paralleled the journey I had made some twenty years earlier, only this young fictional warrior was smarter, faster, and more daring. Yet he had the same anxieties, doubts, and fears as I did; he felt the same crushing responsibility that comes from leading men in combat. He also felt the same rush that comes with surviving mortal combat.

I wrote *SEAL Team One* back when there was only one Navy SEAL writing books—me.

SEAL Team One did well, and is still in print through the Naval Institute Press. I followed this book with *Pressure Point*, *Silent Descent*, and *Rising Wind*—all novels about SEALs and terrorists in more contemporary settings. Each day I arose early, got myself a cup of coffee, and went to my word processor. Each morning I was able to hang out with my imaginary friends for a few hours and do some dashing and daring things. I created bad guys with evil in their hearts who plotted against our nation. To defeat these enemies, I developed SEALs and other special operators who stepped into the breach to counter those threats. Then the folks at Random House came to me and asked if I could write a book on Navy SEAL training—real SEALs and real training. Candidly, it's not easy for a novelist to step back into the real world and write about real people.

Thomas Ricks of *Fiasco* and *The Generals* fame had just written a very successful book on Marine Corps basic training called *Making the Corps*. Random House wanted to know if I could do the same for SEAL training. So I went to the SEAL training compound in Coronado, California, and began my second journey through Basic Underwater Demolition/SEAL training—this time with SEAL Class 228. It was a wonderful experience. Not only was I allowed to revisit an important and formative period in my own journey as a warrior, but I was privileged to meet and share that journey with the next generation of SEALs. Yet a nonfiction work is very different from the make-believe world of writing novels and developing imaginary characters. Following the very real young men through the difficult and demanding ordeal that is modern Navy SEAL training was hard work. A nonfiction book is a 110,000-word term paper. Yet the result, *The Warrior Elite: The Forging of SEAL Class 228*, was satisfying and rewarding beyond my wildest expectations. I'll always be in the debt of Thomas Ricks for helping me to make the transition from novels to nonfiction.

The Warrior Elite, which has recently been updated and rereleased in a special edition, was followed by *The Finishing School: Earning the Navy SEAL Trident* and *Downrange: Navy SEALs in the War on Terrorism*. Then it was back to basic special operations training with *Chosen Soldier: The Making of a Special Forces Warrior*—Army Green Beret training. Following that came *Sua Sponte: The Forging of a Modern American Ranger*, which followed the training of young warriors for duty in the 75th Ranger Regiment. For each of these works, I was allowed to follow some of the finest young men in America as they prepared for war and went into battle in the defense of our nation. I had the high honor to share a part of their journey and to tell their story. This was my second blessing. Perhaps now you can see why I consider myself so fortunate. My time as a special operations warrior is long since over, but I'm now permitted to accompany those preparing for the current fight.

This brings us to *Always Faithful, Always Forward*, the Marine Special Operations Command, and my final work on the training and qualification of American special operations ground-combat warriors. The Marines only recently joined the Special Operations family with the commissioning of the U.S. Marine Corps Forces, Special Operations Command, or MARSOC, in early 2006. In joining this brotherhood at this late date, they were able to learn a great deal from their SEAL, Special Forces, and Ranger brothers. They also had the challenge of standing up their force and immediately deploying that force during time of war. The first MARSOC deployment was a combat deployment. How they did this so quickly and entered the current fight with such professionalism is the story of *Always Faithful, Always Forward*. Once more I am honored to be able to tell the story of the newest of these superb young special warriors.

———

The business of special operations is different and distinct from that of conventional or general purpose military forces. It differs both in the specific mission sets and the scale of military operations. With respect to ground combat, there is some overlap on the periphery of what special operations forces (SOF) and general purpose forces are asked to do, most notably in the increasingly important areas of counterterrorism and counterinsurgency, and the disciplines that relate to these activities. That said, the job of our conventional land army is to defeat enemy armies—to defeat them and to take and hold ground. When general purpose forces try to assume the mission of SOF on their own, they are usually ineffective. When special operations units try to do the conventional, they are almost always overmatched. Yet special operations teams can often be very effective working in concert with general purpose forces—in what we call the "seams of the battlespace." With some notable exceptions, special operations forces are often highly dependent on conventional units for security and support. With this in mind, let's take a look at the special operations mission set and the special operations units tasked with those missions. Briefly and broadly, those missions are unconventional warfare, special reconnaissance, direct action, and foreign internal defense. Each of our SOF ground-combat components has priorities within these special tasks, to include variations and expansions on this basic mission set. The Marine Special Operations Command has certainly done this within their tasking and training, but these are the basics.

Unconventional warfare, or UW, is a somewhat ambiguous term for wresting control of a village, a province, or a nation from an unfriendly government—or an unfriendly nongovernment actor—currently in power. This can be done conventionally with armor and infantry or unconventionally by organizing and encouraging popular opposition to the established order. When we do this "by, with, and through" the efforts of a local, internal opposition, these indigenous forces are often called freedom fighters. Regime change in this fashion is a great deal cheaper than the process of invasion and quite often seen as more legitimate.

Immediately following the attacks of 9/11, it was quickly determined that Osama bin-Laden and his al-Qaeda organization were responsible. It was soon learned that bin Laden and al-Qaeda were being sheltered by the Taliban in Afghanistan—a nation characterized by its mosaic of tribal entities and its historic resistance to outside intervention. Those same tribes had fought the invading Russian army for more than ten years and, with our covert help, defeated them. Now it was our turn to be the invaders. As America debated just how to respond to the attacks of al-Qaeda, there was a great awareness of the difficulties of sending a conventional army into Afghanistan— difficulties we may not have fully appreciated later in our Afghan venture. Memories of the tenacious Afghan mountain fighters and Russian casualties were still fresh in 2001. So we sent no large conventional army; we took an unconventional, irregular approach.

Army Special Forces, the Green Berets, along with CIA paramilitary specialists and a generous dose of American airpower, mobilized an alliance of northern tribes and swept the Taliban from power, although without completely vanquishing them from the nation. This instance of enlisting, arming, and leading local tribes to bring about the expulsion of the Taliban proved to be a classic unconventional warfare operation. This UW effort accomplished in just a few months what the Russian army could not do in a decade, and at a fraction of the cost in both lives and treasury. My vision of that campaign will always be of an Army Special Forces sergeant standing on a hilltop with a Northern Alliance tribal leader at his side, looking down onto a valley held by the Taliban. The sergeant and his tribal counterpart look a great deal alike—both have full beards and both wear native *pakol* hats and are wrapped in *keffiyeh* scarves. Both are filthy from weeks in the mountains. The Green Beret sergeant is on his radio, directing American fighter-bombers as they deliver precision air strikes onto the Taliban positions below. The tribal leader seems always to be at the sergeant's elbow. After a thorough pounding of the Taliban lines, the Northern Alliance tribal fighters move down to mop up the battered and demoralized enemy fighters.

Special reconnaissance, or SR, is the mission to put "eyes on" an enemy position for a future special-operations or conventional targeting. Sometimes an SR mission is a clandestine operation prior to the commitment of a larger force. Navy SEALs conducted a multiday special reconnaissance prior to the Marine occupation of the forward operating base known as Camp Rhino in Afghanistan, a base near Kandahar that preceded the conventional-force occupation of that nation and the capture of Kabul. Sometimes, a special reconnaissance mission is launched for reasons of discrimination. American precision airpower has the ability to isolate, target, and completely destroy almost any given structure on the ground. In both Iraq and Afghanistan, SR teams have been used to observe a target building to ensure that target individuals are inside at the time of the attack and that noncombatants are not. I've spoken with special operators who have spent days in hide sites, under harsh, cold, and miserable conditions, watching remote buildings to confirm that the target individual was there and/or to ensure that women and children were not. With what we've now come to call the Global War on Terror often becoming an insurgent/counterinsurgent conflict, issues of proportionality, restraint, and discrimination are becoming increasingly important. Special reconnaissance may also extend to casual observation in an urban area to assess matters that relate to cultural or political intelligence in an area of interest.

While special reconnaissance is still a core SOF mission, its methodology has changed with recent advances in manned and unmanned airborne ISR (intelligence, surveillance, reconnaissance) platforms and enhanced satellite imagery. Yet ISR platforms have their limitations, especially in politically sensitive environments. Then only the careful observations of someone on the ground can obtain the needed information. In addition, the role of special reconnaissance is changing to more fully address the increasingly important interface between intelligence collection, targeting, and direct-action operations. In its current application, special reconnaissance has as much to do with intelligence collection as with reconnaissance.

Direct action is what most Americans think of in relation to a special operations mission—daring squads of heavily armed men parachuting at night into a remote area to attack an enemy compound, or silent warriors moving room to room with night-vision goggles as they clear a building in order to capture or kill an enemy commander. It's certainly the stuff favored by the media in their coverage of war. If the Army Special Forces mission to mobilize the northern Afghan tribes that swept the Taliban from power embodies the UW mission, then the Navy SEAL raid into Abbottabad, Pakistan, that resulted in the death of Osama bin Laden is the prototype of a direct action, or DA, mission. All of our special operations ground-combat components have the capability to conduct DA missions. It's a SOF mission staple and an extension of basic infantry tactics. The bin Laden raid was one of eleven DA missions carried out that night. At the height of the Iraqi and Afghan campaigns, our SOF units carried out between three and four thousand of those missions each year, with the majority of the raids being conducted by our SOF light-infantry component, the 75th Ranger Regiment. Direct-action missions are certainly the most dramatic and media-genic of the SOF operational taskings and, candidly, a favorite of our SOF ground combatants. It's certainly on the minds of our insurgent enemies. Anytime, anywhere, they may be visited by a lethal contingent of American special operators.

Yet in my opinion, the most difficult, nuanced, and important of the special-operations mission set is foreign internal defense, or FID. Unlike direct action, FID emphasizes the indirect. As it was in Iraq and Afghanistan, the final assessment of whether we ultimately win or lose in these irregular-warfare, often insurgent-contested conflicts lies with our success in the conduct of foreign internal defense.

Foreign internal defense, often called stability operations or village stability programs, frequently seems to pass under the media radar and is overlooked in a conflict. Yet it has been the primary focus of the majority of our deployed SOF personnel over the last two decades. Why is FID so important? Quite simply, it's our ticket *out* of a conflict. If we can successfully groom and train local, host-nation forces to achieve security and stability, then our forces can come home. These efforts in FID helped to bring some measure of stability to Iraq, where at least some of our national objectives were met. Our efforts in Afghanistan and the relentless pressure of the Taliban in their "UW campaign" may have been too little and too late.

When our SOF teams are deployed in a FID role with support of an elected government, as they have been in Colombia, the southern Philippines, and southern Thailand, they can be very effective. They can help local military forces and militias contain an insurgent movement before it reaches a national-level threat. In areas like Africa, where a national government may be weak and resource-challenged, a FID campaign can help even meager local forces to resist insurgent and criminal organizations who oppose a legitimate government and, perhaps, blunt an insurgent movement before it can gain a foothold in that nation. Quite often an effective FID campaign must be waged quietly and for an extended period of time. Following the successful unconventional warfare effort in Afghanistan in 2002, what if we had *immediately,* properly resourced and prosecuted a FID effort there? Might we have avoided the costs in terms of blood and treasury that ultimately led to the buildup a decade later?

In writing *Chosen Soldier,* I stated that the Special Forces soldier was the most important soldier on the current battlefield. My brother SEALs didn't care for that characterization, but I meant it then and I stand by it today. As we will later discuss, just one of the Core Activities of the Marine Special Operations Command is foreign internal defense. Recognizing its importance, the Command has made this core SOF skill an integral part of the training of a Marine special operator. The importance of FID and how MARSOC addresses this SOF skill will be addressed later in this work. As a key component of our nation's irregular warfare capability—one that includes counterinsurgency and counterterrorism—FID will, in my opinion, continue to dominate our special operations posture around the world. That the Marine Special Operations Command has undertaken in their training a robust approach to foreign internal defense is both responsible and advisable.

As our special operations forces regroup and recalibrate from the extended operations in Iraq and Afghanistan, we are going to hear a great deal about the shifting from the direct (DA) to the indirect (FID). As SOF is called upon to work with fledgling democracies and emerging nations to counter undermining threats of al-Qaeda, criminal elements, and drug-related activity, we are going to hear much about efforts to work with host-nation forces and build partnership capacity. This all has to do with foreign internal defense—less about going out and killing bad guys, which we are very good at, and more about empowering local forces to attend to their own security.

———

With this brief overview of the SOF mission set, let's take a quick inventory of the warriors of the U.S. Special Operations Command and their specific mission tasks. With due respect to the many other combat and combat support components of the Command, there are four major SOCOM ground combat components that I'll briefly address here: the Navy SEAL teams, the Army Special Forces groups, the Army 75th Ranger Regiment, and the Marine Special Operations Regiment. There are in fact other Army and Navy ground combatant units at SOCOM that are often referred to as "special mission units." They are special in that they have very narrow, direct-action mission responsibilities, and to be sure, they are highly proficient in that area. These units, their composition, and their specific mission sets are classified and beyond the scope of this work. With that understanding, let's first look at our Navy SEALs.

The Navy SEAL (sea-air-land) teams are the direct descendants of the Navy frogmen of Word War II. At the direction of President John F. Kennedy that all services develop an unconventional warfare capability, SEAL Teams One and Two were commissioned in January of 1962. Currently there are nine active SEAL teams and one SEAL delivery team, with some 2,400 active Navy SEALs, in the SOF force mix. They are well supported by the Navy special boat teams and a professional cadre of special warfare combatant craft crewmen—all special operators. By comparison, there are just over twice as many active-duty Navy SEALs as there are Marine special operators in uniform.

As a maritime proponent of SOCOM, the SEALs train for a host of maritime and littoral missions. Because of their focus in, under, and across the water, the SEALs have the most diverse mission set as it relates to maritime special operations. They are considered generalists across the entire SOF spectrum—direct action, special reconnaissance, unconventional warfare, and foreign internal defense. They have to do it all, and because of their maritime/diving requirements, the SEAL training pipeline is one of the longest of the special operations ground combatants'. Depending on medical and language training, it can take two and a half to three years to a make a deployable, combat-ready U.S. Navy SEAL out of a U.S. Navy sailor. Currently, just getting into SEAL training is a highly competitive business, and the attrition rate is close to 80 percent—only one in five who begin this lengthy training will deploy in harm's way with a Navy SEAL platoon. And while a great deal of media coverage has focused on direct-action missions, much of SEAL work overseas is in foreign internal defense.

The Army Special Forces, or Green Berets, are organized into five active and two reserve Special Forces groups. Each group consists of four operational battalions and a support battalion. Each SF group has an area or regional specialization, with culture and language training tailored to that area. Special Forces routinely deploy in fourteen-man Operational Detachment-Alpha or A-teams. They too are capable of all SOF disciplines and missions, but they are first and foremost teachers of military skills. A-teams currently deploy worldwide in support of the Global War on Terror. Army Special Forces are the SOF specialists when it comes to foreign internal defense and unconventional warfare. With few exceptions, they continue to be deployed to train military, paramilitary, and police units in nations threatened by insurgents; they are specialists in the indirect. Given the critical nature of these FID-related programs in recent conflicts, the Special Forces make extensive use of their two reserve groups. There are some 6,500 active Special Forces soldiers in uniform. It takes from eighteen months to two years to make a Special Forces soldier, and a great deal of that training involves cross-cultural disciplines. I was privileged to spend a year with these fine soldiers, during their training at Fort Bragg, North Carolina, and was with them on operational deployment in Iraq. Our chances for a favorable outcome in insurgent environments depends on the work of these soldiers. They currently field the largest FID-capable SOF ground-combat component. Operationally, they are close to six times the size of the Marine Special Operations Regiment. In further comparison, the Marine Special Operations Regiment is roughly the size of one Army Special Forces group.

The 75th Ranger Regiment and their four battalions of Rangers provide the Special Operations Command and our nation with a unique capability—a superb airborne light infantry. These Rangers do not routinely engage in unconventional warfare, special reconnaissance, or foreign internal defense. They are pure raiders and virtually all their operational taskings since 9/11 have been direct-action missions in Iraq and Afghanistan. There are 75th Regimental Rangers returning to the fight on their *fifteenth* consecutive combat deployment. While their work in the current conflicts has been primarily small-unit, intelligence-driven DA missions, the 75th is the only SOF component that can conduct company, battalion, and regimental-sized operations. Should our nation need to mount an airborne assault to seize an airfield in Africa or a nuclear weapons facility in Iran, we'll send our Ranger Regiment. Unlike the SEALs', Special Forces', and Marine special operators', the basic Ranger training regime for the 75th is very short—only eight weeks. While the training period is short and the mission set comparatively simple, their attention to detail and dedication to their Ranger standard make them a highly disciplined direct-action strike force. My year with the 75th Ranger Regiment taught me a great deal about performing to standard and the warrior ethic of this fine regiment.

This brings us to the Marine Corps Forces, Special Operations Command (MARSOC) and the Marine Special Operations Regiment, which, while still the smallest of our SOF ground combat components, is comparable in size with the 75th Ranger Regiment. It takes between ten months and a year to make a Marine special operator out of a U.S. Marine—longer with language training. This brings us to the tip of this SOF spear and this book. Just who are these Marine special operators? What do they do? What is their SOF mission set and how did they derive that mission set? And why did it take so long for them to join the SOF family? In very short order, they have become a value-added force in the U.S. Special Operations Command force mix. How were they able to accomplish this so quickly? *Always Faithful, Always Forward* is the story of this very special and talented Marine SOF component—MARSOC. As will be repeated throughout this text, they are indeed special or, if you will, specialists, within a larger organization that itself is unique and quite special.

———————

The term "special" has been a source of some debate and controversy within our military, as with other militaries around the world. For every unit that is special, or considers itself so, there is a parent command or brother unit that, by comparison or implication, is not so special. These special units have, by tradition, composition, and mission, been smaller, better trained, better equipped, and more selective in their recruiting than their larger parent-force counterparts. Until recently, they had been used in a supporting or diversionary role—assisting, complementing, or augmenting main-force activities, but never in themselves being a deciding factor. And quite often, these special units found themselves used poorly or underemployed by senior commanders. Senior conventional field commanders deal in regiments and brigades, and they are charged with winning battles, campaigns, and wars. The special units almost always came to the battlespace in company- and platoon-sized increments—seldom reaching the size of a battalion. These specialists might punch well above their weight, but in battle they were unlikely to change the course of the outcome. This was largely true until 9/11.

After 9/11, with the exception of the marginally organized resistance of the Taliban in 2002 and the porous defense offered by Saddam's army in 2003, the enemy had no regiments, brigades, or even battalions. Even when our al-Qaeda, Taliban, or Islamist enemies fielded company-sized opposition, they fared poorly against United States or coalition conventional forces. So our enemies, by necessity, developed robust insurgent capabilities and now use terror, intimidation, and religious fanaticism to oppose our interests. In essence, they are indirect-warfare specialists. They have become adept at controlling local populations—masters of the ancient art of guerilla warfare. In the post-9/11 world, winning the people, by whatever means, is more important than winning battles in the field. Vietnam should have taught us that, but our main-force efforts in Iraq and Afghanistan have reminded us of it again.

I recall the old story of the North Vietnamese Army colonel and the American Army colonel who found themselves in a discussion during the Paris peace talks that brought closure to that conflict.

"You know, don't you," the American colonel is to have said, "that not once did you ever beat us in the field."

The Vietnamese colonel, after a moment's reflection, replied. "That is quite true, we never did. But that was also unimportant in the outcome of this war."

Indirect and insurgent warfare, and the ruthless use of terror to control local populations, are and will be the rule, not the exception, in this century's conflicts. How we respond to these tactics will determine our success or failure on this irregular battlefield. The operational arm of MARSOC, the Marine Special Operations Regiment, is a versatile force, capable of the full range of military special operations. Their training and capabilities include the difficult and demanding discipline we now refer to as indirect warfare, which includes unconventional warfare and foreign internal defense—and, by extension, counterinsurgency operations and counterterrorism. How these Marine special operators train for this and how they bring the expeditionary heritage of their Corps to the business of special operations is the stuff of *Always Faithful, Always Forward*. Before we get to the formative days of the Marine Special Operations Command and the Marines they recruit for their regiment, let's take a brief look at the history of the Marine Corps, and the Marine Special Operations history specifically.

CHAPTER ONE

THE HISTORIES

Come on, you sons of bitches, do you want to live forever?

GUNNERY SERGEANT DAN DALY
THE BATTLE OF BELLEAU WOOD, 1918

A BRIEF HISTORY OF THE CORPS

On February 24, 2006, the U.S. Marine Corps Forces, Marine Special Operations Command, was formally activated at Camp Lejeune, North Carolina. Prior to this official status, the new special operations component began modestly with a small staff that had been known as the Marine Special Operations Advisory Group. Since its inception, MARSOC, as it is now commonly known, has grown into its present configuration as a three-battalion-plus, regimental-sized force capable of a broad range of expeditionary military special operations. In order to better understand the nature of this newest member of the special-operations force mix, let's take a look at the forces that shaped MARSOC. To do this, we need to look at the history of the Marine Corps, the history of Marine special operations, and the history of the U.S. Special Operations Command.

THE MARINES

There have been numerous histories written about the United States Marine Corps well worth the time of any serious military reader. If I had to choose just one, it would be *The United States Marines: A History*, by Brigadier General Edwin Howard Simmons, Ret., Fourth Edition. However, for the purposes of this book, and as a background for our study of MARSOC, I'm going to sprint through the history of the Corps. As you will later see, the history of formal Marine special operations dates only back to the Second World War. Yet the history of the Marine Corps itself goes back to colonial times. And since Marine special operators are first Marines, or Marines first, it's their history as well. The Marine special operators may have been operationally taken out of the Corps, but you cannot take the Corps out of the Marine special operators. They are simply Marines tasked with a special-operations mission.

Our early American military services patterned themselves after European models, and the Marine Corps was no different in this regard. During the latter half of the 1600s, European navies began to train seamen as infantrymen, albeit for naval infantry duty. But it was the British who first saw the need for a professional, onboard, at-sea fighting force. In 1664, the British Navy formed the Duke of York and Albany's Maritime Regiment of Foot. These first marines were recruited from the British Army and trained for shipboard duty. Companies of these naval infantrymen were stationed aboard warships and engaged in ship-to-ship encounters, expeditionary actions, security details, and discipline. Over the course of the next hundred years, regiments of these naval infantry were formed when a crisis arose and disbanded during times of peace. During the Napoleonic period, there were as many as ten regiments serving in units of the fleet. It was the beginning of what was to become the Royal Marines.

The first American Marines served in the British Navy. In 1739 a single, small regiment of Americans were recruited to serve as colonial marines under the command of Admiral Edward Vernon. These colonials served in Vernon's squadron during operations against the Spanish in the Caribbean and Central America and were severely decimated by bad weather, disease, and amphibious actions against the Spanish. They were disbanded three years later, and only about one in ten survived and returned to the colonies. One of those was a Captain Lawrence Washington, a younger half brother of George Washington. Both Washington brothers held Admiral Vernon in high esteem, with the senior Washington naming his home, Mount Vernon, after the British general.

The British continued to employ contingents of marines aboard their warships, and some five thousand were in uniform at the beginning of the American Revolution. By then their role as naval infantry had become more defined. In addition to raids ashore, they served as sharpshooters during ship-to-ship actions where they focused on the enemy officers. Marines led boarding parties, repelled boarders with bayonets, augmented gun crews, and enforced shipboard discipline. As these duties became more specific, the marines aboard men-of-war became more segregated from the sailors.

With the engagements at Lexington and Concord on April 19, 1775, the American Revolution became an open conflict. The colonies had no navy to speak of and relied on the few ships of the colonial navies and privateers to oppose the overwhelming superiority of the British Navy. As the conflict grew, contingents of the new Continental Army were sometimes pressed into service for shipboard duty. A single maritime regiment from the Massachusetts militia, the 14th Continental Regiment, composed mostly of men with maritime experience, became America's first naval infantry. During that first chaotic summer and into the early fall of 1775, George Washington, the newly appointed commander of the Continental Army, made do with a small fleet of colonial ships and the men of the 14th from Massachusetts. It was not until October of 1775 that the Continental Navy was formed and then in name only.

On November 10, 1775, the Second Continental Congress authorized, and funded, the formation of a national corps of marines and laid the framework for what was to become the modern Marine Corps. These American Marines were organized much like their British forebears and were assigned like duties. The new Corps was to be a two-battalion unit and under the command of Captain Samuel

Nicholas—regarded by many as the first commandant of the Marine Corps. The Nicholas family were tavern keepers, and Marine lore has it that the first Marine recruiting station was just outside Tun Tavern in Philadelphia. Officers were small businessmen and merchants, selected for their ties to the local community, and enlistees were drawn from tradesmen and unskilled workers. Again, the legend maintains that the new Corps drew its first Marines from the taverns in and around Philadelphia.

In 1776, elements of the new Continental Marines began serving aboard ships of the Continental Navy. In March of that year, they conducted their first amphibious operation during the Battle of Nassau, seizing large stocks of cannon, powder, and shot. A great deal of what Washington wanted from his nascent Navy and Marine Corps was captured provisions for his under-equipped army. Expeditions into Canada and the Caribbean were largely designed to capture stores and draw units of the British fleet away from their blockade of the colonial coastline. Of historical note, the first Continental Marine killed in action was Lieutenant John Fitzpatrick. He died during an at-sea engagement following the action in Nassau. Also of historical significance, in April of 1776, John Martin enlisted in Philadelphia to become the first African-American Marine.

Following the signing of the Declaration of Independence on July 4, 1776, now Major Samuel Nicholas worked diligently to recruit and train a company of Marines for each of the new Continental Navy frigates that were becoming the backbone of the new Continental Navy and the only open-water challenge to the British fleet. It was not until September of 1776 that the Continental Marines adopted a standard uniform. The color was green, said to be the color of riflemen or, in this case, men with muskets, and their blouses featured a leather collar to protect the wearer from enemy cutlass slashes—thus the nickname "leathernecks." In October of that year, Sergeants William Hamilton and Alexander Neilson were promoted to lieutenant to become the first Marine "mustangs," men advanced from the enlisted ranks to become officers.

Throughout the War of Independence, the Continental Marines continued to serve aboard ships of the Continental Navy, fighting in ship-to-ship engagements and shore raids. They were often pressed into service to fight alongside units of the Continental Army. At the end of the revolution, in 1783, there were some 130 Marine officers and 2,000 enlisted Marines. Both the Continental Navy and the Continental Marines were then disbanded.

Marines have always cited November 10, 1775, as their official and spiritual date of birth. They ignore the gap between the disbanding of the Continental Marines and the establishment of the U.S. Marine Corps in July of 1898. The Navy had also long vacillated on an origin date between October 19, 1775, and the formation of the Department of the Navy on April 30, 1798. In 1972, Admiral Elmo Zumwalt settled the issue by authorizing the October 19 date as the official birthday of the United States Navy. So as a matter of modern historical precedence, the Continental Navy was established almost a month earlier than the Continental Marines.

The early American Marines, the Marines of the War of Independence, inherited a great deal more from their British counterparts than a legacy of difficult duty and a maritime infantryman's job description. All militaries and military service components are cultures, and no American military service is more culturally distinct or tradition bound than the United States Marine Corps. This began during their formative years, when they represented a minority contingent of a ship's company or were fighting ashore alongside larger units of the Continental Army. This naturally bred a degree of separation and the perception of an elite status, both in how these early Marines saw themselves and how other services viewed them. In a word, these first American Marines were "special," and from those early days when the colonial recruiters made their way from tavern to tavern in search of a few good men, the Marines have felt they were just that—special. Their long history of gallant and loyal service to our nation has done nothing to tarnish this perception. Yet in modern times, terms like "special" and "elite" have become contentious within the Marine

Corps when used in making a distinction between one Marine and another.

———————

On July 11, 1789, President John Adams signed into law an act that provided for the establishment and organization of the Marine Corps. It allowed for a battalion-sized corps, primarily as shipboard infantry for service aboard American naval frigates. Lieutenant Colonel William Ward Burrows was made commandant of the new Corps and is by some measures regarded as the first commandant of the *United States* Marine Corps. It is said that Colonel Burrows rode about Washington with President Thomas Jefferson, and together they selected the "Eighth and I" site for the new Marine barracks and commandant's residence. Eighth and I is still the site of the Washington Marine barracks and the home of the President's Own U.S. Marine Band and Honor Guard. Burrows inherited a store of blue uniforms with red piping, which he put into use and which reflected the color of current Marine uniforms. The new Corps's first action was the 1801–1804 war against the Barbary Pirates that featured the (unsuccessful) attack on Tripoli. Yet these Marines made an impression as they stormed ashore on "the shores of Tripoli." The Ottoman viceroy Prince Hamet Karamanli was so taken with these U.S. Marines that he presented a Mameluke sword to Marine First Lieutenant Presley O'Bannon, the sword worn today by Marine Corps officers.

The first extended conflict for the new Marine Corps was the War of 1812. They participated in actions from the Great Lakes to the Battle of New Orleans, where they held the center of the line for General Andrew Jackson. They conducted amphibious operations under Colonel Winfield Scott at Toronto and participated in the famous frigate duels, the only and much-needed American victories at the beginning of the war.

Following the War of 1812, the Marines occupied themselves with pirates operating in and around the waters off Florida and in the

Caribbean until Spain ceded Florida to the United States in 1821. In 1820, the incoming fifth commandant of the Marine Corps took the form of a most influential Marine, both in terms of his transitional influence and his longevity. In addition to serving as acting commandant for six months in 1818–1819, Archibald Henderson served as commandant from October 8, 1820, to January 6, 1859. He's known as "the grand old man of the Marine Corps." During his tenure, Henderson pushed for the Corps to become a more agile force, one that lent itself to rapid deployment and was more suited to expeditionary warfare. His Marines were engaged in the Seminole Wars (1835–1842) and the Mexican-American War (1846–1848). In this latter conflict, the Marines distinguished themselves in several engagements in California and Mexico—most notably, the storming of Chapultepec Castle that protected Mexico City. This difficult and costly assault was made through "the halls of Montezuma." The red or "blood stripe" on today's Marine dress uniform commemorates the heavy losses experienced by Marine officers and noncommissioned officers during the battle for the Chapultepec precipice.

Due to the non-expeditionary nature of the conflict, Marines in the Civil War, on both sides of the conflict, played a very minor role. When war broke out, there were just under two thousand officers and men in the Corps. As with those serving in the Army and Navy, the Civil War forced serving Marines to choose—North or South. Then, as now, those Americans with Southern, rural, and agricultural roots seemed to be proportionally more strongly attracted to military service than those from the urban and manufacturing parts of the nation. Records are vague, but it seemed that about two-thirds of those serving Marines sided with the South and the balance with the North. As with those in the Army who elected to side with the Confederacy, there also seemed to be among the Marines an imbalance in the partitioning of proven ability and leadership that favored the South. Congress modestly increased the size of the Union Marines to meet the needs of shipboard duty for the expanding Federal Navy. The

Confederate Marines also saw a slight increase in their numbers, but they saw only limited action in defensive roles. Priority on both sides was given to fielding large land armies.

The balance of the nineteenth century was an ambiguous time for the Marine Corps. While it was not disbanded, the Corps pressed on with what had been a cadre of Union Marines. As steam gradually took the place of sail, and canonry became more accurate and deadly, there was little need for a shipboard contingent of boarders or a requirement to repel boarders. With the advent of armor plating and the absence of masts and rigging, there was no longer the necessity or a place for sharpshooters. Work for the shipboard Marines became limited to security and the occasional landing-party duty associated with projecting power ashore. The Marines did participate in several dozen uprisings and the quelling of uprisings, including actions that led to the toppling of the monarchy in Hawaii.

Culturally, the Marines continued to add to the lore of their Corps. In 1868, the Marines adopted the famous globe and anchor as their emblem. In that same year, the halls of Montezuma and the shores of Tripoli were incorporated into the Marine Corps Hymn. In 1883 they took up *Semper Fidelis*, or Semper Fi, as their motto—"Always Faithful." Doctrinally, the Marines adopted manuals and codified procedures from amphibious warfare to handling ordnance aboard ship and ashore. In 1880, a young John Philip Sousa became the leader of the Marine Corps Band, and his contingent of musical Marines became nationally popular. It was not until the outbreak of hostilities with Spain that the Marines returned to the serious business of war.

The Spanish-American War (1898) was a short conflict with an overmatched adversary that did much to heal the nation from the divisiveness that still smoldered from the Civil War. Within the Army and the Navy, senior officers and NCOs from both the North and the South fought together. Among the rank and file, there may have been few Civil War veterans. Nonetheless, this short conflict saw soldiers, sailors, and Marines from both the South and the North united under the same flag. The Marines fought in the Philippine Islands, Guam,

Puerto Rico, and Cuba to include the capture of Guantánamo Bay. The Treaty of Paris that concluded the hostilities left the United States in possession of these former Spanish colonies. These new territories created new duties and obligations for the Navy and the Marine Corps.

————

Leading up to the First World War, the elements of the Marine Corps were dispatched to protect legations and foreign settlements in China and conduct a string of engagements in Central and South America, collectively known as the Banana Wars. The United States embarked on a policy of intervention, primarily in Central America and the Caribbean, to include lengthy occupations of Haiti and the Dominican Republic. The big stick of this regional interventionist policy fell increasingly to the Marines. These incursions, while they did little to endear the *Norteamericanos* to the rest of the hemisphere, did much to hone the battle skills of the Marines for the Great War that was to come. The Corps was much smaller than the U.S. Army, yet the majority of American combat experience rested in the Marine Corps. The incursions of the Banana Wars gave the Corps experience in guerilla and counterinsurgency operations that was later codified in the historic *Marine Corps Small Wars Manual* (1935) and was a precursor to the mission of MARSOC in the Global War on Terror.

There are two things that stand out in my mind regarding the Marines on the eve of the World War I—both characteristics that have marked the Corps in their modern history. The first is the emergence of an experienced and professional cadre of noncommissioned officers. At that time, the officer corps of the world's standing military armies and navies was based on family status and position. But in the American military and especially in the Marine Corps, leadership was merit-based. Additionally, being a relatively small, active, and expeditionary force, the Marines did not experience the great expansions and contractions of the Army. This allowed for the development of this talented corps of NCOs. The superb combat leaders that emerged from the ranks proved to be good role models for the younger Marines, and a steady and professional influence on junior Marine officers. The second characteristic is the emergence of the Marine rifleman. With their emphasis on marksmanship and the highly accurate Springfield M1903 rifle, the Marines who entered World War One were simply the best rank-and-file shooters in the world, as the German infantry along the Western Front would discover.

As the nation's most seasoned force, the Marines spearheaded the American Expeditionary Force that entered our First World War on the side of the Allies. They participated in several battles, but it was during the Battle of Belleau Wood that the U.S. Marine Corps established itself on the world stage as a brave and tenacious fighting force. During the three-week battle in June of 1918, a brigade-sized force from the 5th and 6th Marine Regiments were committed to the fight. On June 6, during a single day's combat, the Marines sustained nearly eleven hundred casualties—more dead and wounded than in their entire history to date. Fighting alongside two Army divisions, and elements of British and French forces, they managed to push five German divisions from the area in a decisive Allied victory.

Belleau Wood holds a distinguished place in Marine Corps lore. Again, it served notice to the nation and the world that the Marines were more than a small expeditionary force; they could hold their own and then some in a line-infantry role. At Belleau Wood they displayed a range of fighting skills that ranged from precision shooting to hand-to-hand fighting—from defensive stands against onrushing German infantry to gallant offensive bayonet charges over open ground in the face of murderous machine-gun fire. Following the battle, General Jack Pershing, commander of the American Expeditionary Force, said, "The deadliest weapon in the world is a Marine and his rifle." It was at Belleau Wood that the Marines acquired the name "Devil Dogs." It's unclear whether this moniker came from the Germans, who came to recognize and admire the ferocity of the Marines, or the American press. It was also at Belleau Wood, during the heat of the battle, that then Gunnery Sergeant Dan Daly (as quoted under this chapter heading) was said to have shouted to his Marines, "Come on, you sons of bitches, do you want to live forever?" Following the war, Sergeant Major Daly, twice a recipient of the Medal of Honor, claimed to have said, "For Christ's sake men—come on! Do you want to live forever?" With due respect to this fine sergeant major, I like the popular version.

The Marine Corps on the eve of World War I stood at close to ten thousand officers and men. It was primarily an expeditionary, light-infantry force with a fledgling aviation arm. At the time of demobilization from the "war to end all wars," the Corps stood at just under fifty thousand.

America is, or was, a nation that relied on the citizen soldier in times of war. This called for a near universal conscription during times of conflict, and a dramatic drawdown in the ensuing peace. Because of their peacetime fleet/shore installation security duties and modest expeditionary/intervention requirements, the drawdown affected the Marine Corps far less than the Army or even the Navy. Nonetheless, with the prospect of global war in the wind in 1939–40, there were just over twenty thousand Marines in uniform at the time of Pearl Harbor. This included thirteen squadrons of Marine aircraft.

In the two decades between the world wars, the Marine Corps had five commandants, and perhaps none was more important than Major General John Lejeune, who served a nine-year tenure and for whom Camp Lejeune, North Carolina, is named. Lejeune and other senior officers in the Corps set about developing the amphibious doctrine that was to be key to the War in the Pacific. In 1933 the Marine Corps instituted the concept of the Fleet Marine Force, to better integrate Navy–Marine Corps cooperation in amphibious operations, and pushed for amphibious fleet exercises to develop this capability. More specifically, it helped to focus at least some of the Navy's attention to projecting power ashore rather than preparing only for fleet-to-fleet engagements. In addition to refinements in amphibious doctrine, the Marines developed a significant aviation capability, the only Marine component that was to see significant growth during this between-wars period.

Had there been no Pearl Harbor and had we engaged in another strictly European war, the Marine Corps might have been only another light-infantry unit in the mix. But Pearl Harbor changed all that. With the prospect of a naval war and its attendant amphibious requirements, one that would range across half the globe, the Marine Corps set about an ambitious expansion that would increase the size of the Corps twenty-fold. The Marines saw only isolated duty in Europe, North Africa, and the Middle East; theirs was to be a Pacific war. They were to see action in every significant battle in that theater. The island-hopping campaign across the Pacific is a matter of history, and a gallant one at that—Guadalcanal, Tarawa, Saipan, Peleliu, Iwo Jima, Guam, Okinawa, and a dozen other islands and atolls on the way to Japan. Each of these battles is worthy of a book, and indeed, there have been many on each of them. All were bloody, all were contentious, and all were marked by collective and individual acts of valor. Yet, of all these legendary Marine engagements, Guadalcanal stands out. In most of these island battles, the Americans enjoyed superior air and naval support and an overwhelming logistical advantage. All were difficult and bloody, but the outcome was seldom in doubt. At Guadalcanal, the Marines had none of the advantages of subsequent island campaigns. At Guadalcanal—undersupplied, short on ammunition, and with limited supporting arms—it was Marine courage and stubbornness that won the day. Seven thousand Marines and thirty-one thousand Japanese soldiers died during the six-month campaign. Guadalcanal forced the Imperial Japanese Army to shift from an offensive war to a defensive war, and set the stage for the drive across the Pacific to the Japanese mainland. Perhaps just as important, after Guadalcanal both the Marines and the Japanese knew the vaunted Japanese jungle fighter could be beat.

This drive across the Pacific and the need for Marines caused the Corps to swell to the largest size in its history. By the end of the war there were 485,000 Marines, a number that included an aviation contingent that included 145 squadrons. Just under 20,000 Marines were killed in action in World War II—about the size of the entire Corps at the beginning of the conflict. Some 68,000 were wounded. Eighty-two Marines were awarded the Medal of Honor.

It might be noted here that President Franklin Roosevelt had a special affinity for the Marine Corps. Roosevelt had served as assistant secretary of the Navy from 1913 to 1920. As president, he often referred to "we" when talking about the Marine Corps. At the time of our entry into the war, Roosevelt had been in the White House for almost a decade. He was a consummate politician, and while he listened to his service chiefs, he often took a hand in what might be called their internal military matters. This applied to the Marine Corps, and as we will see, he was instrumental in the formation of what would become popularly known as the first of the Marine special operators.

———

World War II was a true global conflict that resulted in, by some accounts, close to 100 million military and civilian deaths. The specter of the atomic bomb and the primacy of airpower in warfare led many strategists to think that future wars would be fought only from the air. Many argued that these developments made the Navy, the Marine Corps, and amphibious warfare obsolete. The political winds had also changed. While Roosevelt favored his Navy and Marine Corps, President Truman, an artilleryman in the Great War, did not. In the demobilization that followed, all the service components experienced downsizing, with the Marine Corps dropping to close to seventy-five thousand. In 1950, on the eve of the Korean War, the Corps, including their aviation arm, stood at eighty-five thousand.

The brief between-wars period saw the Marines involved in the occupation of Japan and in small, guard-force actions from Southeast Asia to Jerusalem. With the prospect of nuclear warfare obsoleting amphibious warfare, the Marines began to develop a ship-to-shore capability using helicopters.

The Marines were quickly called into action in Korea to help the United Nations forces defend the shrinking Pusan perimeter. When the United Nations forces finally went on the offensive, General Douglas MacArthur, a veteran amphibious campaigner, quickly made use of his Marines in the conflict-changing landings at Inchon. American and U.N. forces were deep into North Korea when the full weight of the Chinese Army attacked them. The American Eighth Army retreated in disarray, but the Marines of the 1st Marine Division fought an orderly retreat that came to be known as the Battle of Chosin Reservoir. Chosin quickly became a symbol of Marine tenacity and resolve when facing numerically superior opposition. Their courage and discipline in that frozen hell is a proud chapter in the battle history of the Corps.

The Korean War did much to quell the notion that the Navy and Marine Corps were obsolete, even with the prospect of a nuclear-weapons buildup among the two superpowers and their allies. The Corps emerged from combat in Korea with a force of just over a quarter of a million Marines, but there was a price for this robust, post-conflict force. More than four thousand Marines lost their lives and some twenty-four thousand were wounded. Forty-two Marines received the Medal of Honor in Korea.

The Marine Corps was to have but a decade of reprieve between Korea and Vietnam. During that time the Corps entertained a series of crisis-management interventions and embassy evacuations, most notably in the Suez/Egypt, Cuba, and the Dominican Republic. The Vietnam conflict was to prove long, difficult, and instructive for the Marine Corps. During what is now our nation's second-longest conflict, the Marines fought counterguerilla actions against the Viet Cong and pitched battles against the North Vietnamese Army. Due to the perceived requirements of the Cold War, the size of the Corps shrank, but not by a great deal. The Marines went into Vietnam with 175,000 Marines—about the size of the present-day Corps.

The Marine experience in Vietnam may be seen through the prism of two battles—the four-day Battle of Hue City and the four-month

Battle of Khe Sanh, both beginning in late January, 1968. In Hue City, a combined force of some twelve thousand Viet Cong and North Vietnamese regulars attacked the city. Defending Hue were three undersized battalions of Marines, two Army battalions, and ten ARVN (Army of the Republic of Vietnam) battalions. Yet Hue City is always thought of as a Marine engagement. In only a few days of bitter fighting, the Marines experienced two hundred dead and fifteen hundred wounded. Enemy casualties in Vietnam were and are hard to quantify, but between three and seven thousand of the enemy died at Hue City.

The Battle of Khe Sanh pitted two North Vietnamese regiments—some seventeen thousand enemy soldiers—against six thousand Marines and the combined muscle of Marine artillery and American airpower. The extent of the battle was difficult to judge, with intense fighting in and around the base at Khe Sanh and blocking engagements in the extended area designed to logistically isolate the Marine defenders. The North Vietnamese commander, General Vo Nguyen Giap, sought to sequester the Marines and bring about a Dien Bien Phu–type encirclement and surrender. However, he did not count on the American supporting arms and the stubbornness of the Marines. The base at Khe Sanh was strategically unimportant; it was a place to test North Vietnamese manpower against American willpower. Whole battalions of North Vietnamese regulars disappeared. Enemy deaths are, again, difficult to estimate, but between five and fifteen thousand NVA soldiers died in the battle—perhaps a great deal more. Two hundred and seventy-four Marines died at Khe Sanh.

Following these two engagements, both tactical victories, much effort was made in the press and by historians, then and now, to present these as strategic North Vietnamese victories. I'll not enter that debate, but one thing is certain: Both can be viewed as lustrous additions to the battle history and lore of the Marine Corps. Today, when I meet a Marine who is a Hue City Marine or a Khe Sanh Marine, I afford him the respect he is owed for having fought in those bitter engagements.

Vietnam was also the first major conflict to see Marines serve in an advisory role. Just as we helped to institute a Vietnamese Army, the ARVN, we also established a Vietnamese Marine Corps. The origin of this Vietnamese-advisory effort goes back to 1954. Over the course of the war the Marine advisory teams expanded the ranks of their counterparts from battalion to division strength. The effectiveness of the Vietnamese Marines in the field was mixed, but their American Marine advisors gained a reputation of working closely with their brother Vietnamese Marines and sharing their barracks space, rations, and hardships in the field. Another advisory effort was the Combined Action Program. This effort saw Marines, from a single Marine to a full squad, embedding with an irregular force platoon of regional or provincial forces in the defense of their village or hamlet. These advisors were among the first Marines to take up what has come to be the special-operations staple of foreign internal defense. While this was the main effort of Army Special Forces, both veteran Marines and SEALs were detailed to this important duty. As a young SEAL platoon leader in Vietnam, I worked with these professional and dedicated Marines. On occasion, one or another would step away from his advisory role and join us on a nighttime, direct-action mission. My platoon SEALs welcomed them on any operation. Invariably, they would show up for the mission operations order with blackened face, a bush hat, their M-14 rifle, and a huge grin.

The Marine Corps emerged from Vietnam and the immediate aftermath with some three hundred thousand Marines in their Corps— up more than one hundred thousand from the beginning of the conflict. Fifty-seven Marines were awarded the Medal of Honor in Vietnam; 13,000 perished in combat and 88,500 were wounded. Oddly enough, this butcher's bill in a pure casualty count was *higher* in Vietnam than during World War II. Advances in battlefield medicine saved more lives in Vietnam, generating a higher relative percentage of those wounded. Though there were less than half the number of Marines engaged in Vietnam than in the Pacific Campaign at any given time, the length of this long war took its toll on my generation of Marines.

A great deal has been made of the difficult times experienced by the military following Vietnam. It was a time of normal, post-conflict downsizing that was given an additional push by the mood of the country. Our armed forces, including the Marine Corps, did in fact experience the effects of the counterculture of the 1960s and early 1970s and the dramatic rise in the use of recreational drugs. It was an extended conflict with the specter of the draft hanging over able-bodied males. That said, 85 percent of those who fought in Vietnam were volunteers. All who served in the Marine Corps were, though it is fair to say that a few were perhaps just a step ahead of the draft. The locus of unrest generated during those uncertain times was on college campuses, involving both students and faculty, and within the media. These were individuals who by and large sidestepped military service. Yet it was largely these same individuals who went on to define the Vietnam generation—my generation. Never in our history have so many Americans who served their nation so well been so misrepresented by those few who did not.

Like all service branches, the Corps downsized after Vietnam. Their numbers shrank to well under two hundred thousand. Throughout much of the 1970s and '80s they were tasked with embassy security operations and the protection of American citizens who found themselves in harm's way, and they participated in the invasion of Panama in 1989. As for the Marine Corps, the most traumatic occurrence of the post-Vietnam era took place during our incursion into the Lebanese Civil War. On October 23, 1983, a truck bomb driven by extremists into the Marine barracks in Beirut took the lives of 241 Americans—220 of whom were Marines. It was, and is, the largest loss of Marine Corps life during a time of peace.

There were two events during the 1980s that tangentially involved the Marine Corps but would be key factors in the establishment of a separate and dedicated special operations command. The first was Operation Eagle Claw in 1980, the aborted attempt to rescue the

American hostages taken from our embassy in Tehran and imprisoned by the Iranians. The second was the Invasion of Grenada in 1983. Both of these actions were marred by a lack of coordination among our service components, miscommunication, and an inability to quickly plan and execute a relatively small military operation that involved intra-service cooperation. These actions led to the Goldwater-Nicholas Act in 1986, which essentially created a fifth service component—the U.S. Special Operations Command.

The 1990s saw the Corps restored to a manning level of approximately two hundred thousand. In the first Gulf War, the Marines were tasked with the liberation of Kuwait while the Army charged into Iraq to humiliate Saddam's Republican Guard. The Corps also saw action in the United Nations intervention in Somalia and embassy/legation missions and peacekeeping duties from Indonesia to the Central African Republic to Bosnia.

The Marine Corps entered the twenty-first century a smaller (approximately 170,000), leaner, and more agile force. Following 9/11, in support of the Global War on Terror, the Corps began a gradual buildup to just over two hundred thousand Marines. Both Afghanistan and Iraq have added chapters in the battle history of the Corps. In June of 2002, the 15th Marine Expeditionary Unit from the USS *Peleliu* (LHA-5) executed a four-hundred-mile penetration/airfield seizure to establish Camp Rhino in the interior of Afghanistan. This longest of amphibious operations paved the way for follow-on coalition forces and the eventual vanquishing of al-Qaeda and Taliban forces. During the invasion of Iraq in March of 2003, the 1st Marine Division drove from the Kuwaiti border, up the Tigris River to Baghdad, helping to rout Saddam's army in the process. Following the defeat of the Iraqi Army, the Marines began the long and difficult counterinsurgency effort in Iraq, primarily in the Sunni province of al-Anbar. They played a key role in the Battles of Fallujah and Ramadi. After our withdrawal from Iraq, the Marines shifted their focus to counterinsurgency operations in Afghanistan. As our involvement in Afghanistan wound down, the Corps, like all the services, was faced with cuts in their budget and troop strength. Yet with all drawdowns, it seems as if there will always be intervening events, like attacks on our embassies in the wake of the Arab Spring, that surface the need for a regionally based, rapid-response force. As America stands away from the demands of regional conflict, there will, in my opinion, always be a need for an agile, expeditionary military response that can move quickly and effectively when our national interests are threatened.

I believe there are two events since Vietnam that have shaped the Marine Corps today and will continue to shape it going forward. The first, of course, was the attack of September 2001. This attack on the homeland created changes in the nature of war for our military in general, but the Marine Corps in particular. Nine-Eleven set in motion a series of regional issues that demand our attention and a need for a focused, limited, and more careful response, which the Marines have been doing for the last two hundred years. Nine-Eleven also made al-Qaeda and the radical Islamists players on the world stage. What President George Bush called the Global War on Terror will, in my opinion, continue to smolder and periodically flare up, demanding the attention of our Marine Corps. The second event was a series of actions by Congress that ended the draft and set our nation on the course of an all-voluntary military. By and large, the draft was a staffing entity for the Army. Yet without the draft and the prospect of compulsory Army service, there might not have been so many volunteers for the Marine Corps. Now a young American must not only qualify for service in the armed forces, he or she *must* be a volunteer. In the Marine Corps, this means these young people must not only volunteer, but step up to the physical, mental, emotional, and professional requirements of this modern band of brothers. In their long history, the Corps has never been more capable or more professional. Yet with every prospect that the Marine Corps will, like the other services, shrink in numbers and funding, the Corps will have to continue to evolve, tactically and professionally, to meet future challenges.

A BRIEF HISTORY OF MARINE SPECIAL OPERATIONS
THE RAIDERS

There are a great many Marines, active and retired—in and out of uniform—who feel that "Marine" and "special" are synonymous. Candidly, a great many of us who served, but not in the Marine Corps, feel the same way. With this in mind, the Corps can trace their *special-operations* history back to the Marine Raider battalions of World War II and the parachute battalions that preceded the Raiders by a year. The story of the Marine Raiders can be viewed through the colorful personage of Evans F. Carlson. It seems as if all our special operations ground-combat units can trace their formation to a forceful and charismatic leader who stood apart from the conventional and put his personal mark on the organization. For the SEALs it was Draper Kauffman. Army Special Forces was shaped by Aaron Bank and the 75th Rangers by William O. Darby. For Marine Special Operations Forces, it was Evans Carlson.

Evans Carlson lied about his age and enlisted in the Army in 1912 at the age of fifteen. He served nine years in the Army and quickly moved up the enlisted ranks. Carlson made company first sergeant and in 1917 was granted a field commission to first lieutenant. He saw action in France, where he received the first of his two Purple Hearts. He resigned his Army commission in 1921 and a year later enlisted in the Marine Corps as a private. Again Carlson advanced quickly, and he was commissioned from the ranks to second lieutenant. In the early 1930s, he was detailed to Nicaragua, where he was awarded the first of his three Navy Crosses.

On three separate occasions, Carlson was posted to China, where he met and soldiered with the Communist leadership that would ultimately wrest control of the country from the Nationalists. While there, he became interested in Chinese guerilla operations against the Japanese, specifically the small-unit, "democratic" leadership model that pushed authority and responsibility down to the most junior levels in small combat units. Carlson traveled extensively throughout

China as an "embed" with the hard-pressed Chinese forces as they opposed the Japanese. He was able to study closely both Japanese and Chinese tactics. In 1939, Captain Carlson resigned from the Marine Corps to write and lecture on what he saw as the Japanese threat in Asia and the Pacific. Prior to Pearl Harbor, Carlson returned to the Corps and was commissioned as a major. His military career was not without its political overtones.

It was in 1933 that then Captain Carlson received orders as executive officer of the security detachment for President Franklin Roosevelt's vacation retreat in Warm Springs, Georgia. There he became an acquaintance and confidant of the president and a close friend of his son, James Roosevelt. This association was to surface again during 1942.

Before World War II there were Marines—infantrymen, artillerymen, logisticians, aviators, and the like. They were, again, special only in that they were Marines. There were, however, also Marines in the Fleet Marine Force, who were assigned to provisional rubber boat companies. These Marines received special training in the use of inflatable rubber boats to make shore landings and served aboard APDs—World War I four-stack destroyers converted to fast transports. These transports could carry a company of these light, amphibious Marines and steam with the lead elements of the fleet.

President Roosevelt, prior to the war and immediately following Pearl Harbor, looked on the British commandos with great interest. At the urging of Winston Churchill, he directed the Marine Corps to develop a "commando unit," along the lines of the British. He was seconded in this request by Admiral Chester Nimitz, who wanted a commando-style unit to conduct raids on lightly garrisoned, Japanese-held Pacific islands. Then Commandant Major General Thomas Holcomb stated that "the term Marine is sufficient to indicate a man ready for duty at any time, and the injection of a special name, such as 'commando' would be undesirable and superfluous." So in February of 1942, he designated two battalions of the 5th Marines as the 1st and 2nd Separate Marine Battalions. At the urging of Roosevelt, Evans Carlson was promoted to lieutenant colonel and given command of the 2nd. In this fashion, the Marine Raiders were born.

In the 2nd Battalion, the forty-six-year-old Carlson began to train his Marines to his vision of a capable light-infantry strike force. He also had the political vision to make one Captain James Roosevelt his executive officer. Carlson implemented the doctrine and tactics he learned from his experience with the Chinese. This philosophy pushed the decision making down to the lowest levels—to the platoon- and squad-level leaders. He initiated the use of fire teams and fire-team leaders as a further breakdown of the infantry squad, the small-unit leadership model that is still used in our military today—both in special-operations and conventional-infantry elements. Many, including this author, credit Carlson with strengthening the role of senior noncommissioned officers as junior combat leaders, paving the way for the relevance and prestige senior NCOs enjoy in our military today.

The Raiders participated in several island campaigns in the Pacific, but for the purposes of this book we'll narrow it down to two: the Makin Island Raid and Guadalcanal. During mid-August of 1942, Lieutenant Colonel Carlson led two companies of Raiders against the Japanese seaplane installation at Makin Atoll in the Gilbert Islands. The Marine Raiders were delivered to the atoll in two transport submarines and made their way ashore in rubber boats. The operation was marked by higher-than-expected surf and a great deal of confusion and miscommunication. The Japanese garrison of some seventy soldiers and that many more who were part of a relief effort were killed at the cost of nineteen Marines killed and eleven captured/MIA. The details of the raid have been well chronicled in Marine Corps histories. The raid was nonetheless one of the first small-unit ground actions of the war for the United States, and a great deal was learned about this kind of raider-type operation. The raid has had, to this day, mixed reviews. A great deal has been made of the confusion, the men who were mistakenly left behind, and difficult command-and-control issues. Yet this was a rather sophisticated mission conducted only *six months* after the Raiders were formed. For their first outing, I think these new Marine Raiders did remarkably well. The immediate aftermath of the operation speaks to the character of Evans Carlson. In his after-action report to Admiral Nimitz, Carlson was surprisingly honest and candid about his own mistakes during the raid, even admitting that he contemplated surrender during the difficult mission. Nimitz was furious and had all reference to the mention of surrender stricken from the record.

The Raider engagements on Guadalcanal were very different. In early August of 1942, the Marines landed on the island of Guadalcanal in the Solomons Group. If the Battle of Midway was the turning point in the naval war in the Pacific, Guadalcanal turned the tide of the Japanese advance on land. As the Marines clung to their foothold on the heavily defended island, both the 1st and 2nd Raider Battalions were pressed into service, this time as light infantry. In the bitter fighting, Carlson and his Raiders were assigned a defensive role. Then in early December, he was assigned a series of reconnaissance missions into Japanese-held territory to the south and west of Henderson Field, the Marine air base that was continually under siege during the battle. Carlson led two companies of his Raiders, 266 Marines, and a contingent of Filipino scouts on what was essentially a monthlong patrol. They covered some 120 miles of dense, humid jungle on this march, killing close to five hundred Japanese soldiers. Of the 266 Marines who set out with Carlson, some 206 of them were killed, wounded, or evacuated due to tropical disease. Carlson was awarded his third Navy Cross, but he was to state publically that the award he valued most was the unit citation conferred on his battalion. Yet, by all accounts, Carlson led from the front. Aside from the courage of his Marines, I have to step back and wonder how a forty-six-year-old man could have been in the field for that long, under those conditions, and still inspire those who fought under him. He was simply an incredible Marine leader.

No reference of the Raiders would be complete without at least mentioning the 1st Raider Battalion and the Battle of Edson's Ridge on Guadalcanal. The battalion, led by Lieutenant Colonel Merritt

Edson, along with two companies of the 1st Parachute Battalion, engaged a regimental-sized Japanese force in close combat. The Marines were dug in on the Lunga Ridge Line and fought off a banzai-style frontal assault by the Japanese in their attempt to retake Henderson Field. Edson's Raiders held the center of the Marine line that saw some of the bitterest fighting. The ridge was later renamed Edson's Ridge in honor of Edson, who along with his battalion exec, received the Medal of Honor—two of the seven such Medals awarded to Marine Raiders in World War II.

The 3rd and 4th Raider Battalions were formed in the fall of 1942, the 4th being commanded by the now Lieutenant Colonel James Roosevelt. The four battalions were loosely organized into the 1st Marine Raider Regiment. The Raiders continued to see action in subsequent island campaigns, primarily as light infantry. As the war in the Pacific progressed, it became a formatted, large-scale island-hopping campaign—one bloody island after another on the drive toward the Japanese home islands. There proved to be little need for lightly armed Marine raiding-type activity. So senior Marines, led by General Alexander Vandegrift, sought to disband the Raiders. The additional training time and special equipment afforded the Raiders were said to be unneeded when they were being used as light infantry or in defensive roles. There was also the lingering issue of an elite force within an elite force. On February 1, 1944, the four battalions of the 1st Marine Raider Regiment were essentially folded back into the Corps.

A great deal has been made of having a special/elite force within the Marine Corps—in regard to tactical utility as well as the morale issue of having some Marines singled out as more special than others. This has led to some speculation that conventional Marine leaders of that day were just not open to unconventional thinking. In deference to senior leaders like Vandegrift and the taciturn General Holland Smith, the Marine amphibious commander in the Pacific, these men shouldered a great burden. They had to send tens of thousands of young Marines onto those heavily defended and murderous enemy-held beaches. Theirs was also the prospect of a costly invasion of the

Japanese home islands. It was a terrible responsibility. I for one am willing to allow them their focus on taking the next enemy beach and on defeating Japan as ample reason for disbanding their Marine Raiders.

The Marine Raider battalions were in existence for scarcely two years, but they would leave their mark on the "specialized" Marine units that would follow. No more than eight thousand Marines and Navy men served in the Raiders during their existence. After they were disbanded, those Marines went on to serve in the amphibious operations in the drive toward Japan that would end the War in the Pacific. By all accounts, these former Marine Raiders served their Corps and their nation well. Three of the men depicted in the famous image of the five Marines and one Navy corpsman raising the flag atop Mount Suribachi on Iwo Jima were former Raiders.

MARINE DETACHMENT ONE

In 1987, when the United States Special Operations Command was formed, selected units from the Army, Navy, and Air Force were seconded to the new command. The Marines did not send such a unit. The commandant at the time, General P. X. Kelley, did not want to release his Force Reconnaissance Marines from their duties as reconnaissance elements for his Marine Air-Ground Task Forces. Additionally, Kelley did not want to place Marines under the operational command of a non-Marine—a sentiment that resonated throughout the Marine Corps and, to some extent, still does today. Of course, there was the lingering issue from the Raider era of creating an elite unit within an elite corps. So the Marines opted out of contributing an element to the new command. General Al Grey, who succeeded Kelley as the commandant in July of 1987, affirmed that the Marines would not participate in the U.S. Special Operations Command. Assign Marine liaison officers to SOCOM, yes. But a special-operations component such as a Force Reconnaissance element? The Marines were not interested.

While the Marines deferred on sending an existing Marine component to SOCOM, or creating a new unit for that purpose, they did elect to enter the special-operations arena in their own way. First, a little background. The Marine Corps can deploy in packages that range from a division-sized Marine Air-Ground Task Force, or MAGTF, to its smallest integrated force, the Marine Expeditionary Unit, or MEU. The Corps has seven MEUs and keeps one or two of them forward deployed at all times. An MEU is built around a reinforced Marine infantry battalion and comes with a complete array of supporting arms to include aviation assets, light and heavy armor, artillery, air defense, logistics, and so on. An MEU is a mobile, integrated, self-contained mini-Marine strike force carried aboard three large amphibious ships and is usually accompanied by a fleet escort. It's a great comfort for policy makers to have a Marine Expeditionary Unit off the coastline of a potential trouble spot—or nearby when an American embassy comes under siege. An MEU is a flexible and versatile force that can project the power of its combined arms or can be used for humanitarian and civic assistance.

Shortly after the establishment of the Special Operations Command, the Marine Corps began to train and deploy MEUs that were "special operations capable." These new MEUs became known as MEU(SOC)s. In addition to their combined air-ground-force projection capabilities, the MEU(SOC)s took on duties such as personnel/embassy staff security, hostage rescue, long-range reconnaissance, airfield seizure, oil drilling–platform seizure, and at-sea shipboard interdiction—missions that were more in keeping with the character of small-unit/special-operations taskings than that of light naval infantry. Many in the special-operations community felt that the MEU(SOC)s could do little in the true nature of special operations, especially in the culturally sensitive areas of unconventional warfare and foreign internal defense.

The invasion of Afghanistan in late 2001 was largely an unconventional warfare effort. However, that UW effort was supported by a forward operating base called Camp Rhino established in central

Afghanistan by the 15th MEU(SOC). This Marine presence at Camp Rhino, as mentioned earlier, was the longest amphibious force projection in history. During the invasion of Iraq in March of 2003, elements of the 15th MEU(SOC) attacked and secured the port of Umm Qasr. Shortly thereafter, the 1st Marine Expeditionary Force began their drive up the Tigris River to Baghdad. I remember watching with some disbelief as tracked Marine amphibious vehicles approached the Iraqi capital—a very long way from the ocean. They, along with their Army brothers from the 3rd Infantry Division moving north along the Euphrates, were magnificent. Following these successful main-force actions, the issues in Iraq quickly became insurgent and tribal, which lent themselves to special operations–centric solutions, with a focus on cross-cultural disciplines and foreign internal defense. The Marines were deployed to the Sunni tribal lands of al-Anbar Province, which saw the fierce fighting in and around Fallujah and Ramadi. It was not until we reached an accord with the tribal leaders in al-Anbar that some semblance of peace was established. However, the Afghan operations and the aftermath of the Iraqi invasion both suggested that this emerging war on terrorism and the accompanying insurgent activity would become increasingly global and would demand a special-operations approach. So the Marine Corps was compelled to revisit their association with the U.S. Special Operations Command. This resulted in the creation of Marine Detachment One.

Under the urging of Secretary of Defense Don Rumsfeld and at the direction of the commandant, General James Jones, Marine Det One, as it became known, was established on June 19, 2003. This detachment was not configured as a raiding force, though they were certainly capable of raiding activities. While the unit drew heavily on Force Recon personnel, it was not structured as a reconnaissance element. Det One consisted of eighty-one Marines and five Navy corpsmen—all carefully selected. By Navy and Marine Corps tables of organization, it was a very senior and experienced group. Its orientation was one of intelligence collection and special reconnaissance, but the detachment also trained in the SOF staples of direct-action unconventional warfare and foreign internal defense/counterinsurgency. In March of 2004, Det One deployed as an incorporated detachment of Naval Special Warfare Squadron One. It might be helpful to point out that an NSW squadron is built around a SEAL team, in this case SEAL Team One. A squadron will normally deploy with some 225 mostly naval personnel with specialists who deal with intelligence, logistics, ordnance disposal, small-craft support, combat close-air support—all in support of some 100 operational Navy SEALs. SEALs and elements of the full squadron normally have an eighteen-month work-up for a typical squadron deployment. For the squadron veterans, much of this pre-deployment preparation is to review and polish skills employed on previous deployments. The Marines of Det One had only eight months from detachment inception to combat deployment. An overwhelming majority of those Marines were combat veterans; they knew their stuff. It was understood at the time that this was to be an initial, perhaps onetime, proof-of-concept deployment of Marines as a special operations detachment.

SEAL Squadron One and their Marine detachment stepped into the middle of the Sunni uprising that took place a year following the invasion and occupation of Iraq. Much of the work assigned to Squadron One had to do with direct-action missions and personal protection for emerging Iraqi political leaders. The Marines were operationally organized into a single task unit, Task Unit Dagger, that operated in and around Baghdad. Additionally, senior Marine officers and NCOs served in intelligence and operational staffing billets in the Squadron One task group organization. By all after-action reports and from the SEALs and Marines that I spoke with, it was an active and successful deployment.

Following the redeployment of Squadron One and Det One in September of 2004, there was much discussion of the future of this Marine detachment—whether it should remain intact and/or whether they should prepare for a follow-on deployment to continue the evaluation process. And there was a far more searching question being asked. What, if anything, could be taken from this proof-of-concept venture to pave the way for the Marine Corps to take a more active and permanent role within the structure of the U.S. Special Operations Command? At the time, a great many folks at SOCOM and in the Marine Corps were waiting to see where this was headed. A study conducted at the Joint Special Operations University in Tampa, the SOCOM educational and doctrinal arm, concluded:

"The trial deployment demonstrated [that] the Marine Corps SOCOM Det could effectively conduct direct action and special reconnaissance. It is reasonable to suggest that the Detachment could also conduct or support foreign internal defense, counter-terrorism, and special activities, selected theater security cooperation plans, and other tasks as required."

———

Deliberations about the disposition of the detachment continued at the highest levels of the Marine Corps, SOCOM, and the Department of Defense well into 2005, even as Det One began to train for the possibility of another deployment. There was some agreement that there was a need for a permanent Marine Corps unit/presence at the Special Operations Command, but not necessarily one that would lead to the commissioning of Detachment One as that unit. As one might imagine, rumors as to the fate of Det One abounded. The lessons of this detachment were discussed, debated, and catalogued, but the detachment itself was disbanded on March 10, 2006, and those special-operations Marines were scattered back into the Corps. As a matter of historical record, Det One was disestablished *after* the formal establishment of MARSOC on February 24, 2006.

Not unlike their Raider forebears, a great deal has been made of the Marine Corps Detachment One. Books have been written about Det One. The experience of Det One added texture to the deliberations on the role of Marines in special operations, especially because of the rise in importance of the U.S. Special Operations Command since 9/11. When I speak with individual Marines from Det One, they all speak well of their "teammates" from SEAL Team One and feel they contributed to the success of Squadron One's deployment. They also express some frustration in that they were a task unit under Squadron One and seldom operated as a stand-alone Marine detachment. The SEALs, to include the Squadron One commander, had nothing but good things to say about going to war with "their" Marines. That's the way it usually works; the turf wars take place in Washington, but downrange, the troops find a way to work together.

Was there rivalry and friction between the SEAL special operators and the Marines? It's my understanding that there was, but it was friendly, both in context and practice, and that which could only be considered as natural between two warrior classes. There was also competition and respect. What I found most encouraging was the perception on the part of senior SEAL leaders that the Marines in Det One were both creative and flexible—traits deeply embedded in special-operations culture but not necessarily found at the top of a list of Marine virtues. At all levels, but especially at the senior and command levels, the SEALs found the Marines to be superbly professional and easy to work with. When it came to getting the job done, the Det One Marines showed a laser-like focus on accomplishing the mission. Did the SEALs on occasion, individually, have issues with the Marines, and the Marines with SEALs? Yes, they did. Yet the commander of SEAL Squadron One had only to remind both factions of the importance of the venture: "Guys," he told them on more than one occasion, "it's good for the nation, it's good for SOCOM, and it's good for the Marine Corps. Let's press on," and they did.

It was my observation at the time that the Marines learned a great deal from their deployment about special operations, and that the "craft" of SOF was well within these Marines' capability. Still there remained the questions of just what form and composition any new Marine entry into the special-operations mix would take, *and* just how was this Marine SOF component to be funded? We'll visit these issues when we get to the formation of MARSOC in Chapter Three.

CHAPTER TWO

THE FORCE

He who is prudent and lies in wait for an enemy
who is not, will be victorious.

SUN TZU

As this book heads off to the printer, the Marine Special Operations
Command is approaching its projected end strength of just under
thirty-seven hundred Marines, sailors, soldiers, and civilians. The
Command is organized into three subcomponents: the Marine Special
Operations Support Group, the Marine Special Operations School,
and the Marine Special Operations Regiment. The Regiment is made
up of three operating battalions. Each operating battalion has four
companies, and each company has four Marine Special Operations
Teams, or MSOTs. Collectively, these forty-eight MSOTs (pronounced
em-sot) are the pointy end of the MARSOC spear and the key individual Marine special operator in the MSOT is the Marine Critical
Skills Operator, or CSO. At end strength, there will be close to one
thousand CSO-qualified Marines, with just under seven hundred of
those dedicated for MSOT duty in the Regiment. The Marine Special
Operations School trains Marines for duty in the MSOTs. The school
also conducts advanced skill courses and MARSOC SERE (survival,
evasion, resistance, and escape) training. The Support Group is home
to two support battalions and a logistics battalion and trains Marines

in combat support and combat service support disciplines. Among other combat support capabilities, the combat support battalions provide an integrated intelligence capability to the MSOTs downrange. In addition to these three branches, there are the headquarters element and headquarters support components that serve the MARSOC commander, a two-star Marine major general. MARSOC is sited on the Stone Bay portion, or "annex," to Camp Lejeune, North Carolina, but also keeps one operating battalion and one support battalion at Camp Pendleton, California. The MARSOC compound at Stone Bay is anchored by an impressive two-story brick headquarters building which, because of its darkened windows, the MARSOC Marines refer to it as the Death Star. The Marine Special Operations School, or MSOS, also a new construction, is a short walk from the headquarters building. Work is under way for new barracks and extended training facilities and a new complex for the two Marine Special Operations Battalions to move onto Stone Bay proper. This is the Marine Special Operations Command as it stands today.

This work will address how the Command finds, recruits, prepares, assesses, selects, and trains Marines to become Marine special operators, primarily Critical Skills Operators. A majority of the text will be devoted to this CSO training, although it will also later address those supporting elements and "enablers" that are vital to the work of the MSOTs and CSOs.

When the Marine Special Operations Command became a standing SOF force in 2006, the commander, U.S. Special Operations Command, directed it to "produce unit capabilities in counterterrorism, counterinsurgency, foreign internal defense, and stability [operations], and to support counter[ing] weapons of mass destruction and unconventional warfare." While this directive did not specifically address the core SOF activities of direct action and special reconnaissance, DA and SR, these are skills that are basic to the conduct of these directed unit capabilities.

To comply with SOCOM direction, the Marine Special Operations Command stated its mission as one to "recruit, train, equip, educate, sustain, maintain combat readiness, and deploy task organized, scalable and responsive Marine Corps Special Operations Forces worldwide to accomplish Special Operations missions assigned by [the Commander] USSOCOM, and/or Geographic Combatant Commanders employing SOF." Later in this chapter we will address MARSOC's approach to these directives and their mission set. And, central to this work, just how MARSOC trains their Marines for these directed and implied SOF tasks—what the Command has identified as their Core Activities. But first, let's take a quick look at the evolution of the U.S. Special Operations Command, or SOCOM, and just how the other ground-combat components of SOCOM took "operational leave" of their parent services to join this new force.

In 1987, when the Special Operations Command was established, it set up its headquarters at McDill Air Force Base in Tampa, Florida. Also located at McDill is the headquarters of the U.S. Central Command, the recent end-user of many of our SOF assets for duty in Iraq and Afghanistan. In 1987, the Army Special Forces, the Army 75th Ranger Regiment, and the Navy SEAL Teams made their way to the new command. It was a controversial time, and all involved were skeptical of this new venture. I remember that we SEALs were very concerned about leaving the protective skirts of the Navy for this unknown organization commanded by an Army general. Many predicted the demise of naval special warfare as we knew it at the time. However, the training, the mission sets, and the deployment rotations remained the same. New SEALs made their way to the teams by way of Basic Underwater Demolition/SEAL training and an arduous Hell Week. The SEAL Teams still trained SEAL platoons and sent them overseas, where they became a part of the geographic combatant commander's force mix. It was much the same for the other SOF ground-combat components. This, in retrospect, was the beauty and vision of SOCOM. They provided guidance and controlled the funding for the special training of their service components, but allowed these separate cultures to train and evolve in their own way. I recently asked Admiral Eric Olson about this issue—this blending of cultures. In 1987, Admiral Olson was then Commander Olson and commanded SEAL Team One, so he was a SOF unit commander from the very beginning. Subsequently, he served as deputy SOCOM commander from 2003 to 2007 and as commander, U.S. Special Operations Command, from 2007 to 2011. Few in uniform have his perspective when it comes to SOF culture and the formation of MARSOC.

"Special Operations had grown to understand that 'jointness' as we practice it here at SOCOM is not about *integrating* the forces, but about ensuring that the force is interoperable, coordinated, and de-conflicted. In fact, it's best if each component is empowered to reach its own peaks of excellence and within its own identity and culture. The essence or art of a joint command is applying each tactical element as it can best contribute to mission success."

So with the formation of SOCOM, the parent services retained an administrative responsibility for these departing SOF units as well as a responsibility to provide the funds to "man, equip, and train" them. Yet this funding only extended to a baseline equipment allowance and standard training. The Special Operations Command now controlled their training and paid for the special equipment and special-operations training. Then as now, funding for a SOCOM unit fell on the parent service for about two-thirds of the cost while fenced SOCOM funding covered the other third of the cost. For those of us in the SEAL community back then, at least at the operational level, this was a seamless transition. The amphibious commanders had some concern about the future reconnaissance and clearance of landing beaches, but there was nothing in the SEAL mission set that seriously affected, threatened, or conflicted with the blue-water Navy.

The relationship of the regular Army and Army Special Forces was a little different. Special Forces is a separate branch within the Army, just like Infantry, Armor, and Engineering, so there has always been an internal competition for officer and noncommissioned officer talent. When a promising young captain or a proven NCO puts in for

Special Forces duty, he will in all likelihood never return to the conventional Army. The migration of the Green Berets to SOCOM changed little in this regard, and those issues persist to this day. The 75th Rangers have enjoyed perhaps the most amiable and symbiotic relationship with their parent service. The Abrams Charter, under which the modern 75th Ranger Regiment was formed, dictates that the officers, and to a much lesser extent senior NCOs who serve in the regiment, will rotate back to the regular Army after a Regimental Ranger tour. So the Army knows when they release a good first lieutenant to the regiment, in a few years they will get back a very capable and experienced captain. When SOCOM was activated, it allowed the 75th Rangers to continue this rotation policy. While the operational transition of these specially tasked units was taking place, the Marines stood on the sidelines. SOCOM welcomed the few Marine officers and senior NCOs the Corps sent them as liaison officers, but no operational Marine units were cross-walked to the new Special Operations Command.

The SEALs, 75th Rangers, and Green Berets also all had the luxury of being fully formed entities with the relatively easy task of adapting their mission set and organization to the new domestic command structure. Overseas, they still received their operational tasking from the geographic combatant commands. It was a soft transition. Individual operators in the Special Forces A-Teams, the SEAL platoons, and the Ranger rifle companies noticed very little change. Another factor that aided this transition, which for most involved seemed more like a command reorganization than a change of command, was that it was done during peacetime. There were issues of terrorism and what we now call asymmetrical warfare on the horizon. However, we were not a nation at war, nor were our ground-combat forces in constant combat rotation. This made the transition from conventional service command to special operations command a great deal easier. Many of the issues were resolved by trial and error. There were a great many mistakes in those first years of SOCOM, but they did not cost lives in combat. It is through this prism of those early days of the SOF buildup and transformation that we can better appreciate the obstacles faced by the Marine Special Operations Command and the dispatch with which they began combat operations.

Because the Marines stood away from an operational commitment to SOCOM for so long and because of the parochial issues of an elite force inside the Marine Corps, the birth of the Marine Special Operations Command was not without controversy and opposition from within the Corps. There were those in SOCOM who wondered just how and in what form the Marines would join their exclusive club. By 2005, it had become clear that special operations would play a far larger role in this war than in any previous conflict. When it was finally decided, the establishment of MARSOC was a top-down decision and one imposed on the Marine Corps in time of war. This did not particularly endear those who supported a Marine SOF component to those senior leaders in the Marine Corps who did not. Yet once the decision was made, all those responsible for its implementation and execution set about the task of making it happen. Having said that, let me quickly add that as those first MSOTs learned their craft and began to apply it in the active theaters, they silenced a great many of their critics—both within the Marine Corps and at the U.S. Special Operations Command. Utility in the battlespace has a way of doing just that.

It would seem intuitive and rather straightforward that in late 2005 and early 2006, when it was finally decided that there *would* be a Marine SOCOM component, Marine Detachment One would form the nucleus of the new command. This was not to be the case. If there was a reason why those eighty-some Marines who had trained and deployed with SEAL Squadron One were *not* incorporated as a unit into the new Marine SOF command, it has never been satisfactorily explained to me. Instead, they were scattered throughout the Corps, and without doubt, some Marine Infantry and Reconnaissance Units inherited some very talented and seasoned Marines. While many of these Det One veterans managed to work their way back to MARSOC, a great many others finished their military careers in conventional Marine units.

The seed corn for MARSOC came primarily from two Marine components—the Marine Force Reconnaissance Companies and the Marine Foreign Military Training Unit. Let's first take a look at the Reconnaissance Marines. In their recent history, the Marine Reconnaissance Battalions have been configured and trained to serve various masters within the Marine Corps, from the division level down to the Marine Expeditionary Unit level. Their primary mission has been to collect intelligence and perform reconnaissance missions for expeditionary Marine operations. They have also been an agile force, capable of a variety of small-unit taskings such as special reconnaissance and direct action. There are three active reconnaissance battalions and one reserve battalion. These battalions are more popularly known as "Battalion Reconnaissance." A prerequisite to serve in Battalion Reconnaissance is the Basic Reconnaissance Course. This sixty-five-day course features amphibious training, small-unit tactics, and long training days and is, in itself, something of a right of passage.

Prior to 2006 "Force Recon" consisted of two stand-alone reconnaissance companies—the 1st Force Reconnaissance Company at Camp Pendleton and the 2nd Force Reconnaissance Company at Camp Lejeune. Usually working in platoons, the Force Recon Marines served the reconnaissance needs of the Marine *task force* commander. Force Recon platoons were typically assigned missions of deep special reconnaissance and direct action. And in a Marine Corps that has an aversion to "special," the Force Recon companies were often considered just that. Prior to 2006, it was common practice for a Marine who finished the Basic Reconnaissance Course to be assigned to one of the reconnaissance battalions. Then after a tour in Battalion Recon, he might move on to serve with one of the Force Recon companies. So in 2006, a great deal of talent and experience in SOF-like skills resided in the standing Force Recon companies. That changed in 2006.

When MARSOC was commissioned, each of the two Force Recon

companies contributed, or was made to contribute, about half of their recon Marines to the new command. The Force Recon companies had served the needs of their Corps well and in many different roles. Now they were asked to send half of their strength to a unit that would no longer be under the direct control of the Marine Corps. The release of these recon Marines left a gap in the Force Recon capability within the Marine Corps, but brought to MARSOC some very experienced and talented Marines. So from the very beginning, the new command had deep roots in Force Reconnaissance. Those Marines also brought to MARSOC the very special recon culture, a culture that has its training roots in the Basic Reconnaissance Course. So it is not surprising that MARSOC has more than a passing Force Recon flavor and is staffed with some very capable and experienced NCOs from Force Reconnaissance.

The decimated 1st and 2nd Force Reconnaissance Companies were then made a part of the 1st and 2nd Reconnaissance Battalions, leaving these battalions to begin the process of rebuilding the strength of their Force Recon companies. As they rebuilt, the reconnaissance battalions sent a few of their Marines to each Individual Training Class. This has served to lend an ongoing recon flavor to the ITC classes and, ultimately, to the MSOTs of the Marine Special Operations Regiment.

The other contributor to the early MARSOC, less visible but perhaps equally influential, was the Foreign Military Training Unit. The FMTU was activated in October 2005 to be an Army-Special-Forces-like Marine unit that could deploy small teams of specially trained Marines to conduct foreign internal defense. In terms of their language and cross-cultural training, they were perhaps the most SOF-like of those Marines detailed to the new command. The FMTU deployed units that were essentially foreign internal defense teams to Africa and South America before being folded into MARSOC. Once a part of MARSOC, they were among the first units deployed by the Command.

Augmenting the Force Recon and FMTU Marines were Marines from across the Corps—some were veteran refugees from Det One, some came from Marine Military Training Teams (MTTs), some from the ANGLICO (Army/Navy Gunfire Liaison Company) Teams, and some were just good Marines who simply had their hearts set on becoming special operators but were waiting for the Marine Corps to give them that option.

Given that close to two-thirds of these SOF starter Marines were from a reconnaissance background and a third were from the Foreign Military Training Unit, two of the original three MARSOC battalions were initially designated as direct-action battalions and one as a foreign-internal-defense battalion. Elements of MARSOC began to deploy in the summer of 2006. Those deployments increased in 2007 and 2008.

At this point, it might be helpful to step back and take a closer look at the Foreign Military Training Unit. The stated mission of the FMTU was "to provide tailored basic-military-combat-skills training and advisor support for identified foreign military forces in order to enhance the tactical capability of coalition forces in support of the Commander, United States Special Operations Command, and the Geographic Combatant Commanders." It's unclear, at least to me, whether this unit was formed in anticipation of the Marines' eventual entry into SOCOM or as an internal Marine capability put into place to forestall that eventuality. It was designed as a Special Forces–like, purely FID organization that was to stand up twenty-four eleven-man teams, each headed by a major. The teams were to deploy with duties paralleling those of a JCET (joint combined exchange training) deployment, but it had yet to be determined if the funding for these deployments was to be borne by SOCOM or by the Marine Corps—or by the Department of State. There was even some question as to whether the FMTU was to be inside SOCOM or inside the Marine Corps.

Whatever the reasons for its origination or its intended role in the force mix, some very dedicated and experienced Marines poured a great deal of hard work into the concept of this unit. While the FMTU had a very short tenure and deployment history, their inclusion assisted the new Marine SOF component to comply with the SOCOM directive that MARSOC develop capabilities in foreign internal defense and counterinsurgency. Something on the order of a hundred Marines from the FMTU came to MARSOC, and many of them brought with them a native ability in languages.

Both Force Recon and the FMTU were integral to the forming of MARSOC. Yet during my time at Stone Bay with MARSOC, I was constantly reminded that the deepest roots of the Command seemed to be Force Recon. While at the training pool or at one of the medical, communications, and tactical training venues, or on the shooting ranges, it was always easy to find an instructor with a Recon background. The training conventions and customs were very much in keeping with those of Force Recon, especially during the first three phases of the Individual Training Course. With a few exceptions, it was not until the final phase of the course, the irregular-warfare phase, that I was to see more of the former-FMTU Marines.

======

Once the decision was made at the most senior levels of the Department of Defense to fund and establish a Marine Special Operations Command, things began to happen rapidly. The new command was established at Camp Lejeune with a mandate for a brigade-sized force. Without getting into rice-bowl issues and the senior-level wrangling that accompanied those issues, the start-up funding and manning of MARSOC came from monies taken from the Marine Corps budget and Marines taken from the Marine Corps end strength. Neither the funding nor the manning were terribly popular with the senior Marine Corps leadership at the time.

Always Faithful, Always Forward is about MARSOC today and the journey a young Marine must take to be a part of this special operations corps. That is the focus of this work. Yet I felt that it was necessary to mention, however briefly, the issues that surrounded the founding of MARSOC and the forces that helped to shape it during those early days. There was a great deal of both opposition and insistence regarding a dedicated Marine component within SOCOM, and

I can only imagine the heated discussions that took place at the very top echelons of the Marine Corps, the Special Operations Command, and the Department of Defense. It's fair to point out that those senior leaders, civilian and military, were all variously passionate and committed to their duty *and* to the defense of our nation. The stakeholders who fought for their respective agendas have all stepped down from senior command and responsibility. I can only hope they can now take some measure of comfort and pride in what MARSOC has become today, and its contribution to both SOCOM and to the Marine Corps. With respect to the often contentious climate that sometimes marked the Marines' entry into SOCOM, I don't wish to minimize or overstate those formative issues. They are simply a matter of history and have a diminishing impact on MARSOC going forward.

There were also the early agendas, perspectives, and experience that the more junior leaders brought forward, and as with the senior leadership's issues, they were addressed with a great deal of passion and vigor. At the troop level, how was this new force to be organized? How were Marines for the new force to be identified and taken into the new command? Most importantly, given the latitude afforded the Command by SOCOM in defining their missions, how were they to train for this new and diverse SOF mission set? These junior Marine leaders were tasked with building an organization in which they would serve and which they would then leave to the Marines who would come behind them. The mandate that would bring MARSOC into existence was one thing. Just *what* it would be and *how* it would function were another matter. Regarding the stated mission and the mission set, I have spoken with a great many Marines who participated in the early evolution of Marine special operations and the birth of the Marine Special Operations Command. A surprising number of them were involved while they served on active duty and as civil servants after their retirement from active service. My research has led me to conclude that the mission set of MARSOC evolved from (1) what those first Marine special operators could do at the time, (2) how those Marines thought their MARSOC could contribute to the Global War on Terror in the future, and (3) the pressing needs of the current battlespace—which at the time was still centered in Iraq. Regarding this latter issue, keep in mind that in 2006, Iraq was very active and very much in play. The Marine Corps efforts there were focused in al-Anbar Province, and they were fully engaged with the Sunni-backed insurgency in that large western province. The Battle of Fallujah had all but leveled that city, and the pivotal Battle of Ramadi was just taking shape. Al-Anbar was also the focus of much of the SEAL and Special Forces in-theater assets. The Marine special operators that began to deploy in the summer of 2006 were well received during those uncertain and dangerous times. It's sometimes hard to recall, in light of our more recent and hurried exit from Afghanistan, that the Global War on Terror was Iraqi-centric and a seemingly kinetic war without end.

Before moving on to issues that relate to the recruiting and screening of Marines for MARSOC, let's talk about the mechanics of forming this new force. Specifically, just how did those early Marine special operators build their new force in time of war and immediately begin making combat deployments? How did they select and prioritize their missions? In retrospect, what they were able to do in so short a time was nothing short of amazing. Again, their accomplishments might best be viewed through the lens of the existing Army and Navy SOCOM components. The SEALS, Special Forces, and 75th Rangers all had existing combat and combat-support organizations. They were variously dependent on general-purpose forces overseas for basing and security, but they brought with them a command structure, battle staffs, intelligence specialists, a combat support or enabler cadre, and in some cases, a modest logistics train. At their home stations, they had mature, well-established training pipelines. Physically, they had everything from existing barracks facilities to office space to word processors. They had armories filled with automatic weapons and SOF-specific tactical gear. These special operations units often shared shooting ranges, chow halls, and security arrangements on conventional military installations that were supported by established host/tenant relationships that had been in place for years.

These "grandfathered" SOCOM components also brought two other things that are difficult for a new SOF component to orchestrate. The first of these was a job. These existing SOCOM units were in deployment rotation of one form or another and enjoyed pre- and post-9/11 history with their battle-space commanders. They had work, and when they went on deployment, they were going *back* to work. They trained, prepared, and deployed under SOCOM guidance; as events unfolded after 9/11, their contributions as special operators simply became more central to the conflict. The second thing the existing SOF components brought with them to the current fight was their respective cultures. As previously mentioned, culture is very important to a military unit and to a SOF unit in particular. It defines us—tells us who we are. Those first Marines who began to collect at Camp Lejeune brought with them various levels of combat experience from Iraq and Afghanistan, and in some cases, this was combat experience in special operations. Some brought Recon culture, others FMTU culture. Yet collectively, they brought with them their Marine Corps culture. From the beginning, Marines were who they were; special operations was simply the business in which they were now engaged. Perhaps most importantly, they brought Marine Corps standards and Marine Corps values.

MARSOC immediately began operational rotations, modestly in 2006 and more robustly in 2007 and 2008. These first deployments, in the opinions expressed by those Marines who were on those deployments, were sometimes clumsy affairs and often did not match the deploying MARSOC unit capabilities with the needs of the battlespace. As one Marine veteran put it, "On those first rotations, we were basically a large security force with a light-infantry capability and a good bit of direct-action experience. They were more of a learning experience for us than a value-added capability we brought to the battlespace commander." Yet in many ways, the MARSOC units were able to contribute. There were Marines with FMTU backgrounds who were trained in foreign internal defense; they even had some experience in FID, if not an extended deployment history. Most of the

Reconnaissance Marines were combat veterans, and many of those had experience in working with partnership units of the Iraqi and Afghan military. Given a target folder, they knew how to assault an enemy compound and run a targeted enemy combatant to earth. While the muscle memory of the new Marine special operators was heavy on direct action and reconnaissance, the most pressing requirements of the active theaters was clearly in the area of foreign internal defense and counterinsurgency. The theater commanders, and by extension the SOCOM providers, were looking for FID teams to train the locals to deal with what was increasingly becoming an insurgent threat to regional stability. Along with this pressing need, there were Special Forces and SEAL FID teams in the battespace, ready and able to help the new Marine special operators. As one MARSOC senior NCO told me, "There was plenty of work for everyone—more than enough to go around. So there was never an issue that we were taking work from someone else. When we showed up and offered to help, we were made welcome by the other special-operations and general-purpose forces alike."

It was during these formative times—balancing the immediate needs of the current battlespace with their future utility in the Global War on Terror—that the new Marine SOF component identified what were to be their Core Activities. It is these Core Activities in which they currently train their force, in accordance with the guidance provided by SOCOM. The activities are:

Foreign internal defense
Counterinsurgency
Direct action
Special reconnaissance
Counterterrorism
Support (for) counter-proliferation
Support (for) unconventional warfare
Support (for) information operations

In the early days, it was the urgent need of the theater commanders for foreign internal defense and counterinsurgency that drove the MARSOC deployments–work they quickly adapted to in 2007 and 2008, and for which they formally train today. And as has been discussed previously, FID and counterinsurgency (COIN) are the most difficult and training-intensive of all the SOF mission sets. A future conflict may put a premium on other Core Activities, but in Afghanistan and Iraq there were never enough teams skilled in foreign internal defense and counterinsurgency.

As the early MARSOC Marines stood up their organization and began to deploy Marine Special Operations Teams, they quickly realized that two issues had to be resolved for the long-term benefit of their new force. The first was that MARSOC Marines had to have their own separate military occupational specialty, or MOS. The second, which is central to this work, was the need for a formal process that recruited, screened, assessed, selected, trained, and certified Marines to a uniform standard for duty in MARSOC. Both of these would lead to a trained, professional Marine special operator who could be retained or "closed looped" in MARSOC on an indefinite basis. The first formally assessed and selected Individual Training Course convened in October of 2008, which meant the first formally trained CSOs did not enter the force until May 2009. The 0372 Marine Special Operations MOS was approved in January of 2011 and implemented in October of 2011. These measures were incorporated into the new command with close attention to how the other SOF ground-combat components trained and qualified their special operators, and how they prepared them for combat rotation. Before moving to issues of recruiting, selection, and training, it might be instructional to look back to how MARSOC functioned before there was an Individual Training Course and before there was a MARSOC MOS—before there was a formal process that sought to find the right Marines for this duty and to train them to standard. As someone from the outside looking in, I often wonder how they did it. How did they "jump-start" this process and deploy MSOTs before there was a dedicated MOS and before there was a formal training and qualification process? The short answer is that they were Marines—veteran Marines who were assigned a task and simply got the job done.

Those first deployments were made with Marines who had Force Reconnaissance and/or FMTU experience but little in the way of traditional SOF training. There were no codified tactics, techniques, or procedures in place. There was minimal administrative and logistics support in place. And no set criteria by which a Marine was said to be qualified as a Marine special operator. I've spoken to those Marines who were at Camp Lejeune in those early days, and candidly, their accounts vary. The consensus and my conclusions are that those first Marine special operators simply saw the mission requirements and adapted themselves to the task. Force Reconnaissance NCOs drew on their Recon experience and did what they felt was required of a special operations NCO. The platoon sergeants, now team sergeants, knew all about leading Marines; they just took the new mission sets as they were assigned to them and drove on. There were Marines from the FMTU who pushed long and hard for a Marine role in the areas of FID and COIN. Now they got their chance in the active theaters. The junior Marine officers usually had combat experience and, if they were lucky, Recon or MTT (advisory) experience. For the field-grade officers and up, it was more of a challenge. Many of them had the experience of a staff tour at SOCOM or one of the Theater Special Operations Commands, so they understood what a special-operations organization should look like and had an understanding of SOF mission requirements. But there was a great deal of learning on the job. In summary, it was a rare blend—a perfect storm if you will—of Marine talent, vision, dedication, versatility, and perseverance that carried the day and set the stage for what has become the Marine Special Operations Command. They all contributed, yet I have to give special credit, as in my dedication, to those senior NCOs who first came to MARSOC, made those initial ambiguous deployments, and stayed on to lend their passion, experience, and professionalism to the infant command. They held the line until the formalities of a dedicated MOS and a formal training program began to bring the modern MAR-SOC to parity with the other SOCOM ground-combat components.

That MARSOC could, in such a short time and in time of war, come this far and this quickly, can be attributed to the fact that they are Marines. They had only to, if you will, take on the new skill set of special operations. As the reader will see in the next chapter, the MARSOC corporate model is built around proven talent, carefully selected.

CHAPTER THREE

THE SELECTION

Out of every one-hundred men, ten shouldn't even be there,
eighty are just targets, nine are the real fighters, and we are lucky
to have them, for they make the battle. Ah, but the one, one is a
warrior and he will bring the others back.

HERACLITUS

CRITICAL SKILLS AND MULTIDIMENSIONAL OPERATORS

The Critical Skills Operator and the Individual Training Course are the focus of *Always Faithful, Always Forward*. It is the process by which a Marine becomes a special operations–trained Marine—or in the convention I have been careful to use in this work, a Marine special operator. The Critical Skills Operator is the building block of the Marine Special Operations Team or MSOT and the expeditionary Marine special-operations deployment package. It takes, *at a minimum*, four and a half years to create a Marine CSO. This is because a Marine must have served at least three years in the Corps before he can put in for CSO training and duty in MARSOC. Past initial screening, there is the six-week assessment and selection process and, after a possible change-of-station move, the thirty-four-week Individual Training Course. Past the ITC, there may be follow-on training, to include language training, before our special-operations Marine joins his operational team.

Three years or more of duty as a Marine infantryman, amphibious vehicle driver, systems analyst, or air controller may not seem germane to the business of special operations, but a tour of duty in the Marine Corps adds maturity, socialization skills, teamwork, and basic/specialized military training to the résumé of the Marine special-operations prospect. Also there are the cultural imprinting and core values that come from building a special-operations force from a universe of fully formed Marines. As previously noted, MARSOC is the *only* SOF ground-combat component that *does not* recruit civilian volunteers as potential candidates for their force. They begin the process with Marines. When the process is complete, they are still Marines—Marine special operators.

The SEALs and the 75th Ranger Regiment receive the vast majority of their SOF trainees directly from Navy and Army basic training—sailors and soldiers who only a few months earlier were civilians. The Army Special Forces have more of an even balance between veteran soldiers and those recruited from the civilian population at large, but they still have to build their training pipeline around those new soldiers fresh from basic infantry and airborne training. Yet MARSOC first asks for a successful tour of duty in the Marine Corps before a Marine can apply for MARSOC duty. No other SOF component has such a universal prerequisite.

Once assessed and selected, our Marine must then negotiate the Individual Training Course conducted by the Marine Special Operations School. The school also conducts a variety of advanced training courses, but the ITC is the primary training venue there. This CSO training is the counterpart of the Q(Qualification)-Course for Special Forces, the Ranger Assessment and Selection (RASP) for the 75th Rangers, and Basic Underwater Demolition/SEAL (BUD/S) training and SEAL Qualification Training (SQT) for SEALs. At the successful completion of this ITC, an enlisted graduate will have earned the Primary Military Occupational Specialty (PMOS) 0372 designator. He is no longer an infantryman, amphibious vehicle driver, systems analyst, or air controller; he is a Critical Skills Operator or, by my convention, a Marine special operator. From there, our newly minted CSO will join one of the three battalions of the Marine Special Operations Regiment on the way to his Marine Special Operations Team. Depending on the needs of the battalion, the battalion deployment cycle, and the aptitude of the individual CSO, there could be thirty-six to fifty-two weeks of language training in his immediate future. Selected CSOs may receive additional individual and collective training in engineering, communications, and weapons. Others will receive SOF-focused training in specific skills such as sniping, breaching, and close air support to name just a few. In addition to the deployment-cycle predeployment training, there may be other advanced schools and training courses sandwiched between his operational tours. In the life of a CSO, training and cross-training are never over. There is always something new to learn or a technical application/update of an existing skill.

The path of a MARSOC officer initially parallels that of the enlisted Marines. Officers will go through the same selection process and the same thirty-four weeks of the Individual Training Course, plus an additional four weeks at the Team Commanders Course. Following his successful completion of his ITC/TCC training, the graduating officer, a junior captain at this point, will become a Marine Special Operations Officer (SOO) with an Additional Military Occupational Specialty (AMOS) code of 0370. Depending on timing and the operational requirements of his battalion, he may be sent to language school and/or more advanced training.

In support of the CSOs and SOOs is a contingent of Marines that are loosely categorized as the "enablers." They too are selected and trained for duty in the Marine Special Operations Regiment.

The first of these supporting Marines are the Special Operations Capabilities Specialists, or SOCSs. These Marines bring combat support in the form of MOS-specific skills. They support the MSOTs with specialists such as intelligence analysts, explosive ordnance disposal technicians, dog handlers, and fire control specialists. SOCS Marines may receive additional training in critical SOF supporting skills to include language training. They are an MSOT force multiplier and often serve side by side in the field with the CSOs. "When an operational MSOT overseas gears up for a mission," an MSOT team chief said of the Capabilities Specialists, "you really can't tell the difference between them and us." The second group of these enablers is the Special Operations Combat Service Specialists (SOCSS). These Marines, like the SOCSs, routinely deploy in support of the MSOTs; they bring transportation and logistics support to Marine special operations. The Capabilities Specialists and the Combat Service Specialists are carefully recruited and screened. They attend their own special operations training courses to prepare them for deployment with the operational teams. These MARSOC enablers all receive training in SOF communications, foreign weapons, basic tactics, and a variety of other SOF-related skills. Later in this work we will cover the training and duties of the important MARSOC Marines tasked with these special capabilities and combat service support.

There is yet another group that serve alongside the CSO-trained Marines and are standing members of an operational MSOT. These are the Navy corpsmen who serve as combat medics and on occasion, in the battlespace, as medical practitioners. They have a long training pipeline and serve a key role on their MSOT. They are a rarity in that their core training and qualification training is done by the Navy, Army, *and* the Marine Corps. The training and MSOT duties of the team combat medics will also be addressed later in this work.

All Marines and the Navy corpsmen assigned to MARSOC are trained within the guidelines of the MARSOC mission statement to carry out MARSOC Core Activities. Collectively, they are designated as Marine multidimensional operators. CSOs who earn the 0372 PMOS will serve indefinitely within the MARSOC and serve primarily in the Marine Special Operations Regiment. Much of their operational life will be as members of an MSOT, and they will spend a great deal of that life away from home. The Capabilities Specialists will serve in the MARSOC for a projected sixty-month tour, or longer, before rotating back to the standing Marine Corps for future duty. The Combat Support Specialists have a projected minimum tour at the Command of thirty-six months.

Marine Special Operations Officers have a separate and distinct service rotation from their enlisted, CSO-trained teammates. Their designation as a 0370 is an additional or secondary specialty; they retain their primary designation as an infantry, armor, or logistics officer, or whatever is their primary MOS. Yet a large majority of these Marines are infantry officers. They arrive for MARSOC training and duty after three to four years in their primary specialty. Their projected tour with the Command is four to five years. Currently, most have at least one or perhaps two overseas rotations and most have seen duty in Iraq and/or Afghanistan. This initial MARSOC tour will allow for a year of training and three to four years as an MSOT commander. For a few, their time at MARSOC will include a deployment rotation as an MSOT commander and another as a deputy company commander. The expectation is that many of these SOO-qualified Marines will, after a subsequent tour or two with the conventional Corps, rotate back through MARSOC, first as a company commander and perhaps later as a battalion commander. In this fashion, MARSOC has modeled their officer-staffing philosophy after the 75th Rangers', rather than that of the SEALS and Special Forces. SEAL and SF officers remain in SOF command, operational, and staff billets for their entire service careers.

Regarding this 75th Rangers/MARSOC officer rotation policy, there are advantages and disadvantages to this career path for these Marine SOOs. Among the disadvantages is that the practice of the irregular-warfare disciplines of foreign internal defense, counterinsurgency, and unconventional warfare are considered by many (especially those in Special Forces) to be a full-time job—especially in today's complex irregular-warfare environment. It's an exceptional officer who can master these SOF-related disciplines at these various levels of command and leadership and step away from them for three or four years for a tour as an infantry officer with an MEU or some other Marine unit. This is far easier for an infantry officer with the 75th Rangers whose non-SOF duty with the 82nd Airborne or the 3rd Infantry Division is not terribly dissimilar from a tour with the

Ranger Regiment. Our Ranger Regiment is a light-infantry force that executes a far more narrowly defined mission set than do SEALs, Army Special Forces, or MARSOC.

On the positive side of this officer rotation policy, the SOOs who leave MARSOC take their training and experience in direct and indirect special operations back to the Marine Corps at large. The Marine Corps, by the very nature of their expeditionary, Marine Air-Ground Task Force (MAGTF)–orientated deployment orientation, often find themselves in an insurgent or irregular-warfare environment and in a position to use these SOOs to good advantage. And there is every possibility that at some point in the future, the MSOTs will effectively serve as enablers to condition the battlespace for the engagement of an MEU ashore. So these highly capable SOOs may in the long run prove effective ambassadors for Marine Special Operations Forces and create greater interoperability between the regular Corps and MARSOC. As a side note, I do know that the Ranger model as adapted by the Marines for the rotation of MARSOC officers was another of the hotly debated issues at the senior Marine Corps and U.S. Special Operations Command level. Many at SOCOM wanted commissioned, career Marine Special Operations Officers. This issue seems to have been resolved in favor of those in the Corps who wanted to retain some measure of control over those officers who serve in MARSOC—at least for now.

———

Having identified a "corporate model" for their personnel needs and their SOF mission taskings, MARSOC set out to recruit, select, assess, and train Marines to those taskings or Core Activities. Regarding those Core Activities, the Marine Special Operations Command has, in my opinion, taken a bold step in their approach to training their Marine special operators in the indirect SOF disciplines. Much of SOF tasking in the way of direct action is but an extension and refinement of basic infantry tactics. Most of this is found, in one form or another, in the *Fleet Marine Force Manual* and the *Ranger Handbook*. Regarding the direct-action skill set, all Marines get some exposure to these fundamentals in Marine basic and advanced training, but these skills and tactics have to be well learned in order to execute them as a small unit and teach them to others. Yet close to a quarter of the training time in the ITC and an even greater portion of the training dollar go into indirect-warfare training. This indirect-warfare training sets the MARSOC apart from all but Army Special Forces in preparing Marine special operators for duty in the insurgent and asymmetrical environments that are so much a part of the Global War on Terror. In constructing their training in this fashion, I believe MARSOC has acted wisely, for both current battlefield utility (read that as post–conventional force withdrawal in Afghanistan and indirect operations in Africa) and what in all probability will be a future SOF skill set in high demand. The media and the growing legion of former special operators who have taken to writing books will continue to focus on direct action. It plays well in the press and on the History Channel. But as far as the prosecution of our nation's interests overseas and seeking favorable outcomes in ongoing and future conflicts, I put my money on the skills associated with indirect special operations, primarily foreign internal defense. We'll be addressing indirect special operations in some depth during Phase Four and the irregular warfare portion of the ITC and the Team Commanders Course.

If the Marines are looking for a few good men, MARSOC is looking for a few good Marines—those with the ten desired traits of a Critical Skills Operator. We'll get to those ten shortly, but three of them—initiative, adaptability, and interpersonal skills—are essential for success in indirect operations and to be really good at foreign internal defense. So how do we find those individuals who are predisposed to these three traits? How do we identify Marines of proven ability who also enjoy the study of other cultures, do well in languages, and are comfortable in ambiguous situations? The answer is threefold: First you screen and test for it. Then you assess and select for it. And finally, you train for it. With this understanding, let's talk about how MARSOC finds the right Marines for this work.

RECRUITING FROM THE CORPS

Since MARSOC Critical Skills Operator training is open only to serving Marines, the Marine Corps has already made the first cut. From
this pool of candidate Marines, MARSOC recruiters now impose the
next screen, one that is made on paper or, in today's world of electronic
administration, by computer. A Marine wishing to screen for CSO
training must have a minimum score on the GT (General Technical
Knowledge) Test of 105. This test, a derivative of the Armed Services
Vocational Aptitude Battery, or ASVAB, puts a premium on verbal
and mathematical ability. The CSO prospect must then have scored
a minimum of 225 on the Marine Physical Fitness Test and be eligible
for a secret-level security clearance. All MARSOC candidates must
pass the Naval Special Warfare/Special Operations physical, more
commonly known as the jump and dive physical—one that clears them
for parachuting and scuba-diving training. There are time-in-grade/
time-in-service requirements as well. MARSOC is primarily looking
for Marines of any MOS with between three and five years' time in
service—specifically, senior lance corporals, corporals, and junior
sergeants. The Command is no longer accepting staff-sergeant requests
for CSO training, although there may be a few sergeants still in the
pipeline who will be promoted to staff sergeant between the time of
their selection and beginning the ITC. For officers seeking CSO training, MARSOC looks for unrestricted ground officers—career designated first lieutenants and those captains with a year and a half, or
less, time in grade. For both officers and enlisted Marines, there are
requirements that address conduct, professional performance, and
additional medical criteria. Within these established guidelines, I found
there were exceptions made for a particularly talented or exceptional
Marine special-operations candidate. At one time, MARSOC was
looking exclusively for Marines with the infantry/infantry-related
MOSs. This proved too restrictive, so MARSOC duty is now open to
all Marine MOSs. Opening MARSOC duty to all Marines has proved

to be a blessing, especially within the enlisted ranks. Now the deployed MSOTs have Marines with a range of prior military specialties from vehicle maintenance to data processing to advanced communications.

The MARSOC MOS accomplished two important things for the new Command. The first is that they can now retain their 0372 enlisted Marines indefinitely; they are effectively close-looped for the majority of their Marine Corps career. Secondly, MARSOC recruiting is now assisted by Headquarters Marine Corps to help promote the career opportunities for Marines interested in special operations. Internal MARSOC screening teams conduct recruiting/screening forums at Marine installations Corps-wide. These events bring targeted Marines, voluntarily and involuntarily, together to hear a recruiting pitch on MARSOC.

These recruiting sessions, while sponsored by Headquarters Marine Corps, are staffed with MARSOC recruiters and presenters. The one I attended at Camp Lejeune featured a packed house of some 350 Marines—a virtual sea of Marine corporals with a few lance corporals and sergeants sprinkled in. The MARSOC presenters laid out the basic qualifications for entry into the CSO pipeline and talked about the MARSOC mission. There was a slick video followed by an energetic PowerPoint presentation. The "What are we looking for?" slide covered the ten attributes of a CSO candidate:

Effective intelligence
Adaptability
Determination
Dependability
Integrity
Initiative
Stress tolerance
Interpersonal skills
Physical ability
Teamwork

This recruiter focused on two of them: effective intelligence and physical ability—problem solving skills and a strong and persistent desire to be physically superior.

"You have to want this training," the recruiter told the assembled Marines, "both the training and the lifestyle, which will keep you away from home and on deployment a great deal of the time. You will shed your current MOS when you begin the Individual Training Course. If it doesn't work out for you, then you'll probably be sent back to your same MOS, but there are no guarantees."

Following the hour-long program, the assembled Marines were asked to form two lines on either side of the room—those who had questions or further interest in MARSOC on one side and those who had no interest in MARSOC on the other. It was a one-third/two-thirds allocation. The two-thirds in the no-interest line were primarily corporals who were getting out of the Marine Corps. The occasional holdover was a corporal who was happy in his current MOS or a sergeant who wished to remain in the Corps for drill-instructor duty. The recruiter wished them well and checked them off the list. On occasion, he handed one of them a card with an offer to call him should the Marine change his mind. I spoke with several of the one-third who had questions or were interested.

"I want to be in a unit where everyone wants to stay in and not get out," one corporal told me. He was in an infantry battalion.

From another, "I wanted to be an infantryman when I enlisted, but they made me a truck driver. I joined the Marines to fight, and this is a chance to be in an outfit that will be in the thick of it. And to be honest, I'd take any 0300 [infantry/infantry-related] MOS."

"My MOS is closed to advancement due to the downsizing in the Corps," said another corporal. "Any other MOS that is now open to me is very restricted. I want to stay in the Marine Corps. This is a chance for me to stay in and to get promoted."

There were Marines who were variously interested in the additional pay, the physical challenge, duty in a small unit, the special equipment afforded Marine special operators, the chance to serve with an elite unit, and so on. One young sergeant told me, "I just made sergeant, and I'm in for the long haul. But I have a wife and a baby. I'm interested, but I have some questions about the time away from home. I know the MARSOC guys are gone a lot, and I need to know more about that."

As I looked at those in the two lines, the Marines in the line interested in MARSOC stood a bit taller and seemed to be more focused; they seemed to have a better sense of themselves. The difference was slight, but it was there. Perhaps the selection for MARSOC duty had already begun, or perhaps I was only seeing only those individual Marines who were looking for a better way to serve their country.

The officer SOO candidates are screened by a different metric. Officers interested in serving in MARSOC submit packages that detail their duty status, fitness evaluations, standard performance scores, letters of recommendation, and a personal biography. These packages are reviewed and formatted and then sent to the Command. There they are reviewed by a panel of selected members from the school and the Command at large and chaired by the executive officer of the Marine Special Operations Regiment. This panel balances the qualifications of these officers with the needs of the Command and the availability of officer slots in the training pipeline. I'm told that there is an ample supply of quality officers who wish to serve in MARSOC, more than there are billets to begin the assessment and selection process, so this panel has its work cut out for it.

Formally stated, it is the mission of the Command recruiting section to "recruit, screen, and assign qualified candidates from the Marine Corps to attend the MARSOC Assessment and Selection, Preparation and Orientation Course (ASPOC) and Assessment and Selection Course (A&S), with follow-on assignment to the Individual Training Course (ITC) in order to fill Critical Skills Operator billets." The recruiting/screening process is the gateway to ASPOC, and ASPOC is the gateway to A&S. A Marine must successfully complete both ASPOC and A&S to begin the ITC.

To do this MARSOC recruiters first screen and select the best qualified candidates for ASPOC or "the Prep Course" as it is called. The Prep Course at one time was optional for officers and senior NCOs but is currently mandatory for all Marines who attend Assessment and Selection. The three-week Prep Course is immediately followed by A&S, which is approximately three weeks in duration. Marines who qualify to begin this process come to Camp Lejeune on temporary assignment for the six weeks of the ASPOC/A&S cycle. Those who are selected for the ITC will return to their units to await change-of-duty orders that will bring them to MARSOC and Camp Lejeune. For the enlisted Marines, it could be two to six months or more, depending on class convening dates and availability. For the officers, it could be a year or more. Those Marines who are not selected will return to their current duty assignments. The ASPOC and A&S are currently conducted three times a year to meet the requirements of the Individual Training Course, which is currently conducted twice each year. First the ASPOC.

THE MARINE ASSESSMENT AND SELECTION, PREPARATION AND ORIENTATION COURSE

MARSOC recruiters try to enroll 140 qualified enlisted Marines in each Prep Course, which will seek to annually prepare 420 Marine corporals and sergeants for the formal Assessment and Selection Course. There is space for 160 Marines in each ASPOC class, leaving room for as many as 20 officers in each class, or 60 officer candidates annually. All Marines screened and assigned to the Prep Course are strongly advised to have completed the *A&S Ten-Week Preparation Guide* which will condition them for the physical demands of the ASPOC/A&S process. This guided conditioning regimen is a graduated, multilevel fitness program that includes running, swimming, scaling obstacles, and cross-country movement while under a rucksack. The guide is an excellent primer for the demands of MARSOC training, and it addresses more than just targeted physical activity. It's a modern, professional approach to the demands of the military athlete, with movement preparation or warm-up, selected calisthenics, post-workout regeneration, and guidelines for nutrition and hydration. It's simply the best guide I've seen to prepare an individual for the demands of special-operations training.

The goal of the twenty-one-day ASPOC is to physically, mentally, professionally, and emotionally prepare these student Marines for the ordeal that is the MARSOC Assessment and Selection Course. By convention, Marines are referred to as students at ASPOC; when they get to Assessment and Selection, they will be addressed as candidates. The Prep Course is designed to build their confidence, situational awareness, and mind-set for the formal selection process. It's also a time to educate these Prep Course students on the roles and missions of MARSOC, as well as the Command history and heritage, and to condition them to think like a Marine special operator rather than solely as a Marine.

As a historical average, close to three of every four students who attend the three-week Assessment and Selection Preparation and Orientation Course move on to the formal Assessment and Selection Course, which will ultimately determine which Marines will attend the Individual Training Course.

———

At 0800 on Wednesday, January 16, 2013, 120 Marines assigned to ASPOC Class 1-13 begin their check-in process at Camp Lejeune. There are 12 officers and 108 enlisted Marines, so this class is a little smaller than average, especially in the officer ranks. There are no outward distinctions. No one in this course, or in the follow-on assessment course, will wear rank insignia; the captains and the corporals will be evaluated the same. ASPOC Class 1-13 is the first ASPOC/A&S cycle of 2013—again, the first of three. A good amount of time during this first day is given over to insuring that the Marines' service records are in order and that they have been medically screened.

This should all have been completed at their current duty stations, but that's not always the case. At 1730, they muster in the auditorium of the headquarters building, their first formal evolution.

"Welcome to the ASPOC Course. Everyone glad to be here?"

"OOH-RAH!"

This response, variously described as an evolution of the Devil Dog growl or a derivative of the claxon in a diving submarine—AARUGHA—is a universal Marine response in the affirmative. With Class 1-13, it was soft acknowledgment, more sounding like a gutturally pronounced "earl."

"My name is Staff Sergeant Stacey and I will be your chief instructor for your ASPOC training." Stacey is tall, trim, and recently selected for promotion to gunnery sergeant. He is dressed in a golf shirt with a MARSOC logo and creased cargo pants, as are the ASPOC instructor staff in the back of the MARSOC Headquarters auditorium. Yet there is no mistaking that he is the Marine in charge.

"This will be your in-briefing for the course, and before we get to the dos and don'ts of this training, let's talk about why you're here—what we expect of you. First of all, this can be a fun course if you came prepared. If you followed the *Ten-Week Preparation Guide*, you're going to do just fine. If not, then you're going to struggle and some of you may find that what we ask of you is a little more than you bargained for. We are here to teach, train, and mentor, and to encourage you to do your very best as you prepare for the Assessment and Selection Course. We are not here to crush you, nor are we here to babysit you. But we do have expectations. Remember that you are all competing for the limited number of slots in the assessment course. So do your best. Just doing the minimums will not get you into Assessment and Selection; we will choose those who give us the best effort and are most suited to move onto selection, clear?"

"OOH-RAH."

Staff Sergeant Stacey introduces his sixteen ASPOC instructors. Six of them are active-duty Marines with operational MSOT experience. The other ten are former special operators—Special Forces, SEALs, Rangers, and SOF Marines. It's difficult to pick out those still on active duty from those who are not. After a brief course overview and housekeeping issues, Staff Sergeant Stacey pulls up the first slide of a PowerPoint presentation.

"Gentlemen, this is the greatest job in the world, but it's not for everyone. For some of you, the difficulty of this training or the time we are away from home for training or away on deployment may be just too much. That's just the way it is. If at any time you feel this is not for you, then tell your instructor, and he'll take it from there. No angst and no push-back, okay? Now, I don't want to insult your intelligence, but I'm going to read this slide as it's very important. We call it our statement of understanding:

I UNDERSTAND IT IS MY CHOICE AND MY CHOICE ALONE TO BECOME A CRITICAL SKILLS OPERATOR (CSO). I AM AWARE OF THE COMMITMENT THAT IS INVOLVED WITH BECOMING A CSO WITHIN MARSOC. I UNDERSTAND THAT I WILL BE SACRIFICING PERSONAL COMFORTS AND TIME BY CHOOSING TO BE A CSO. IF I AM SELECTED AND CONTINUE ON TO ITC, AND FURTHERMORE TO THE OPERATIONAL FORCES, I UNDERSTAND THAT THIS IS A COMMITMENT FOR THE EXTENT OF MY MARINE CORPS CAREER.

I UNDERSTAND THAT I MAY BE REQUIRED TO SPEND EXTENDED PERIODS AWAY FROM MY FAMILY AND MY HOME. I AM PREPARED TO SACRIFICE TIME WITH LOVED ONES DUE TO TRAINING AND OPERATIONAL COMMITMENTS. IF I AM MARRIED, I WILL ENSURE MY SPOUSE UNDERSTANDS THAT THIS DECISION IS A COMMITMENT FROM HER AS WELL.

I UNDERSTAND THAT I MUST BE MENTALLY PREPARED TO JOIN THE MARSOC COMMUNITY AND MAKE

THE SACRIFICES REQUIRED TO FULFILL MY COMMIT-
MENT TO THIS ORGANIZATION AND THOSE MARINES
AND SAILORS WITHIN THE COMMAND.

For these Marines, the first several days of the Prep Course are relegated to orientation, briefings, gear issue, and testing. They must again pass the standard Marine Corps Physical Fitness Test, or PFT, with a minimum score of 225. They must complete a pass-fail swim assessment that entails jumping from a six-meter platform in utility uniform (as in an abandon ship drill), swimming three hundred meters, treading water for ten minutes, and then conducting a five-minute survival float using knotted clothing as a personal float. During these first few days, and indeed throughout the Prep Course process, the ASPOC students are treated to gradations of swimming, running, physical training, and ruck marches. These initially modest evolutions ensure that all the Prep Course Marines are at least meeting the minimums and that they've not let their conditioning slip between when they put in for MARSOC training and their arrival for the Prep Course. The *Ten-Week Preparation Guide*, if followed carefully, will easily get a candidate through these initial physical requirements. Of special note are the hikes, in boots, detailed in the guide. A candidate must not only make these relatively easy timed marches carrying a loaded rucksack, but his feet must be conditioned so he can complete subsequent marches—during the Prep Course and during Assessment and Selection.

ASPOC classroom evolutions include programs on nutrition and hydration, ruck technique, foot care, and sports psychology. There are presentations on the Marine Special Operations Regiment, the Marine Special Operations Support Group, MARSOC history, and the roles and missions of the U.S. Special Operations Command. The students are introduced to the Personal Resiliency, or PERRES, Program and the associated exercise regimes designed around the combat athlete. They are also introduced and tested on KIMs games—keep-in-mind games that evaluate an individual's ability to observe and then recall his observations. Items are scattered over an area, and the students are asked to note them for a period of time. Then, after leaving the area and at a later time, they are asked to recall in detail what they saw. There are timed runs, but the bulk of time is focused on pool drill, ruck marches, and land navigation.

The ASPOC students will spend close to ten hours in the pool. This is to assess their level of watermanship, but also to let them know that the in-water requirements of CSO training are at a level that many of these Marine special-operations hopefuls have not anticipated. On the ruck marches, they will move under a combat load of seventy-plus pounds for a total of thirty-two miles, beginning with a four-mile ruck and ending with a twelve-miler. Two and a half days are given over to land navigation and land-navigation practical work. The Marine special-operations trainers have taken a page from Army Special Forces preparation and assessment and set up a challenging land-nav course. In spite of the advent of miniaturized GPS receivers and individual tracking systems, there is something about making one's way over unfamiliar terrain armed with only map, compass, and one's pace count that speaks to the intelligence and decision-making ability of a Marine special-operations prospect. To one degree or another, all these Marines have trained in land navigation, and land navigation is a part of the Prep Course and the Selection and Assessment Course. Their ability to make their way from point to point on their own will become a part of their assessment package.

The Marines who attend ASPOC arrive in various stages of preparation and physical conditioning. A great many of them arrive in superb condition, others not so much. Yet they are a far different group from those young men who arrive for basic Marine Corps training at Parris Island just to the south of Camp Lejeune in South Carolina—or for that matter, those soldiers and sailors who begin at other SOF training/qualification venues. The average age of these Marines is twenty-five, and on average, they have two deployments behind them. About half of them are infantrymen and well over half of those have been in active combat. The average GT score is 117 and the average

PFT score is 250. On the final twelve-mile ruck march, they will average well under three hours. Of course, there are a few who due to duty assignment, the constraints of their former MOS, or individual inattention to their conditioning, are only making minimums. Yet most of these Prep Course students seriously want to become Marine special operators. They have prepared themselves accordingly and perform well above minimum standard. For ASPOC Class 1-13, there were five students who scored a perfect 300 on the initial Marine Physical Fitness Test. The best time on the PFT three-mile run was sixteen minutes, thirty-five seconds, and one very fit Marine did thirty-five pull-ups. The first student across the line on the first ruck march, a four-miler, was clocked at just under thirty-two minutes. Those in the ASPOC cadre not involved with timekeeping and record keeping do the timed and graded physical evolutions, including the ruck marches, with their student Marines.

The attrition begins immediately for this ASPOC, with eleven men dropping on the first day. "We get a few Marines who come here to get away from their assigned units," John Miller told me. John comes from a Recon and MARSOC background, and is a retired Marine master gunnery sergeant. Shortly after his retirement from active service, he assumed duties as the director for both the ASPOC and the A&S Course. "Then we get a few of those who somehow felt they could come here and we would get them in shape for selection. Others have just let their conditioning go between the time they met the qualifying standard and their coming here; they just didn't take it seriously. And there are those few Marines who struggled to meet the minimums, and they are just physically unsuited for the rigors of this training. We are also religious about our standards here. We follow Marine Corps guidelines pertaining to all aspects of the Marine Physical Fitness Test. To ensure uniformity and fairness in counting all exercises, we calibrate our staff on what is and what is not acceptable with each exercise in the Marine Corps PFT. A pull-up, for example, is with the chin up over the bar and down to a dead hang with the arms straight—or it doesn't count.

"Students that drop from the course are counseled by the ASPOC senior NCO," John continued. "Through these counselings we've learned that some students who volunteer for MARSOC were dissatisfied with their MOS or their former units and were looking for a way out. Once here they find that we're a Marine unit with a special mission—that perhaps, like their current unit, we too uphold the highest standards of the Marine Corps. And that we also uphold the highest standards of the SOF community."

Not all the screening is physical. During the Prep Course, students also undergo a psychological evaluation that will be part of the screening and evaluation process. The students are individually evaluated on three levels: psychological testing, demographics, and interviews—all of which are designed to measure the student's psych profile against the ten desired characteristics of an effective CSO. The Prep Course students are formally tested with three psychological instruments. The first is the Wonderlic Cognitive Ability Test, which is used to measure learning ability and problem solving. Next, the NEO Personality Inventory tests for extroversion, agreeableness, conscientiousness, neuroticism, and openness to experience. And finally there's the Minnesota Multiphasic Personality Inventory, a standard test that is said to identify personality structure and psychopathology. The MMPI is widely used by the military and government agencies for security-clearance screening.

This battery of tests is used to identify those strong or dominant tendencies in an individual that may prove to be strengths or weaknesses in his character or performance. The psychological assessment team likes to see low scores on traits like anxiety, anger, and depression and on a tendency to be overly self-critical. Traits like cautiousness, responsibility, organization, discipline, leadership, and self-motivation the assessors like to see score high. On occasion, the testing can surface some pathology or personal issue that makes an individual unsuitable for this training or for duty in MARSOC, but this is rare. The results of these tests become a part of the prospective CSO's assessment package.

Demographics seemed an ambiguous concept to me, but the command psychologist, Dr. Carroll Green, explained it like this: "The demographics have to do with a Marine's early environment, family values, perhaps a history of abuse, cultural opportunity, and education. These characteristics are not in themselves positive or negative but speak to the background of the individual. For example, someone with a history of family abuse or dysfunction may be looking for order and fairness, and strive to achieve this in his personal and professional life. This makes for a good Marine and a good Marine Critical Skills Operator."

An issue or combination of issues may lead a staff psychologist to call an individual Marine in for an interview. "These consultations are to probe an issue more thoroughly or to address a trend that falls outside our norms for a prospective Marine special operator," Dr. Green said of the interviews conducted during the Prep Course. "Unvariably they get resolved by talking it over with the Marine, and he continues with the Prep Course. We interview maybe 10 to 15 percent of the Marines in a Prep School class. Every Marine who is selected for the ITC at the A&S Course will be interviewed by someone on our staff or one of the contract psychologists."

The second week for Prep Class 1-13 is shortened by Martin Luther King Day. Following the holiday observance, the class receives classroom work in land navigation, nutrition, and physical training. The days are long, beginning with morning chow at 0430 and with the last evolution ending at 1900, or 7 p.m. These long days, the prep students are told, are how it will be over the course of the ITC. "It will be a marathon," Staff Sergeant Stacey informs them of the CSO training, "not a sprint." The second week is a continuation of the first and finishes with two days of daylong land-navigation field exercises. These map-and-compass evolutions are done with the same seventy-pound rucksack and equipment load as on the timed ruck marches.

"It wasn't as bad as I thought it might be," one of the Prep Course students told me. "On the first leg I got lost and paid for it by retracing much of that leg of the course. Carrying the pack added to the time and pain. But the instruction they gave was very good. I'm a little concerned about doing this at night, so we'll see how that goes."

The final days of the ASPOC are devoted to PERRES workouts, physical training, pool-training evolutions, medical and nutritional counseling, endurance runs, and longer ruck marches. There is a final PFT and swim assessment to calibrate/assess any change in student performance over the course of ASPOC. ASPOC Class 1-13 is individually close to 20 points stronger in the PFT at the end of the Prep Course than at the beginning. On the final PFT, six students score a perfect 300.

One-Thirteen closes out the Prep Course with a twelve-mile ruck march they are expected to complete in three hours. The first Marine student crosses the line in an hour and forty-eight minutes. That's a nine-minute-mile pace with a load of more than seventy pounds. The slowest ASPOC Marine finishes in two hours, fifty-two minutes. Thursday afternoon and Friday are given over to a final medical record review, gear turn-in as needed, barracks cleanup, and the selection process—just who will and will not move on to the formal Assessment and Selection Course.

Attrition or "self deselection" goes on throughout ASPOC. Most of those who leave do so voluntarily. A few of those come to realize that they haven't the desire or the mental toughness to stay with this program. The prospect of the long days over the many months of the ITC causes them to rethink their goals. Others, on learning more about the life and deployment commitment of a MARSOC Marine, conclude that this is not how they want to serve their country. Still others, while they are still making minimums, realize that minimum standards, even if they are selected, are not enough to get them through the ITC. So by the time ASPOC is drawing to a close, most of those not suited for CSO training have left the course.

As the course director, John Miller convenes a review panel along with the senior NCOs from both ASPOC and A&S cadres to determine those students that will be recommended as "no-gos" for the A&S Course. These recommendations are based on overall performance and cadre observation comments. There are three critical graded evolutions. Failing to swim three hundred meters in thirteen minutes or less, scoring below 250 on the final PFT, and finishing the twelve-mile hike in more than three hours are all below acceptable standard. Failure in two or more of these three events, along with cadre comments, are the data points on which the commanding officer of the Marine Special Operations School will make his final decision regarding these marginal students. Those student Marines who will not be moving on to Assessment and Selection are counseled by the cadre and out-processed to be returned to their units. Some are encouraged to go back to their units, work on their deficiencies, get stronger, and return for a future ASPOC. Others are not. From Class 1-13, twelve Marines are brought before the review panel to address their shortcomings. Four of them, having been made aware of their marginal performance, are allowed to move on to A&S. In total, 79 of the original 120 ASPOC Marines will move on to the Assessment and Selection Course.

THE ASSESSMENT AND SELECTION COURSE

The Prep Course and the Assessment and Selection Course could not be more different. The Prep Course is all about conditioning, educating, mentoring, and otherwise predisposing candidates for success in A&S. At A&S, the candidates will be stressed, tested, and evaluated to see if they have enough of the ten desired attributes of a CSO to be selected for the Individual Training Course. There is no coaching or mentoring. Of those ten attributes, adaptability, initiative, stress tolerance, interpersonal skills, and teamwork are closely examined. Whereas the instructor staff in the Prep Course were helpful and approachable, those at A&S are detached. They are there to conduct an assessment of these candidates, not to help them. Who can think on their feet and who cannot? Who can deconflict the ambiguous? And who, when he's tired, sleep-deprived, and hurting, can still be a good teammate?

These are the kinds of things the Assessment and Selection Course seeks to find out.

"We have well-defined roles in this process," Gunnery Sergeant Adam Parker said of preparation and selection. Gunny Parker is the senior noncommissioned officer in charge, or SNCOIC, for the ASPOC and A&S Courses. "On the ASPOC side, we do all in our power to prepare a Marine for the A&S Course. In the A&S Course, our job is to assess and select Marines for the Individual Training Course. Neither of us, at the ASPOC or A&S, are selecting Marines to become CSOs; we don't make that cut or that determination. That's for the Individual Training Course cadre and trainers. Our job is to first find the right Marines to enter the assessment arena and, from there, to find the right Marines to enter the ITC training pipeline.

"I think we do a pretty good job of this," the gunny continued. "We go to great lengths to make sure that the Marines who come to Selection get a fair and equitable chance to show us they have enough of the ten traits of a successful CSO to move on to the ITC. To that end we've created our own confined world of sorts, a vacuum if you will, that's free of external influences and distractions. It's a very level playing field. We put these candidates in situations that allow them to show us they have what it takes to succeed. In some ways it's impersonal and clinical, but so is it fair—one that allows each candidate to individually succeed or fail within the framework of our evaluation process."

All special-operations components have their particular testing rituals, rites of passage, and component/service-centric gauntlets by which they assess and ultimately select those individuals they will admit to their band of brothers or their band-of-brothers in training. And there seems to be a good supply of young men who wish to serve in these SOF brotherhoods. It's the same with these fine Marines seeking to earn their admission slip to MARSOC training. In some ways, these vettings may seem like a rite of passage. In the past, these rituals have been, to various degrees, mindless, abusive, and arbitrary.

It's been my experience over the past fifteen years of close association with special-operations training venues that the dysfunction that may have accompanied these SOF-component selection programs in the past no longer exists. They are, by and large, highly focused sorting processes. They are programs that quickly test and identify those individuals who have the potential to be trained to function within the mission set of that particular SOF component—nothing more and nothing less. This does not mean that they are easy or, from an outsider's perspective, terribly compassionate or even humane. Yet the medical oversight is ongoing and comprehensive. The candidates are tested—physically, psychologically, professionally, and morally, often to their personal and emotional limits—to see if they have the right stuff. The process for which they voluntarily submit themselves has value. It tells the candidate himself if he *really* wants to do this, and it tells the organization if the candidate *really* has that special something inside him to perform in a hostile, ambiguous, demanding environment. And it's terribly revealing. Few processes in our culture, military or otherwise, lay bare the physical, psychological, and emotional worth of an individual as do our SOF evaluation programs. It is a rendering for the essentials of the human spirit.

The managing partner of a large and prestigious law firm once told me there are intelligent and gifted law-school graduates who come to him every year and want to be lawyers. Then there are those modestly talented, hardworking law-school graduates who really want to practice law. "I first look for those in the latter category," he told me, "then I sort through these few to find those who have it within them to win cases in favor of their clients—no matter what it takes or how long it takes. Then I hire 'em." It's not a lot different from selecting special-operations candidates, although MARSOC screening seems to recognize and select Marines with intelligence and talent as well as other traits. Yet they must still have that drive to succeed—the will to win.

MARSOC, in the process of establishing their Core Activities, has determined the kind of Marine they are looking for to train to these

Core Activities. That Marine must have the same ten essential elements identified earlier as a prerequisite for the making of a Critical Skills Operator.

In the development and implementation of their assessment and selection process, the Marine special operators visited other SOF selection programs and saw how the other components selected their personnel. There was a great deal of useful information to be gained in seeing how others conduct their assessment and selection—especially the Army Special Forces process. This seems only right in that Marine special operators and the Green Berets share an indirect-warfare focus in their training pipelines and their mission taskings. Yet those veterans who constructed the ITC were mindful that there were differences in the making of a MARSOC Marine. One of those is that they are in the business of what I will call "expeditionary SOF" in that their operational teams need to be versatile and capable of a broad range of SOF and maritime SOF disciplines *and* they have to deploy and operate with a minimum of support. Those who are selected for the ITC were, are, and will always be Marines—able to live hard and with minimal creature comforts.

This "a Marine first" theme carries strongly through the selection process and for good reason. Since the Marine Corps is much smaller than the Army, and will remain America's premier expeditionary, small wars–capable force in the future, those in MARSOC have been careful to remain close to their parent Corps. I think this is also for two other reasons. One is that they see nothing incompatible between being a Marine and being a Marine special operator. On the contrary, they see the alliance as a great positive. And secondly, they feel that the Marine Special Operations Command has a role to play both in our nation's special-operations force mix and in support of the Marine Corps.

As for the MARSOC assessment and selection process itself, I found it to be focused, well organized, and with a great deal of attention to detail. Close to one hundred contractors, cadres, and training specialists are involved in the conduct of a single A&S Course. The review process that makes the final determination of who will and will not attend the ITC is formal, formatted, and supported by a state-of-the-art evaluation software package that is used throughout the ITC. The final board is chaired by the Marine Special Operations School commanding officer, Colonel James Glynn. He is joined on the board by the school's master gunnery sergeant, the regimental sergeant major, the regimental operations master gunnery sergeant, and the ASPOC/A&S SNCOIC, Gunny Adam Parker. Collectively, they represent well over a century of Marine Corps service.

The board selects ten officers and thirty-five enlisted Marines from ASPOC/A&S Class 1-13 to attend the ITC. Following the final selection, as is the practice, the school commanding officer collectively congratulates those who successfully completed the Assessment and Selection Course. He also individually counsels those officers who were not selected, just as the school master gunnery sergeant does for the enlisted non-selectees. This particular class, Class 1-13, experienced a lower selection rate than has been the case with previous classes. It is the policy of MARSOC going forward to look for more junior Marines from the pool of qualified corporals and junior sergeants. There were no staff sergeants in ASPOC/A&S Class 1-13. The relatively junior composition of this class may have contributed to the low percentage of selectees for the ITC. It would seem, at least to this writer, that the CSO attributes of adaptability, dependability, interpersonal skills, and stress tolerance are marginally easier to find in a twenty-six-year-old Marine than in a twenty-two-year-old Marine. So it would appear that the ITC standards are being met by the younger Marines selected, even as the percentage of those selected is lower. It just may take a few more of them to begin the screening and selections process in order to find those with the desired traits.

I'm most fortunate to have been allowed to closely observe all the major SOF ground-force assessment and selection programs. While these venues are highly scripted and well supervised, they are also private and what takes place there is often closely held. It's not that these programs are classified, but rather that ambiguity is a part of the process. I was asked not to write about what takes place during the (ambiguously approximate) three-week MARSOC Assessment and Selection Course.

"We feel that the less these candidates know about what is in front of them the better," John Miller said of his course. "We do this at a remote location, and the conditions under which we select our Marines for the ITC is austere, challenging, and dynamic. We feel that the uncertainty and isolation help us to focus in on those ten traits that are essential in the Marines we select. We learn a great deal about these candidates during our selection process, and they learn a great deal about themselves. It's a work in progress, just like the other SOF assessment and selection venues. We receive continual feedback from the leadership at the Individual Training Course, and from the candidates themselves. Using this feedback, we are able to make minor adjustments to the course without changing the basic dynamics of a program which has historically served the Command well."

It's not my intention to compare the MARSOC assessment and selection process with the other SOF components'; each is carefully designed to meet the specific needs of that individual SOF component. Yet like the other SOF unit admission criteria, MARSOC asks that a prospective special warrior give 100 percent of himself during this process and that he care for his teammates as much as himself. Each candidate must look into himself and inventory his personal commitment to the goal of joining this brotherhood. *Do I really want to do this?* and *Am I personally willing to pay the price?* The School Training Branch master gunnery sergeant remarked on this when he spoke to the candidates of Class 1-13 shortly after their arrival at ASPOC: "During this assessment and selection process, you will work in teams, but you will be assessed individually. Each of you must show us individually and as a teammate that you want to be here."

Those forty-five Marines selected from Class 1-13 for the ITC will return to their current duty assignments, complete their tours, and then return to begin their journey through the Individual Training Course. Not all will return. Approximately one in ten will choose not to accept orders for the ITC. For some, a more careful reflection with time and distance will cause them to change their minds about coming to MARSOC. Other talented and capable Marines will, perhaps with some encouragement from their present command, choose to stay with their current duty station in a position of increased responsibility. Before we move on to the ITC, a word about those Marines *not* selected. In most cases, those Marines deselected themselves. They found that the demands of this calling were just too great, or once they came to a better understanding of what the duties of a CSO in MARSOC entailed, they felt they could better serve their nation and their Corps somewhere else. Not unlike other SOF selection processes, the ASPOC and A&S cadres see their role as one of not only finding the right Marines for selection or the right Marines for ITC training as the case may be, but to ensure that those who do not screen for the ITC are better Marines for the experience. With that, let's move on to the heavy lifting of creating Marine Critical Skills Operators from these well-assessed and highly selected Marines.

=====

Author's note: Again, it is not my intention here to compare the methodology of MARSOC in their selection process with other SOF components, or to evaluate or validate their program in finding the right Marines for their Core Activities. Their ten essential traits seem well articulated and appropriate for the Marine special-operations brand, and their recruiting, screening, preparation, assessment, and selection seem to sort and find those individual Marines best suited for CSO training. I do wholly agree with their philosophy: find those most suited for your mission set, train them to a high standard, and release those that are not selected back to their parent units the better for the experience so they can continue to serve their country.

Over the past two decades, I've been a student of special operations and, more specifically, a student of special-operations training. I'm often asked, what does it take to be a Green Beret—or a SEAL or a soldier with the 75th Rangers? I'm sure to be asked to compare CSO training to that of the other SOF components. In fact, that question is often put to me by MARSOC students and cadres alike. SOF selection venues have a great deal in common, yet each is looking for those special and sometimes unique qualities that are compatible with their mission set and their culture. In the course of my work, I have identified five characteristics that I find common to all successful special-operations training candidates. They are presented here as a comparative exercise. I'm happy to say that there is nothing exclusive or incompatible between my five attributes and the MARSOC ten.

1. Physical Toughness. While it is intuitive that any special-operations candidate has to be fit, that requirement is not so easily met as one might think. Young Americans now grow up neither eating as well nor exercising as much as previous generations. Fast food and sedentary lifestyles have rendered many young males unfit for the physical demands of basic military service. It's been my observation that apart from all-around fitness, "durability" is the key component in the physical makeup of a SOF warrior. Durability in military-speak is hard to define, but carrying an eighty-pound rucksack on an all-night forced march and being able to fight throughout the following day is a good start. Being a star high-school athlete does not always make a young man durable. Many young American males are simply physically unsuited to basic entry-level military training, let alone the elevated standards of a serving special operator.

2. Intelligence. Special operations is not brain surgery, but I contend that intelligence is a key factor in nearly every endeavor, whether you're a counter jockey at Burger King or a paralegal in a law office or a special operator. The single most competitive commodity for those looking for new hires is smarts. A large body of evidence suggests that the best barbers, waiters, policemen, health-care workers, computer programmers, and warriors are the smart ones—those who learn quickly and are able to apply that learning

to operational tasking. The armed forces are generally prohibited from giving IQ tests, but they do use certain testing instruments to identify aptitudes and certain predispositions—from which intelligence can be inferred. Along with intelligence are the related mental abilities like judgment, problem solving, and decision making. A great many attributes that make for a good soldier, sailor, or Marine can be taught through drill and conditioning. Unfortunately, intelligence is not one of them. The SEALs, the 75th Rangers, the Special Forces, and MARSOC are all looking for candidates who are smart. Those charged with the assessment and training of special operators use personality and psychological testing instruments as indicators. But the final measure of who makes it and who does not is the candidate's ability and his desire to measure up to a physical and professional standard.

God-given intelligence aside, a great many Americans have been pushed through a primary and secondary educational system that has left them intellectually unsuited for even basic military training, let alone the intellectual requirements of a special operations unit.

3. Mental Toughness. This is a difficult attribute to measure and it's different from intelligence, but drill sergeants and military trainers the world over recognize it when they see it in a young recruit. Perhaps it is a blend of confidence and determination. I believe it comes from a young person's parenting. Parents who have raised their children with high expectations and discipline have predisposed them to mental toughness. Mental toughness can also be as simple as a pattern of finishing what you start. It conditions a young person to expect success and not to be a quitter. This can be a powerful force for success in basic military and special-operations training. I've been to more than a few SOF-component graduations and have made it a point to meet the parents of those young men I considered mentally tough. These were proud parents, but without exception, none were surprised that their son had

completed a difficult and highly selective training regime. It's how they raised all their children.

Mental toughness and intelligence seem to be qualities found in those who set goals and accomplish them. There is also a very high degree of success in those young men who are smart enough to clearly see their goal and have the mental toughness to persevere in achieving that goal.

4. Ethical Maturity. On today's insurgent battlefield, right conduct and strict adherence to specific rules of engagement are becoming increasingly important. The target demographic for military service is a video- and online-centric generation. While that may predispose them to be good with computers, it also exposes them to a great deal of video violence, often gratuitous video violence. Military special operations deal in real violence, not video violence—big difference. Sometimes, the decade or so of video games, reality TV shows, and the farce-fighting of professional wrestling in the life of a twenty-year-old leaves an imprinting that's at odds with reality. To the extent that it exists, this imprinting has to be overcome before a SOF candidate can become a warrior. SOF warriors are in the business of taking life and exercising the moral restraint to not take life—often on the same operation and perhaps in a single engagement. Ethical grounding is as important as professional combat-arms skill. Young special operators have to exercise proportionality and restraint along with the courage and professionalism to engage in mortal combat. Fortunately, there are young men who can do this—who understand right and wrong in the real world. Many others have simply spent too much time in front of the TV or playing video games and cannot.

5. Patriotism. We don't often think of this as a warrior-requisite skill, and certainly not as one that is reserved for warriors, but for those serving in ground-combat roles, it is most important. It's not an attribute conferred by waving the flag or a conservative political persuasion. It's not just a willingness to serve one's country,

although that's important. This kind of patriotism is a deep-seated belief that a warrior, in uniform and in the service of his nation, has the moral authority to take human life. The military in general and special operators in particular are in the business of killing people. For those who fly drones or employ standoff weapons, killing is almost an abstraction as they are physically far removed from the battlefield. Not so for a special operator; it's up close and personal. A dead insurgent fighter is part of the job; so is the unintended and unfortunate death of a noncombatant. In casual soldiers' banter, killing can be trivialized or the enemy can be so demeaned as to appear less than human. If this casual banter goes to motive, then the warrior is potentially on a slippery ethical slope. Patriotism is the primary moral armor of our ground combatants. Their professional skill gets the job done and gets them home physically intact. Patriotism—the belief in a righteous fight—is what returns them home mentally and morally intact.

It's been my experience that those seeking to serve in SOF-related units with no patriotic grounding usually do so for some misplaced personal agenda, macho reason, or to prove something to themselves or someone else. These men are usually incomplete and ineffective warriors. Patriotism leads to self-sacrifice and team orientation—both solid SOF attributes.

———

With this understanding of the MARSOC selection process, let's move on to the training of Critical Skills Operators.

CHAPTER FOUR

THE ITC: BASIC SKILLS

We must remember that one man is much the same as another,
and that he is best who has training in the severest school.

THUCYDIDES

IN PROCESSING

At 0555 on Wednesday, November 14, 2012, Individual Training Class 1-13 stands at their ease in formation behind their dated, two-story brick barracks. The barracks and the formation area are just outside the gated MARSOC compound on the Stone Bay portion of Camp Lejeune. Stone Bay itself is a mini-base separated from Camp Lejeune proper by the New River. It has a chow hall, two small gyms, a tiny base exchange, an extensive series of rifle ranges, and the MARSOC headquarters complex. On the MARSOC grounds proper, there are academic facilities, shoot houses, a paraloft, a diver-training tank, rappelling towers, and physical training fields. Class 1-13 has just come from the chow hall, taken a few minutes to straighten their barracks spaces, and now wait in four distinct groups. There are seventy-nine of them; three twenty-man student Marine Special Operations Teams and a single student MSOT with nineteen. They are dressed in standard green Marine woodland-pattern camouflage utility uniforms, or MAR-PATs. The only thing out of the ordinary is that each student has a twelve-foot length of black climbing rope, doubled and carried across his torso. The rope is worn around the nape of the neck, looped down over the front of each shoulder, then underarm of the opposite shoulder, and tied in the small of the back with a double sheet bend knot.

Dawn is not far off, but for now the new ITC class is bathed in the iodized wash of the nearby streetlights. A brisk western breeze pushes a few dead leaves across the tarmac of the formation area. It's a moist, chilly wind with a bite to it, yet it serves to hold off the fog hovering over the broad reach of the New River just to the east. Rain is in the forecast, and the absence of stars serves to document the low overcast. The assembled Marines talk quietly as they await the training cadre who will direct them on this first day of their nearly nine-month journey to become Critical Skills Operators. A great many of these ITC students know each other from the Assessment and Selection Course, though not all of them are from the same A&S class. Nearly all are new to the ITC, but there are a few refugees from Class 2-12 or previous classes, held over due to an injury or performance issues. Class 1-13 will share their barracks building with Class 2-12, who are midway through their Phase Three training and have already begun their training day. Class 1-13 is the tenth MARSOC ITC class and will be the first to graduate in 2013. There are twelve Marine officers and sixty-seven enlisted Marines in the class. The students, as they are referred to in the ITC, have been checking into the barracks over the last several days—some for the past several weeks, depending on duty location and duty rotation. Those who arrived early were detailed to the MAT platoon—Marines awaiting training. There they were assigned light support duties and allowed time to continue their physical preparation for the ITC. This is 1-13's first formation as a class.

The training for this ITC class will be structurally different from that of Class 2-12. The Basic Skills Phase, which they begin today, was for 2-12 called Phase One. For 1-13 it is Phase Zero or Basic Skills. Phase Two of the course was once a more lengthy phase titled Small Unit Tactics. For Class 1-13 this phase has been sectioned into two phases: Ground Combat and Amphibious Operations being one phase, followed by Special Reconnaissance, which is now a phase of its own. The phase content, while modified and expanded, is much the same. Yet no two ITC classes are alike; with each class come enhancements and refinements. Indeed all SOF training venues are continually being refined and updated to meet the changing requirements of the operational end users.

A Marine with starched desert-pattern utilities and an air of authority steps in front of Class 1-13. He is a slim six-footer with an open, boyish manner that seems at odds with his focused intensity. His Navy-Marine Corps jump wings and Marine combatant diving badge mark him as a special operations Marine, and in this case, a former Recon Marine.

"Good morning, Marines."

"GOOD MORNING!"

"My name is Gunnery Sergeant Patterson, and I will be your proctor for the Individual Training Class. I hope to be there with each of you on graduation day, 5 August, 2013, and to congratulate you on successfully completing this course. These gentlemen behind me are your TACs [pronounced tacks], and they will be with you during this initial phase of your training." Behind Gunny Patterson are four staff sergeants who introduce themselves in turn. They are dressed in boots, tan MARPAT utility trousers, and black cadre sweatshirts. In the Army, TAC stands for training and counseling; in the Marine Corps, it means tactical advisory cadre. The class will be broken down into their four student MSOTs for training, administrative, and accountability purposes, with one phase TAC assigned to each student MSOT. The student leadership and student chain of command will flow through the student officer team commander and the student enlisted team sergeant—the team's senior officer and senior sergeant. By convention, there is no student class leader. The ITC students will remain in these same teams throughout the course except for an occasional rebalancing that might be needed due to attrition in the class.

The tactical advisory cadre Marines are experienced staff sergeants who have stepped out of operational rotation from their Marine

Special Operations Battalion for a tour with the Marine Special Operations School. Once at the MSOS, they were screened and selected for duty as ITC TACs. Some of them serve as TACs full-time, while others split time between duty as TACs and duty as subject-matter experts in other phases of training. Most have served as MSOT element or squad leaders and bring current MSOT operational experience to the training. These TACs have had at least two MARSOC deployment rotations before coming to the school and many have had three. In terms of the recent rotations to Afghanistan, this translates to somewhere between fourteen and twenty-four months of combat in an MSOT. Most of them have had multiple combat rotations before coming to the MARSOC. For Class 1-13, there are two TACs from the 3rd Marine Special Operations Battalion and one each from the 1st and 2nd. As if to document the heritage of the MARSOC as well as its youth, neither Gunny Patterson nor any of his TACs attended the ITC; they are all former Force Recon Marines who came to MARSOC and, after the pre-deployment training cycle, went immediately into deployment rotation.

Staff Sergeant Jamie Baker is from the 1st Marine Special Operations Battalion at Camp Pendleton in California. Baker is from Texas, twenty-nine years old, and has been a Marine for eleven years. He has had three overseas rotations prior to coming to the MARSOC, the last as a Recon squad leader in Ramadi. Since then, he has made two combat rotations with a 1st Battalion MSOT, both to Afghanistan. Staff Sergeant Baker is balding, stocky, and has the physique of a weight lifter. Yet he has an easy smile and is unfailingly polite. Baker arrived at the school just six months ago along with his wife of just eight months. Both are still making the California-to-North Carolina adjustment.

"Okay, bring it in," Gunny Patterson says, and the class breaks formation and collapses in around their proctor. Staff Sergeant Baker and the other TACs stand off to one side. "This is a long course and a difficult one. In some ways it will feel like your last [overseas] workup as you'll be working long hours and traveling to remote training locations. I expect 100 percent from each of you. Give it your very best, and you'll succeed here. These first ten days of In Processing are designed to take care of the admin issues and to get in some of the preliminary indoctrination and routines before the core instruction of Phase One begins. We'll also get in some good morning physical training. These In Processing days will also get you into the daily rhythm of the ITC. We start early and often work well into the night. That's just the way it is. Keep in mind it's a long school with long training days. The main portion of Phase One will begin on 3 December. Between now and then, there will be a lot of hurry up and wait. Nevertheless, pay attention to what we teach you during this Basic Skills and In Processing period. It will get you better prepared for when we begin the core training."

Class proctors are E-7 gunnery sergeants carefully selected for the role of managing and mentoring a class during the ITC. Gunnery Sergeant John Patterson, recently promoted to E-7, was a TAC for Class 2-11 as a staff sergeant. He is a Massachusetts native who attended college for two years at two universities. He's been a Marine for just under twelve years. After his third change of major, he decided to put aside his college studies and joined the Corps. When the first airliner slammed into the first World Trade Center tower he was in his Marine advanced infantry training in 29 Palms, California. Following infantry training, Private First Class Patterson was posted to Okinawa, where he sat out the initial Marine actions in Afghanistan and the push into Iraq. Disappointed at missing these first campaigns of the new war, he put in for Marine reconnaissance duty. Following his graduation from Basic Reconnaissance Training, he was posted to the 2nd Reconnaissance Battalion at Camp Lejeune. From there, he was later assigned to the 2nd Force Reconnaissance Company, where he made two deployments to Iraq.

"I was lucky," Gunny Patterson said of his coming to the MARSOC. "I was in 2nd Force Recon when my Recon platoon was posted en masse to the MARSOC. One day I was in Force Recon and the next I was in the MARSOC. Timing is everything," he says with a grin. "A lot of guys in Force Recon wanted to come to the MARSOC. I just happened to be at the right place at the right time."

After two tours with an MSOT to Afghanistan, he rotated from the 2nd Battalion to the school. He is married and has two children. As a relatively junior gunnery sergeant, he was selected to proctor Class 1-13. Except for the uniform, Gunny Patterson still looks like the college student he was more than a decade ago. Well, perhaps now more like a graduate student. He's a very quiet-spoken Marine, and all eyes in Class 1-13 are on him. Patterson pauses to survey his students and consult his clipboard.

"A few things to keep in mind. All Marine Corps uniform and grooming standards apply while you're here. That means a clean and proper uniform always, a clean shave each day, and a weekly haircut. I expect you all to be in the barracks or on base during nonworking hours, Monday through Friday, unless there's a training evolution that takes you to a remote training location. Keep your barracks clean and your lockers locked. No cell phones during the working day—leave them in your barracks. If you have a personal issue, get it fixed. If you need help, use your student chain of command or your TACs. Don't let a personal problem get to a point that it affects your performance in this course. If you have a problem, let us help you get it solved; that's our job.

"You all know about DORs?" The students nod collectively. "Drop on request, right? If you find this training is not for you, then take off your rope. That rope stands for more than just practicing your knots. It's a symbol of your commitment to work hard and do your best here—to become a Marine Critical Skills Operator. If for whatever reason you want to quit, take off your rope and give it to your TAC, and he'll take it from there. Basically, you take off your rope and you're done."

I've seen these same coiled lengths of line around the torsos of other SOF students and candidates, but never as a symbol of commitment—meaning that its removal is an overt act of quitting. This length of climbing rope serves much the same purpose as the bell in Navy SEAL training—one designed to work in favor of keeping a struggling trainee in the program. Sometimes the shame of quitting publicly can serve to get that trainee past the pain of the moment and get him through the evolution or through the day to where he can make a better decision. The rope itself has its origins in the Raider and Recon battalions, where the Marines posted to those units carried lengths of rope for training and operational tasks. New men, when checking in and setting up their kit, were issued similar ropes and called "ropers."

Following a morning of administration and individual counseling, the class again musters in the large classroom of the MARSOC Academic Facility, a sprawling single-story complex within the MARSOC compound that houses the Marine Special Operations School. The school is also home to the Special Operations Training Branch that is directly responsible for the ITC.

"Attention on deck!"

There is a scraping of chairs as the seventy-nine members of Class 1-13 come to their feet. A tall, neat officer makes his way to the front of the classroom.

"Take your seats, men. Welcome to the Marine Special Operations Command, and thank you for choosing to be a part of this great organization. My name is Lieutenant Colonel Dodd and I'm the commander of the Special Operations Training Branch. First off, let me say that we want and we need you here. We worked very hard to get you here, and I know each of you worked very hard to get here." He pauses to frame his words. "Your Marine Corps and your nation have invested a great deal of time and money to get you to this point in your career. In this training we will continue to invest more. It costs in the neighborhood of $150,000 to get just one of you through this course. And close to nine months of your time and ours, and that's for just the basic course. You'll quickly find that in this business, you never stop training. We've selected you to come here because you've demonstrated that you have those ten attributes we're looking for in a Critical Skills Operator. Each of you has earned the right to be here.

But you have a lot to learn before you step up to your duties as a member of an operational Marine Special Operations Team.

"We currently have about one-third of the force forward-deployed, and right now most of those are in Afghanistan. That's currently where we're needed. Tomorrow that will probably change. As a serving member on a Marine Special Operations Team, you may be called on to serve just about anywhere in the world in any number of roles and missions." The colonel displays a slide with the MARSOC missions and Core Activities and talks about each one. "When we say today will be different, we mean that—here in the training command and later on when you begin operational deployments with your teams. On any given day, and on very short notice, you may be sent overseas to carry out a SOF mission. So what does it take to get through this training and to take up your duties with an MSOT in the Special Operations Regiment? You have to work hard, and you have to listen to your TACs and instructors. Probably never in your Marine Corps career will you ever be exposed to the quality, density, and experience of the staff we've assembled here at this school. Take advantage of them; they're here to help you to learn what it takes to be a CSO.

"A few things to keep in mind as you go through this course. There will be areas where, due to your ability or experience, you will do very well. In other areas, perhaps not so well. Work on your weak points. Secondly, be a good teammate. Help the Marine next to you if he's having a problem, and he will help you. And finally, never forget that you're a Marine and all that being a Marine entails. Marines are who we are; special operations is what we do. In each class we seem to lose someone because they forget they're a Marine, and they do something stupid, either during training or off duty. Look out for each other; don't let that happen in this class.

"And finally, if you have a personal issue during this course, let us help you with it. Your proctor and your TACs are here to help you with any problems—personal or otherwise. I'm here to help you with them. Handing me your rope doesn't solve the problem. Don't let a personal issue come between you and your goal of becoming a Critical Skills Operator." The colonel again measures the class. "You are the tenth class to come through since we began the Individual Training Class. That's a milestone for us and this training will be a milestone in your career as a Marine. Now, any questions for me? No? Then let's get my master guns up here to say a few words."

The Special Operations Training Branch senior enlisted leader is shorter than his branch commander, perhaps a little less refined, and certainly more direct. Master Gunnery Sergeant Derrick Denard came to the school from the 1st Marine Special Operations Battalion. Before coming to MARSOC, Master Guns Denard had spent more than a decade in Force Reconnaissance. He has a deceptively soft manner and chooses his words carefully. As do most Marine master gunnery sergeants, he exudes authority and experience.

"Welcome aboard. I met a great many of you during selection, and it's good to see so many of you back for the real thing. For those I haven't met, I'm Master Gunnery Sergeant Denard, and I hope to see all of you at graduation, but between now and then, it's a good thing if you can manage to stay out of my office. If you get to my office, to my level, then something is very wrong, and you're probably on your way out the door. If it comes to me, then I probably can't get you out of the trouble you're in. So to prevent this, as the colonel said, get any issues to your TACs and your proctor. Gunnery Sergeant Patterson was hand-picked to be your proctor. Stay close to him, seek his guidance, do what he tells you. He will be with you from now until graduation. Let him help you through this course. Understand what I'm saying?"

"OOH-RAH."

"Remember, you will be constantly evaluated, 24-7, while you're here—on duty and off duty. Remember that you are first and always a Marine. Think about that. Past classes tell us that close to a third of you will not graduate. However, you all have the potential to graduate or you wouldn't be here. Think about that as well. Good luck and stay out of my office."

"OOH-RAH."

The balance of the first week involves testing, screenings, and evaluations while individual issues such as security clearances and medical concerns are brought up to ITC entry requirements. One of the screenings is the Functional Movement Screening. There are three strength coaches and a nutritionist assigned to the Training Branch to serve the needs of the school and those in the ITC. There are a like number of these civilian specialists assigned to each of the three operational battalions of the Marine Special Operations Regiment.

Functional Movement Screening is part of a commercial exercise philosophy called the Functional Movement System. Its techniques and philosophy are used by professional athletic teams to provide an evaluation of an individual's predisposition or susceptibility to injury. Once this is identified, then the individual is given a series of exercises to strengthen that muscle group or that part of the body that's been identified as at risk. The screening itself is seven simple movements that register inflexibility or an asymmetry in one part of the body or another. The student MSOTs of Class 1-13 are brought in and screened, then divided into groups with similar injury-prevention, exercise-strengthening needs. A strength coach works with each group showing them what they need to do on a daily or pre-exercise basis to improve in these areas.

The screening test itself takes about ten minutes, with each of the seven specific functional movements evaluated. The screening seeks to isolate asymmetry, restrictive movement, or pain in a muscle group. Those who score low are said to carry a higher potential for injury, and those students are strongly counseled to begin a focused program of injury-prevention exercise. My screening surfaced some pain issues in my lower back and some inflexibility in my hamstrings, so my Functional Movement Screening was below the average. I now know what to do to fix those problems. Now if I could turn the clock back, say at least forty years, I'm good to go for a crack at the ITC.

Following the functional screening, the coaches take the students outside for an exercise primer—exercises that are a part of the Personal Resiliency or PERRES Program. "There is a lot to learn about how to exercise and the exercise regimes we follow," Gunny Patterson pointed out as we watched one of the coaches put A Class 1-13 MSOT through their paces. "It's a lot different than the PT exercises these Marines are used to. A lot of it stresses agility and coordination. They have to learn the routines and the use of weights, primarily the kettle weights, so there's an exercise learning curve. During In Processing, we do as much as we can to get them ready for the formal PT training that will begin in earnest in a few days. This program of injury prevention and exercise routines designed around combat activity has been a success, and more than just here at the school. The feedback we get from the operational battalions is that it's valuable in conditioning the MSOTs, both during the pre-deployment work-up period and while on deployment. It was just getting to the battalions and MSOTs when I was there, and we could see that it was going to be beneficial in getting us ready for combat."

"We have a set of exercises we have them do before any physical training," one of the strength coaches told me. "Most of them relate to preparing them for more strenuous exercise routines and exercises that relate to combat movement—holding a weapon, carrying their combat load, or carrying a buddy who's been injured."

I asked about the fifty-pound kettlebell weights that are used frequently. "We find the use of kettlebells is a good way to strengthen the core muscles in the back and stomach, and the connective tissue throughout the upper body."

Among their training-equipment issue is a hard rubber rifle that has the size, weight, and feel of a real M4 but can be used for other training, including PT. This also gets the students used to always having their rifle on them or nearby. Sometimes they have their rifles slung during warm-up exercises and sometimes the exercises involve moving tactically while in a shooting position, looking over the top of the rifle. This will help them on the combat shooting ranges during Phase Three and, ultimately, in combat.

The early physical training sessions serve to get the students familiar with the PT routines they will follow throughout the ITC. There are also timed qualifications that will set a baseline for students in the ITC to measure their progress while in training.

I was expecting to see the Marine Physical Fitness Test given to the new ITC class, but I was wrong. Instead, I watched as Class 1-13 completed the Marine Combat Fitness Test, or CFT. There are three parts to the CFT. The first is a half-mile run wearing boots and utilities. The second part has a student pressing a thirty-pound ammo can from under his chin to a full extension over his head as many times as he can in two minutes. The third event of the CFT is movement under fire. This has a student moving over a three-hundred-yard course that features a belly crawl, a high crawl, a zigzag sprint, push-ups, a grenade toss, running with sixty pounds of weight, and dragging, then carrying, another Marine for a part of the distance.

This CFT is relatively new to the Marine Corps, having been required of all Marines beginning in 2009. In this class, the best half-mile time was 2 minutes, 32 seconds. The max ammo-can lifts were 152, and the best three-hundred-yard movement under fire was 2 minutes, 21 seconds. "The Marine Physical Fitness Test and this Combat Fitness Test are Marine Corps requirements," one of the TACs told me, "and we do it because it's a requirement. We use other texts more central to the requirements of a CSO to get the full measure of combat fitness during this training."

Most training days begin with reveille at 0430 and PT at 0500. On occasion, they will sleep in until 0530. The PT program is designed to both strengthen and teach. The strengthening aspect is to make these Marines perform better on the battlefield and become more effective warrior-athletes. The teaching aspect gives them the exercise tools they can take with them when they leave the ITC. Yet while they are here in the school, they will be led in PT by the strength coaches, or by their TACs and proctor under the supervision of the coaches. In other SOF training venues that I have observed, PT is cadre-led or student-led. Here at the ITC, physical training is largely driven by a staff of professional trainers.

"Much of the initial PT is not graded," Staff Sergeant Baker told me, "but it gives us a chance to see who's fit and who may be a little out of shape. Usually we don't have to say anything. If a Marine can't keep up with the others in his team, then he knows he has to step it up. It's a matter of pride, and for the most part, these guys came here to succeed. If they didn't, then it will show up in areas other than PT."

From another TAC, "During the In Processing period, we will time them and test them, but most of the PT time is given over to set exercise procedure, specialty exercises and work with weights—especially the kettlebells. A lot of these guys spend time in the weight room, but few of them have used weights to battle-condition their bodies. There's a great deal of technique associated with these weights and with the targeted exercises. That's why we have these strength coaches with us to ensure we do these exercises properly."

The students alternate between starting the training day on the PT field or at the pool. PT sessions last two hours; the pool evolutions, three hours. In-water training is an important part of the ITC, and twice each week the class is in the pool for water conditioning. This water work is to prepare these students for the amphibious portion of the ITC, which will take place during the next phase of training. As a former Navy SEAL and one who writes about current SEAL training, I found the in-water work throughout the ITC surprisingly robust. The initial pool session has a single goal—ensure that all students meet the Marine Corps advanced swim qualification. The Marine Corps has three levels of swim qualification—basic, intermediate, and advanced. CSO students must perform, at a minimum, at the advanced level. All of the students should be at this level prior to getting to the ITC. However, the staff has them in the pool and puts them through their paces to make sure they are current. The qualification calls for an abandon-ship drill, swimming, and a survival float, much the same as they performed during the ASPOC or Prep Course.

"We do this again here," the lead pool instructor told me, "for several reasons. We want to make sure these Marines are still making at least the minimums of what we require. It also allows us to see them perform in the water and make note of any who can do the minimums but are struggling a bit. And we're looking for any phobias. On occasion, we get a Marine who has the grit and who powered through the swim qual, but who really isn't comfortable in the water. Given the amphibious portion of this course, a guy has to be both strong and comfortable in the water.

"We also use pool and open-water drill as a form of conditioning and the application of stress. These guys will probably never again tie knots underwater at fifteen feet, but in the process of performing underwater tasks while holding their breath, they gain a measure of ease and confidence that we're looking for. Some of these guys will go on to be scuba trained, others will not. They'll all have to fin ashore at night in an over-the-beach exercise with a combat load. Our basic timed distance with swim fins and combat load is two thousand meters. They will do the two thousand meters many times on the clock, and they'll do longer fins for conditioning." I quickly learned that "swimming" means swimming without fins, and "finning" is swimming with fins, the standard U.S. Diver rocket fins. I also learned that if an ITC student has on fins, he will also be in combat utilities and have with him his combat load and weapon. He will never swim with just swim trunks and fins. "We're not SEALs, but for a Marine special operator, water is a means to get to the target or is a refuge, not an obstacle."

"And if a student is having trouble?"

"We remediate him. If for some reason we can't get him to an acceptable level of water competency, then we can't take him into the open water for training. So before he leaves the Basic Skills Phase, he has to be performing to the advanced Marine Corps level and show us he can be safe in the open water. If a student is having difficulty in the water and wants to improve, we'll work with him. But if he can't perform, he can't be in the class. And this is just a baseline. He'll have to continue to show improvement if he is to survive the more rigorous pool drills and open-water requirements of Phase One."

As I watched Class 1-13 go through their paces, I could see there were a range of abilities. There were those who clearly had been competitive swimmers on one level or another. Six of the Marines in the 1-13 class were qualified Marine Corps water survival instructors. Most had a mastery of the sidestroke or breaststroke and seemed comfortable in swimming lengths of the pool or in the abandon-ship drills. Those few who were having trouble seemed to lack technique or were so densely muscled that they had to kick extra hard to stay afloat. All but one student from Class 1-13 successfully completed the advanced Marine swim qual on the first day, and this lone straggler managed to meet standard on the second day at the pool.

With the class having met the in-water minimums, the instructors begin a series of pool conditioning exercises designed to make them proficient combat swimmers in the open water. I found these pool-conditioning sessions rigorous by any standard. The students were made to do push-ups and flutter kicks at poolside, then swim length after length fully clothed in MARPAT utilities. Then they tied knots in fifteen feet of water and retrieved weights from the bottom at fifteen feet. While most of the pool drill, or pool conditioning, was individual, some of it was team-centric. The one I found interesting was when a student MSOT, in utilities, was asked to tread water and deal with one or two ten-pound weights. Ten pounds of lead will take any one man down, so it has to be passed around—quickly. One student would take the weight and kick madly for a second or two, before the load was taken up by a buddy. It became a conditioning event and a team event.

Not all of the pool training was conditioning. The swimming instructor staff also worked with individual students who needed help with their strokes and getting comfortable in the water. Again, some of them perhaps failed to take seriously what they were told during the Prep and Selection Courses–that proficiency in the water was to be a staple during the ITC. So they struggle in the pool.

The school nutritionist has the class for an hour to cover how to eat right and the effects of diet on performance. Aside from a proper balance of the right kinds of foods, there is emphasis on when to eat and the advantages of eating often with smaller meals and snacks between meals. He also emphasizes the importance of eating before and immediately after a workout. And of course, there are the cautions against trans and saturated fats. This nutritionist has a master's degree in his subject and worked with performance diet requirements for professional athletes before coming to MARSOC.

"Professional sports has taught us a lot about the role of hydration, diet, sleep, and personal habits as it relates to performance," he tells the class. "For the military athlete, carbohydrates are very important and necessary. A lot of you think protein is the key to strength and performance. But the carbs are very important in maintaining a proper blood-sugar level while you're exercising or operating. Regarding alcohol, it's a poison to the system that overworks the liver, promotes dehydration, and hinders muscle repair after exercise. An ounce or two a day is probably okay, but anything more than that and it is detrimental to your performance."

"As for the use of tobacco, there is nothing about tobacco that is good for you. Smoking is detrimental to performance and will cut your life short. So is dipping." Glances are exchanged around the class. A great number of these students, as well as their cadre sergeants, use smokeless tobacco. "You may get a rush from it, and it might keep you alert when you've been awake and on the move for a while. And I know it's something of the big boy's drug of choice, but it's simply not good for you. Right now, as you begin this training, might be a good time to quit. It will not make you faster, stronger, smarter, or a better warrior. Just the opposite."

In addition to the various administrative requirements, lectures, and classes, the new ITC students draw a full measure of training and operational gear for the course. They work and train in their green woodland-pattern MARPAT utilities and use their tan desert MAR-PATs for PT. In addition to the uniforms and personal items on the packing list of what they were to bring with them, they are issued a daunting ITC training allowance. There are some one-hundred-plus items that include shooting glasses, body armor, canteens, rocket-type swim fins, ammo pouches, warbelt suspenders, a pistol holster, and assorted cold weather/wet weather gear. On the list of highly account-able items is an M4A1 rifle supported by an LA-5 target pointer/aiming laser. Also on this sign-out, sign-in accountability list is an AN/PVS-15 night-vision device and an M45 CQBP .45 caliber pistol. Getting to the right place, at the right time, and with the right equipment issue will punctuate the daily life of these CSO students.

At the end of the first full week of the In-Processing period, 1-13 is down by two Marines. One brought with him an injury he acquired between his ITC selection and the convening of the class that prevents him from continuing. The other had a security-clearance issue that could not be resolved in time for him to remain with the class. All MARSOC Marines must hold at least a secret-level security clearance. The second week of In Processing is designed to continue with the conditioning, attend to any last-minute personal or equipment issues, and to get the students into the mind-set of their duties, challenges, and opportunities as Marine special operators. One that I found par-ticularly interesting was a briefing by Lieutenant Colonel Dodd and Master Gunnery Sergeant Denard for the twelve student officers—all captains.

They met in a conference room around a large table in the Aca-demic Facility. This was the first of these officer-only training meet-ings, but not the last. As I was to learn, a great deal of attention is afforded these student officers and their role as future MSOT com-manders. The meeting began with a discussion of the preconceptions, misinformation, and impressions that might have followed these cap-tains from their last command. Most were, at one level or another or at one time or another, discouraged from coming to MARSOC. The colonel assured them that a tour with the Command would not hurt their promotion chances within their peer group. He then went on to talk about their duties during the ITC and beyond.

"We expect you to be both students and leaders here," Dodd told his captains. "When it's your chance to lead, we'll be evaluating you on the decisions you make and how timely you make them. We'll grade you on how you lead. Here, and especially when you get to your operational team, we expect you to direct others and let them carry out your direction. As a student team leader and later as an MSOT team commander, you will make the final decisions. Your decision might be heavily swayed by those on your team and your team chief, and you may even have to sell your decision rather than issue a proclamation, but in the end it's your decision and you own it. Giving direction doesn't mean that you then do it for them. Let them do it; they learn by doing. When you are not in a leadership position, lead by example and support those who are making the decisions.

"Regarding your enlisted Marine classmates, we expect you to help them get through this course. You have knowledge and experience they don't; use it to *their* advantage. If there's a problem with another student, call it to the attention of the staff. Especially if it relates to safety. A lot of these Marines have been the best in their platoon or company at their previous duty station. Here, they may be average or below average, and that may cause them to get discouraged. Your job is to motivate the Marines on your team and to mentor them. That's a part of your job, understood?" There is agreement around the table. "Now for some serious talk. This is not an attrition-based school. However, there will be attrition, and in the previous nine classes, attrition has been the heaviest in the officer ranks. This is a difficult business, and we hold you to a high standard. In that regard, it's more of a calling than a career. Some of you may not be right for this duty. You may come to that realization at some point in the course on your own, or we here on staff may come to that conclusion. Then we'll have a very honest conversation about it. That's just the way it is; no drama, no hardship, and no apologies. The duties of an MSOT commander will be difficult and demanding. We are here to train you and to certify that you are ready to meet that challenge. Okay?"

More somber nods around the table.

During the course of the meeting, Colonel Dodd asked each man to stand up and give a two-minute biography of himself. Dodd wanted to know these officers individually and to see how they handled themselves on their feet. The Marine captains of Class 1-13 are a diverse and valuable mix of experience. All but two have an infantry/infantry-related 0300 MOS. Two are Naval Academy graduates. Eight are from the East, two from the South, and one each from the North and West. Three have prior enlisted experience, two as enlisted Marines. About half had some civilian job experience between college and attending the Marine Basic Officer's Course. All have had multiple rotations to Iraq and/or Afghanistan, and all but two have seen active ground combat. Most have had two, some have had three combat rotations. One has had five. The youngest is a twenty-seven-year old signals intelligence officer who physically tests off the chart. The oldest is a forty-one-year old captain who came up through the ranks. He's a former Recon company commander, hard as nails, and his seniority and age in this training are rare. One common thread that runs through all twelve is that they have all had some experience in working with local populations overseas—partnership forces, advisory duty, civil affairs, village stabilization operations, or some duty with the Iraqi/Afghan military or police units. Most cite this as a reason they put in for the MARSOC. More than a few have worked with MSOTs in the battlespace and that influenced their decision as well.

Following Lieutenant Colonel Dodd's remarks, Master Guns Denard weighed in. "Some of you may have questions about your interaction with the enlisted Marines in your class. How close or how distant do you get with your enlisted classmates? It's no different here than in the [Marine Special Operations] Regiment, or wherever you came from. We expect you to inspire and control these Marines. In some ways it's an older brother–younger brother relationship. Yet, as an officer, you are always in command. And always set a good example; hold yourself and them to a Marine standard."

"This is a tough course, but it's a rewarding course," Lieutenant Colonel Dodd tells the class captains. "It's a chance to exercise a span of control in the battlespace well above your pay grade and to serve your country in a way more meaningful than you ever imagined. Keep that in mind and good luck."

Captain Andrew Fraker is twenty-nine years old and has been in the Marine Corps for six years. He grew up in Oak Ridge, Tennessee, and has a degree in criminal justice from the University of South Carolina. He's an infantry officer with two combat deployments, one in Iraq and one in Afghanistan. He has also been on a training deployment with a partner force in the Caucasus. He is a serious triathlete and, like nearly all the captains in 1-13, is in superb condition. He comes to the ITC from a company commander's tour at the Marine Corps Mountain Warfare Center. As did several other Class 1-13 captains, he just completed the Army Maneuver Captains Course at Fort Benning, Georgia.

Regarding the ITC, "I've dreamed of doing something like this since I was a little kid," he says with a grin. "I want to do my best and I want to serve with the best."

Later that evening, these captains hold similar meetings with the enlisted Marines in their student MSOTs. There they ask each of their Marines to stand up and tell his teammates something about himself. In doing so they learn more about these already-special Marines they will be expected to lead through the ITC.

Sixty-seven enlisted Marines began with Class 1-13. Nine in the class are staff sergeants, and this class will be one of the last to have student staff sergeants. There is a single corporal, who is soon to pin on his sergeant's chevrons. All others are E-5 sergeants. By MOS, they are a diverse group of Marines, yet as with previous classes, 0300 infantrymen dominate the class; there are twenty-eight of them. Of the twenty-eight infantrymen, seven are staff sergeants and five are Recon Marines. Six in the class come from a communications background and five each from the artillery, the aviation community, and the motor pool—those latter Marines being mechanics and truck drivers. There are three amphibious vehicle crewmen, three IT/data-management technicians, three administrators, and three military-police/security specialists. Two in the class are logisticians and two are heavy equipment operators. There is one small-arms repairman and one Marine Corps Band drummer. Among these enlisted CSO candidates are five Marines who were rolled back from a previous class for injury or administrative issues. One Marine in Class 1-13, a truck driver, is a combat services support specialist from the Marine Special Operations Support Battalion. He has deployed twice with the Regiment in support of MSOTs in Afghanistan. Now he wants to return to the fight as a CSO.

Four Marines are reservists, having come through the selection process while in the reserves and come back on active duty for the ITC. The ITC is the portal through which these reservists will return to active duty in the Marine Corps. Currently, there is no MARSOC reserve component, only the standing, active Marine Special Operations Command.

Nearly all of these Marines have been deployed overseas and nearly all of them have been in the active theaters. Most of them have been in combat. The oldest Marine is a thirty-four-year old landing support specialist; the youngest, a twenty-one-year old artilleryman. The average age is just under twenty-six years. A few of the younger Marines come to the ITC with only three and a half to four years of service, while Marines with five years' service or more are not uncommon. The average time in service is just under five years. As with the class officers, about half of these enlisted Marines are married and about half of those married have at least one child.

One of those Marines from a non-infantry specialty is Sergeant Brad Hansen. He is from Texas, twenty-four, and by MOS, a cyber network operator. This means Sergeant Hansen is trained in data transmission and secure communications and would also suggest that he is a very smart Marine. He's also a martial arts instructor. Hansen had attended five semesters of college and was working at Home Depot before he decided he wanted to be a Marine. He's married and has been in the Marine Corps for four and a half years. His MOS has taken him on deployment to Haiti, Kuwait, Jordan, and Djibouti, yet he's looking for something more from his Marine Corps experience, which he shared with me.

"I've always wanted to be in the infantry community, and this is my chance to be in a ground-combat unit. I also want to push myself.

The MARSOC is where the Marine Corps is heading, and I want to be a part of it. I feel very fortunate to be here."

––––––––––

The second week of In Processing, like the first, is punctuated with more PT, pool evolutions, knot tying and rope management, equipment issue, security briefings, and last-minute administrative details. There is an evening program for the married students and their wives on family assistance and family support programs. The Marine Corps has a very robust outreach program for the families of their Marines. So does the U.S. Special Operations Command for their personnel. In this regard, MARSOC Marines and the Marine Special Operations School students are doubly blessed. The School commanding officer, Colonel James Glynn, Lieutenant Colonel Dodd, their master gunnery sergeants, and Gunny Patterson are at the evening program to reinforce this commitment to family. There is a sober admission to the families of the class Marines that the ITC is a difficult and stressful time for families, and that the Command and the school stand by to help in any way and at any time.

Physically, there are two key timed evolutions prior to the end of In Processing. Neither is a criterion for being dropped from the course, but both are indicative of who is fit and who is really fit. One is a timed five-mile run and the other a ten-mile ruck march. The five-miler is in shorts, T-shirt, and civilian running shoes. All but one student is under the forty-minute minimum standard. The first Marine crosses the line in twenty-eight minutes, thirty-three seconds on a very cold morning. The ruck march is in utilities, boots, and a soft cap with a forty-five-pound rucksack, ammunition vest, canteens, and a weapon. The average student loading is between seventy and seventy-five pounds—much like their ruck-march equipment loading during the assessment and selection process. While on the march, which is more of a run than a march, the students have to keep both hands on their weapon at all times. The first student comes in with a time of one hour, thirty-nine minutes, forty-two seconds—the second fastest time ever on this ten-mile course. The next man is five minutes behind this very fast Marine. Both of their heads are bathed in frost as their sweat froze to their hair. The times are recorded and the rucks weighed. Those that are at forty-five pounds or just over are told to add a few more pounds to the forty-five that is the minimum for their ruck.

"Anything *less than* 45 pounds is an integrity violation," Gunny Patterson tells those close to the threshold. "So you don't want to be anywhere close to that. Be safe and tuck in a few more pounds."

About half of the class is under the two-hour mark, which is considered excellent, and all are under the two and a half hours that is the course minimum. But then the ITC is not about just making minimums. Other than the fast times posted by the lead students in each event, I was taken by the close attention and formatted exercise regime before and after each event. One of the civilian strength coaches was there to lead the class in a comprehensive series of warm-up and cool-down exercises. And the TACs all made the run and ruck march with their students.

As for the ruck march, there was more on the line than who was fast and who was faster. The slowest student MSOT must, as a team, carry two man-sized, two-hundred-pound dummies around to each training evolution. The second- and third-place teams have to port a single dummy. The team with the lowest collective times have to deal with neither—until the next competitive ruck evolution.

With the completion of the ruck march, Class 1-13 is all but finished with their ten days of In Processing. There remain only the formalities of any lingering administrative, equipment, or medical issues and two more briefings. The first of those briefings is delivered by John Dailey, a civilian who is the deputy director of the Special Operations Training Branch. In a great many ways, John Dailey is the architect of the ITC. Dailey is a retired Marine master sergeant with a long Recon résumé and a history with Marine Detachment One. He came to the MARSOC early on and was with the first MSOTs to deploy in 2006. One day, he came to work in uniform, and then, following his end-of-service leave period, he returned in a short-sleeved shirt and tie. His duties keep him at a desk, but as most of the physical training takes place between 0530 and 0800, he is there for that as well. John is short, stocky, forty-three-years old, and deceptively fit. On the five-mile run, he finished in the middle of the pack; on the ruck march, very close to the front of the pack.

"John Dailey?" one of the TACs said of the branch deputy. "The guy was born about five hundred years too late. He should have been roaming medieval Europe with a battleaxe, killing the king's enemies until someone tougher came along and killed him, which would not be all that easy. He's the eternal warrior."

"There are three things I want you to keep in mind." Dailey tells 1-13 during their course overview briefing. "The first is to do things our way. Many of you come with some experience in what we teach in this class, and that's fine. But do the skills as we teach them here; it's how they will be done in your MSOT. That's also how we will be grading you. Secondly, you have to be thinking all the time; stay alert and keep your head in the game. How many of you have heard of John Boyd and the OODA Loop?" Most of the hands go up. "Most of you, okay," He quickly covers the decision-action mechanics of the famous Air Force fighter pilot, John Boyd—Observation, Orientation, Decision, Action. "We make hundreds of decisions a day. With the skill-based training you will get here in the ITC, we will expect you to make those see-decide-do decisions faster and faster. When you get to your MSOTs and into combat, you will act faster than the enemy, and this is what allows you to win the fight. John Boyd was able to outthink his opponent, then out maneuver him, and shoot him down. It's the same for us. Our training allows us to act quicker than the other guy and kill him before he kills us. It's really that simple. And finally, this is a physically demanding course. Physical toughness leads to mental toughness. We are here to extend you physically and mentally, and give you the tools to dominate your personal battlespace and the battlespace of your team."

Dailey is followed by Colonel James Glynn. "Welcome to the ITC, gentlemen," Colonel Glynn says to the class, as he strides to the front of the room. His responsibilities include SERE school, language training, and the Special Operations Training Branch, which in turn is responsible for the ITC and the preparation and assessment of candidates for the ITC. The colonel is a slim, energetic Naval Academy graduate with dual master's degrees, in military studies and national security affairs. He is an infantry officer. In addition to seeing combat in Desert Storm, he has made four MEU(SOC) deployments. Colonel Glynn came to the school following a tour with the Special Operations Command, Africa, where he served as the director of operations (J3) and as director of strategy and plans (J5).

"Let me echo what Mr. Dailey had to say and add that we have great expectations of you—here at the school and going forward as members of an MSOT. While a great deal of your training will be skill-based, keep in mind that much of our work overseas is relationship-based. Working with the local populations and achieving our objectives using a by-with-and-through approach is as important as closing with the enemy." The colonel paces as he talks and expands on the expectations and demands that will be made of 1-13 during the ITC. "There are three external things that can affect you while you're in this course and can cause you to fail. They have to do with alcohol, money, and family issues. Don't let alcohol come between you and your goal of becoming a Marine Critical Skills Operator. As for money and family problems, there is help for those issues. We have a very accomplished family-support group, so let them help you before they become a serious problem.

"Past that, do your best while you're here. Our expectations are high and our standards are clear—they are Marine Corps standards and SOCOM standards. Stay focused, work hard, and these fine instructors at the ITC will help you to reach your maximum potential as a Marine and as a Marine special operator. I'll be back to talk with you as you progress through the course. Good luck to each of you."

Seventy-six Marines from Class 1-13 will begin the formal training portion of the Basic Skills Phase of this Individual Training Course. One more of the original seventy-nine left training due to a family issue—one that could not be resolved by the Command. If previous classes are an example, there will be more, as injuries and the pace of activity begin to take their toll. At one time or another, nearly all of these students will have to perform when they're hurting. Past the physical, there is the mental. It's not just the recent pace of activity that is so intimidating. There's knowing that the pace will go on for another eight months and that, at times, it will get a great deal more active and more stressful. With the In Processing period behind them, the class moves on to medical and communications training and to the MARSOC Survival Evasion, Resistance, and Escape Course— SERE school.

TACTICAL COMBAT CASUALTY CARE

On what is considered the first real day of training, student MSOTs Three and Four are in the classroom of the Academic Facility for the medical portion of the ITC while Teams One and Two are off for their three weeks of SERE training. For this training, I will be with Three and Four. Tactical Combat Casualty Care, TCCC or Triple-C, is taught at this basic level for all SOF units. Nearly all of the instructors teaching SOF combat casualty care courses are 18-Delta qualified, which is to say that they have attended the Army's twenty-four-week Special Operations Combat Medics Course and the twenty-two-week Special Forces Medical Sergeants Course. Most of them have a great deal more medical training as well, to include treating combat wounded. On this first day of training for Class 1-13, they are greeted by the lead TCCC medical instructor, who was born in the United States but carries a pronounced British accent. He is 18-D qualified and a retired Navy senior chief petty officer. For Teams Three and Four, their training begins with a video of the D-Day scene of *Saving Private Ryan*, with lots of bullets pinging off steel beach obstacles and a lot of casualties.

"Okay," the lead instructor begins, "how many of you have received triple-C training before this?" Well more than half the hands go up. "Good. This will be a review for most of you and some new information for some of you. But you will all have to pass the practical application on Thursday, so pay attention. More importantly, this information can save a life, perhaps your own.

"We'll be focusing on three things," the former senior chief says, "but they all have to do with getting oxygen to the body where it needs it. First and very quickly, we have to make sure there's enough blood in the system to carry that oxygen from the lungs out to the tissues in the body. Secondly, we have to have a clear airway to get oxygen to the lungs. Then we have to make sure the lungs function properly to get that oxygen into the bloodstream. Keep the blood inside the body, keep the airway clear, and keep the casualty breathing, making sure the lungs can do their job, right? That's the procedure, but you may have to do it in the middle of a firefight. Tough to apply a tourniquet when you're in the open and getting shot at."

He goes on to talk about what has to happen before treatment begins. "You have to first win the fight. The best initial medicine is fire superiority. Then you can move your casualty to safety and begin treatment." He walks them through the steps of what to do first, and how. "If he's not breathing and he's bleeding from a hole in his femoral artery, what do you do first? Someone, anyone."

"Stop the bleeding."

"Right. Doesn't do much good to open the airway when he's going to bleed out. Take a minute or two to throw on a tourniquet, then see about his breathing."

The format is classroom presentation, demonstration, then practical application. For breathing they learn how to check the airway of a casualty and, if it's obstructed, get it cleared. This includes the insertion of a nasopharyngeal airway when required—the insertion of a lubricated rubber tube down one nostril, which the students do to each other. They are trained in chest needle decompression to treat a condition known as tension pneumothorax. This results from a gunshot or shrapnel wound that pierces the chest cavity. When this happens, air enters the chest cavity, collapsing one or both lungs and interfering with the victim's breathing and his heart pumping blood—a life-threatening condition. For this practical application, they use a test dummy. I've talked with soldiers who have had this done after they've been shot, and the pain that comes with this pressure buildup in the chest cavity is excruciating. As bad as the idea of sticking a large, vented needle between your ribs sounds, the relief is immediate, not to mention life-saving. For bleeding there are a host of prepared field pressure and hemostatic dressings. And of course, there are tourniquets. On surveying just these two student MSOTs, I see that six of them have used tourniquets in combat and two of them have had tourniquets used *on* them in combat. That's eight of these thirty-eight Marines who don't have to be told of the importance of this training.

"Fifteen percent of all preventable battlefield deaths are due to bleeding from the extremities, or failure to get air to the lungs or from the lungs into the bloodstream," the instructors tell them. "If you practice good Triple-C, these deaths can be prevented."

After the classroom lecture and classroom practice, the two Class 1-13 MSOTs are ready for their field practical work in preparation for their practical exam. The following day they meet at a roughly constructed combat town on the Stone Bay range called Dodge City. There they begin drills in five- and six-man teams as they treat casualties under simulated fire. There is an instructor medic with each team and a patient who has fake rubber stumps to simulate a missing hand or foot. The teams run drill after drill where they set security so they can drag the wounded man to cover. Then a single student medic treats him. The instructor calls out the trauma.

"His left leg—bleeding, bleeding, bleeding."

"His breath is shallow and rapid. What are you going to do?"

"He was talking to you; now his speech is slurring and he's losing consciousness."

"Okay, he's stable; now what? Right, reassess, reassess, reassess. Get him ready for transport."

The students follow the MARCH protocol in the priority of their treatment: Massive bleeding, Airway, Respiration, Circulation, and Head wounds. "You've got a minute or two, maybe less, to control massive bleeding," the lead instructor tells his students, "and another few minutes to clear his airway and get him breathing before brain damage sets in. Once you've done that, sit back and take a quick breath, then look for any breathing problems or signs of a tension pneumothorax. Tend to any minor wounds and keep reassessing him—get him comfortable, keep him warm, look for shock."

Each student is graded on a final run through the trauma lanes for his TCCC certification. For this graded pass, there is more attention given to the moulage of the victims. There are liberal amounts of fake blood splashed on them and they are equipped with bladders of the fake blood to simulate arterial bleeding. And there's a movie set–like sound system that plays loud Arabic music punctuated by gunfire and explosions to add to the chaos. The student medics are graded on a 100-point system with 80 as a passing grade. Those who fail on the first pass are remediated and retested. It's as real as it can be, without an actual casualty and real blood. That's reserved for the final day of training.

There's a single day of medical training in the ITC that is uniquely different from other basic SOF medical training venues. It is a day of medical training with live tissue—i.e., with animals. This is a controversial issue so I will cover it briefly and only by way of its mention. It is similar in practice to the training conducted for physicians-in-training at the nearby Duke, North Carolina, and Wake Forest schools of medicine. While this instruction is focused on the treatment of trauma and battlefield care, the same considerations for the humane treatment of the subjects are observed while they are at the civilian medical training facilities.

"I've had to treat battle wounds in Afghanistan," one of the student sergeants told me, "and this is as close as it gets to the real thing."

"This is outstanding training," Gunny Patterson said of the live-tissue training. "This hands-on experience will save Marine lives and the lives of civilians who otherwise might die from collateral damage due to getting caught in a cross fire. There are no doctors in some of the places we operate, and either we save that life or the person dies."

COMMUNICATIONS

While student MSOTs One and Two continue with SERE, teams Three and Four begin their two-week block of communications training. After the normal Monday team-centric PT session, the two teams are in the classroom to meet with their communications instructors. The instruction will follow a format of studying radio theory, communications format, and the individual radios in the classroom, then going outside for communications practical work. The lead communications instructor is a retired Recon master sergeant who prowls the classroom as if he were still in uniform amid a group of Basic Reconnaissance Course students.

"In the next two weeks you will learn to operate and troubleshoot our three primary radio systems, and you will be tested on two of them. Your training will cover transmission, reception, power supplies, and antennas. We will cover HF, VHF, UHF, and SATCOM (high-frequency, very-high-frequency, ultra-high-frequency, and satellite) communications on our field radios. You'll also get training on signal propagation, field expedient antennas, and radio procedures and etiquette. These are the radios you will use on a daily basis with your MSOTs overseas. There are extended communications capabilities at the company and battalion level, but at the team level, these are the radios you will have to know, and know them you will, good to go?"

"OOH-RAH."

The first weekday of instruction gets the students up to speed on the Microsoft Office software and its interface with the communications systems. Data and text in transmission are handled with ruggedized notebook computers called Toughbooks. They are also introduced to the AN/CYZ-10 or "crazy ten" data transfer device that is used to install encryption into the field radios. "All our communications are encrypted," the lead instructor tells them. "The current enemy may not have the ability to tap into our radio traffic, but there are a great many potential enemies out there that do."

Their first radio is the AN/PRC(Army-Navy/Portable Radio Communications)-150 radio. The 150 is a multiband HF and VHF manportable radio that is the primary HF, long-haul radio for special operations teams in the field. This radio can handle encrypted voice and data transmission and has a range up to thirty miles or more. The radio, with its battery pack, weighs about fifteen pounds and interfaces with a Windows-based Toughbook computer. This AN/PRC-150 is also a standard Marine Corps radio, so most of the students in the class are familiar with it or have used it on deployment.

The second radio that the class learns and is tested on is the AN/PRC-117F, which is the primary SATCOM radio used by the deployed MSOTs and a great many other U.S. and foreign militaries. This radio provides a secure and reliable, over-the-horizon capability for voice and data transmission. It's similar in size and weight to the 150 but with a collapsible, directional antenna that can be field-deployed. If the radio is relatively easy to deploy and use, the interface with the satellite "bird" is a bit more complex. It must be planned for and programmed in advance. The students are tested individually on both the 150 and the 117F.

The radio that these ITC students know, have used on deployment, and were issued at the beginning of the course is the AN/PRC-148, also known as the multiband inter/intra team radio, or MBITR (pronounced em-biter or me-biter). This is an encryption-capable radio that was developed by SOCOM in the mid-1990s and is now perhaps the most widely used tactical radio among U.S. and NATO forces. It is a versatile, handheld device with line-of-site range and is compatible with most other PRC-type radios. In the student MSOTs and the operational MSOTs overseas, everyone carries this MBITR radio, but perhaps not for too much longer. The AN/PRC-152, while not currently taught at the ITC, is rapidly replacing the venerable 148.

"For most us, this was a review," one of the student infantrymen told me, "but it was a very thorough review. Overseas, most of us rely on the platoon commo guy to handle everything but the MBITR. Here we had to do it all on our own and make commo within the allowed time. That made us all pay attention. When test time came, it was on you to make it happen."

SERE TRAINING

After the Christmas break, Class 1-13 returns to Stone Bay to take up their duties. All deployable MARSOC personnel, and this includes support and combat support personnel as well as the CSOs, have to attend survival, evasion, resistance, and escape (SERE) school. SERE originated for combat flight crews who needed this training in the event they bailed out over enemy territory and were taken as prisoners of war. This training is still a requirement for these crews and has long since been a requirement for ground-combatant special operators. CSOs and their enabling cadres often operate well away from the reach and support of conventional military forces. This makes them more vulnerable to capture. Basically, they have to know how to best conduct themselves if they are taken by the enemy, and the current enemy comes in many forms and gradations.

The MARSOC SERE School has been operating since October of 2008 and trains all MARSOC multidimensional operators. In this group are the female Marines of the Cultural Support Teams assigned to MARSOC. They too must complete SERE training to be fully deployable.

"This school is a full-spectrum SERE school," the school officer in charge said of his training. "We provide training in the event they are captured and classified as prisoners of war. We also address those situations where a serviceman may be detained, say if they were picked up by the police in Pakistan or Equador. Then there's the issue of being taken hostage by a non-state group, and we all know what that entails. Each of these forms of capture or detainment require different techniques, and we teach them all. They are with us for three weeks.

The first part of the training deals with survival. We begin in the classroom and then move into the field. The second part has to do with evasion so they're out there in the woods with their teams, moving toward an objective and using the evasion skills they have learned. The last portion of the training is the resistance and escape portion of the course, and here we dial up the intensity and the realism. They get a taste of what it might be like should they find themselves being detained, taken as a POW, or they find themselves held hostage by a terrorist group."

The scenario played out in the resistance and escape portion of the training relates to an insurgent situation where the United States is coming to the aid of a friendly but weak democracy. SERE students are introduced to a rather elaborate, irregular warfare scenario that will be an integral part of the later phases of the ITC. In this construct, the United States is giving aid and military assistance to the Republic of Abyssinia, a nation that in our scenario physically encompasses Camp Lejeune, the southern coastal area of North Carolina, and all of South Carolina. To the south is the Kingdom of Aksum (state of Georgia) that gives sanctuary to the Sword of the Right Hand, a terrorist group that supports an insurgency in Abyssinia. To the north is the failed state of Sumal (most of North Carolina), where the Sword of the Right Hand operates with impunity. The United States has deployed MSOTs to Abyssinia to train them in foreign internal defense. It is in the context of this scenario that the SERE students, as deployed American service personnel, must first evade capture. Once captured, in this scenario by Sumal militiamen, they must conduct themselves with the skills they learn in this training.

"Once you become a prisoner or a detainee," the lead instructor tells his students on the first day of training, "you have two primary goals." This SERE class has twenty-seven students from ITC Class 1-13 and ten students from the Marine Special Operations Support Branch. "Those goals are to survive and to return with honor. We will teach you the techniques of survival, evasion, resistance, and escape, and how these techniques apply in the various forms of capture. But just remember, a thousand days of survival, even under the most austere conditions, are better than a single day of captivity."

"This course will challenge you mentally, physically, and spiritually. You will be cold, tired, confused, and angry. You will hurt; you will want to quit. Don't. Just suck it up and continue on. We good on that?"

There are reluctant nods around the classroom. These Marines know they are in for an ordeal. "Now, on your feet. Gentlemen, [this class has no females] this is the Code of Conduct." A colored graphic of the Code slides onto the large flat screen at the front of the room. "It's the foundation of what we teach here and what will be expected of you should you find yourself in the hands of the enemy. Let's recite it together."

I am an American, fighting in the forces which guard my country and our way of life. I am prepared to give my life in their defense.

I will never surrender of my own free will. If in command, I will never surrender the members of my command while they still have the means to resist.

If I am captured I will continue to resist by all means available. I will make every effort to escape and to aid others to escape. I will accept neither parole nor special favors from the enemy.

If I become a prisoner of war, I will keep faith with my fellow prisoners. I will give no information or take part in any action which might be harmful to my comrades. If I am senior, I will take command. If not, I will obey the lawful orders of those appointed over me and will back them up in every way.

When questioned, should I become a prisoner of war, I am required to give name, rank, service number, and date of birth. I will evade answering further questions to the utmost of my ability. I will make no oral or written statements disloyal to my country and its allies or harmful to their cause.

I will never forget that I am an American, fighting for freedom, responsible for my actions and dedicated to the principles which made my country free. I will trust in my God and in the United States of America.

This is not the last time these SERE students will orally recite the Code in unison, and as the class progresses, they will do so with a great deal more passion and understanding. Sometimes the recitation will be with the SERE cadre and sometimes not. Those who administer, teach, and conduct this training are like no other. SERE instructors are among the most talented and colorful of all military trainers. A great deal of what takes place during SERE training is classified or restricted information. But here is what a few in Class 1-13 had to say of their SERE experience.

"It's the most professional course I've attended in the Marine Corps," Captain Andrew Fraker said of the training. "I've been to some good survival courses and had a lot of experience in moving quietly and undetected in the field. But I learned a great deal from these instructors; they were terrific. As for the period in confinement, it was a learning experience and then some. It was only for a few days, but it gave you a perspective on what Senator McCain and Admiral Stockdale went through."

Sergeant Brad Hansen agreed. "We were hungry, cold, and isolated for what seemed like a really long time, but in some cases, it was only for a few hours. Yet it was a good taste of what it might be like. It was educational, but it was not fun."

I had to ask the proverbial SERE school question, "How much weight did you lose?"

"I lost about fourteen pounds," replied Sergeant Hansen. "And I plan to put a lot of it back on as soon as I can get to the chow hall."

"I went from 172 to less than 160," said Captain Fraker, who was one of the more fit students in the class. "I haven't seen that weight since I was in middle school."

"It was a real eye-opener," said Sergeant Kerry Irving, one of the more senior sergeants in the class. "It's the best training I never want to have to do again."

After a day's rest and three good meals, the SERE students are back where they started, in the classroom, for a comprehensive, in-depth individual critique of their performance in SERE school.

===

Over the duration of the Basic Skills Phase, the days are long and intensive. A typical day begins with reveille at 0430, with the student teams kitted up and in formation for PT at 0500. Days end with barracks study or an evening evolution and lights out at 2200 or 2230. That's six or seven hours of sleep to support a seventeen- or eighteen-hour work day. Those in the field portion of SERE get much less sleep than that. The weekends are for catching up on sleep, laundry, gear overhaul, and study. And a break from the routine to let sore bodies regenerate.

Physically, they are tested, retested, measured, and ranked in a number of different ways. At any one time throughout the ITC, the student times and rankings are posted on a bulletin board outside the TACs office. They are ranked individually and by student team on the obstacle course, a strength test, the five-mile run, the ten-mile ruck march, the Marine Combat Fitness Test, the Marine Physical Fitness Test, the five-hundred-yard swim in utilities, and the five-hundred-yard swim with fins and full kit. The postings are color-coded—green, yellow, and red. For the team codings, the green team is the one whose collective scores are the highest and times the lowest. The second and third place teams are yellow, while the red-coded team is last. The students are also individually ranked. Those who score in the outstanding range are coded green, yellow for acceptable, and red for unsat. At a glance, everyone knows who is performing well and who is not. On the non-graded days, the PT can be reasonable, with a long run, a conditioning workout with weights, agility training, and shuttle runs, or swimming laps using different strokes while swimming coaches work to improve technique. Then there are the crushing PTs. In the pool, the Marines will swim a lap in utilities, hop out, and do push-ups; then swim a lap, hop out, and do flutter kicks; swim to the bottom, tie a knot, hop out, and more push-ups—over and over. This was one of the few times the students were made to do push-ups. Push-ups have little combat utility, so they are seldom a part of the physical training.

All timed evolutions are factored into the student's overall class standing. But for ongoing and periodic evaluation of student performance over the length of the entire ITC, there are four timed events that mark their physical progression: the five-mile run (in boots), the five-hundred-yard swim in utilities, the double O-course (a short obstacle course run twice in succession), and the ten-mile ruck march.

One morning I watch as the teams did breakdowns. The student MSOTs are kitted up with a full combat load, rucksack, water, and weapons so they are packing seventy-plus pounds of gear. Each team must also carry a two-hundred-pound, man-sized dummy; five fifty-pound kettlebells; and four five-gallon jerry cans of water—each weighing about 50 pounds. That's 620 pounds of weight that, if evenly distributed, add about 35 pounds to each student's load. That's the challenge. The extra weight really can't be evenly distributed, and the added pounds are incrementally more difficult to carry. It's a race, and the teams begin with a mile-and-a-half lap carrying everything. The fastest teams are those who most efficiently manage the extra poundage. At the end of the first lap, the teams can shed one class of extra weight—the dummy, the kettlebells, the jerry cans of water, or their rucks. The rucks collectively weigh the most, but they are the easiest to carry. Next in total pounds are the kettlebells, which are easier to carry than either the water or the dummy, and so on. After each lap, the team leader must decide what kind of weight they will discard, what they will carry and how, and press on. Oh, and the team leader cannot speak; the team must remain tactical, and the team leader must use hand signals to tell his team what he wants them to do. After four laps and six miles of this competition, they head to the barracks to change clothes and stow their gear. The winning team runs to morning chow with only their ropes and rubber rifles. The three non-winning teams must port their two-hundred-pound dummy to chow and for the rest of the day's training.

During their final week, the student teams make their first open-water fin. For 1-13 it was a cool morning with the air temperature in the high thirties. The good news is that the water is warmer, but the not-so-good news is that the water temp is in the low fifties. As with finning in the pool, if a MARSOC student dons his fins, he is also in utilities and kitted-up for land warfare. In addition to their fins, students wear wet suits under their utilities and, strapped over them, their Rhodesian ammo vests, life vests, and rifles. On the vest are two quarts of water, dummy magazines for the weight, a knife, and a radio pouch. Their rucks average fifty pounds, are waterproofed and positively buoyant, and are pushed through the water ahead of the amphibious Marine finner.

The distance is the course standard, open-water, two thousand meters. All MARSOC students are expected to fin this combat load over this distance in an hour or less. In addition to the time in the water, each student must enter and exit the water in the proscribed, tactical manner, both of which add to his overall time. On this first of their open-water timed fins, and on this one fin, they swim as individuals and are timed as individuals. Based on these times, they will be paired with swim buddies of comparable ability. As it's their first open-water fin, the class strings out a great deal. The first student emerges from the water, ruck on his back and porting his rifle at the ready position in fifty-one minutes, twenty-four seconds. Six students are under the one-hour threshold. The others will have ample opportunity to bring their times up to the course standard. One of those making standard on this first swim is Sergeant Kerry Irving.

Sergeant Irving is twenty-eight, married, and has two children. He came from a training command on Camp Lejeune, so his family is close. He grew up in Virginia Beach, Virginia, and his father is a retired Navy chief petty officer. Irving is five eleven, slim, and has a mature way about him. As with many of the older sergeants in 1-13, he is very fit and very focused, and he has a long résumé of Marine Corps schools and instructor qualifications. And as with many of these more senior class sergeants, a great many of his peers and senior NCOs from his previous company wondered just what he was doing by volunteering for MARSOC training. Being a Marine is not the easiest of callings in the best of times, but the respect, status, and authority of a Marine NCO is, in itself, special.

"A lot of my fellow squad leaders in my old company, along with my first sergeant and company commander, wondered what I was doing. They thought I was crazy to trade where I was to come here and be a basic student again—along with the killer PT sessions and long swims. I guess I'm not ready to settle into that comfortable company routine; I want more. When it's all over, I don't want to look back and say that I never did my best or served with the best. This is where I want to be."

One of the last evolutions for Class 1-13 is the peer process. This takes place twice in each phase—once mid-phase and once at the phase conclusion. At the ITC, the Marines in each student MSOT rate the Marines, including themselves, in each of the ten characteristics of a CSO: integrity, effective intelligence, physical ability, adaptability, initiative, determination, dependability, teamwork, interpersonal skills, and stress tolerance. There are five rating marks: Among Top of the Class, High Average, Average, Low Average, and Among the Bottom of the Class. There is also a category for "who on your team would you most like to deploy with" and another, "who would you least like to deploy with." This information is entered online in a confidential database that can be accessed by the cadre and displayed in any number of ways. It's the same proprietary software used in the assessment and selection process.

"Early on, this information is of little value except for flagrant issues of integrity," Gunny Patterson said of the peer-review process. "But as the class progresses, a trend will emerge. Who do these Marines want to serve with and who do they wish not to serve with? When we're not around, who is a good teammate and helps in the barracks and who does not? On occasion, we think a guy is doing well, but his teammates see him when he cuts corners or shirks his duties in the barracks. And it can change. Sometimes a guy who is good in the classroom and a stud in the physical evolutions is not so good during the field problems or when the team hasn't slept in a few days and still has to perform as a team. It's a valuable tool for us."

———

The out-processing of Class 1-13 from the Basic Skills Phase is a formal, individual review of each student's performance to date. At the head of the big conference table is Lieutenant Colonel Dodd, with Master Gunnery Sergeant Denard close at hand. Also attending are Gunny Patterson and the senior leadership for the Ground Combat/Amphibious Phase or Phase One. The Basic Skills Phase TACs are aligned along one side of the table and the Phase One TACs on the other. On the big flat screen, a picture of each candidate is brought up accompanied by his rank, age, time in service, time in grade, GT score, his language ability score, and a score for his personality inventory. Below this information is listed his most recent PFT and CFT, his marital status, and any pending family issues. This data is displayed along with a computer graphic that details his performance in academic testing, physical testing, TAC character evaluation, and peer evaluation. This display in the form of a scatter diagram has room for future performance data as the course progresses.

Close to two-thirds in Class 1-13 are performing well above standard and coded green with a green border around their photos. About a third are coded yellow as they are deficient or just making minimums in one category or another, but succeeding overall. There are two or three Marines in each team that are struggling to keep up with the class performance averages. They are coded with a red border. It was my sense that this board was convened not to drop any of the Marines from the course, but to allow for the Basic Skills TACs to talk about their problem Marines and for the Phase One TACs to make note of who was having difficulties.

"He has the potential and he's improving, but he's still weak and failed the double-O course twice."

"Sergeant Smith is strong in the team PT and everyone likes him, but he's just getting by on the runs and has trouble keeping up."

On one of the red-flagged students, "He doesn't take correction well. I get the impression that he only really puts out when someone is right there watching him."

I heard comments that ranged from timid to assertive to awkward to arrogant to hardworking to unengaged. Lieutenant Colonel Dodd allowed the discussion to flow before summing it up. "I want to thank you TACs from Basic Skills for bringing these Marines this far. For you new TACs, you have your work cut out for you. Some of these students need a good heart-to-heart talk about the standards we expect and the ground they will need to cover to reach those standards. This is not a board to put anyone out of training, but a few of these Marines are going to have to pick it up during this next phase or they will not fare as well at the next board."

Following the two-hour meeting, I found the team TACs two by two, the old and the new, huddled up to talk about their student Marines. Seventy-one Marines from Class 1-13 clear Phase One and move on to Phase Two. Of the original seventy-nine, one was a medical drop and one left for a security-clearance issue. Of the six DOR—drop on request—Marines, only one did so for a compelling family issue, and he alone will be allowed to join the next ITC class. And Class 1-13 has reinforcements. Four Marines who had to leave previous ITC classes for legitimate medical or personal reasons will join the class, bringing 1-13 back up to seventy-five Marines—twelve officers and sixty-three sergeants.

CHAPTER FIVE

PHASE ONE: GROUND COMBAT AND AMPHIBIOUS OPERATIONS

The battle, sir, is not to the strong alone, but it is to the vigilant, the active, and the brave.

PATRICK HENRY

Phase One is tactically challenging and perhaps the most physically demanding of the four instructional phases of the Individual Training Course. The days are very long and there are a number of military disciplines that come at the students with little break in moving from one of these skill sets to the next. It would seem that those with an infantry background would have an advantage, but that's not always the case. In this phase, the students will move from mission planning, to basic tactics, to amphibious operations, to weapons, to fire support, and so on. The 0300-MOS Marines in the class may be more familiar with some of these infantry-based skills, yet perhaps not as they are applied in a special-operations environment. Additionally, many of these combat-veteran infantrymen have had those basic-infantry tactics so modified and adapted to the specific requirements of combat in Iraq and Afghanistan that they've moved well away from the basics. Many will need to relearn these fundamentals as they relate to standard infantry tactics and as they are employed by a Marine Special Operations Team. The phase concludes with a fast-moving, integrated exercise that will call on the student teams to use some or all of their

ITC skills in scenario-based training built around our notional nation of Abyssinia. This field training exercise is also something of a gut check to see if these Marines have the physical stamina, mental discipline, and personal commitment to perform in a dynamic tactical situation when they are tired and sleep-deprived. For the ITC cadre, the serious business of evaluating the students as special operators begins. In addition to the phase subject matter, they will also continue to monitor these Marines for those ten characteristics of a Critical Skills Operator.

MISSION PLANNING/MISSION PREPARATION

Before these student Marines get to the practice of infantry skills or tactics, they will first learn how to plan. The heart of operational planning, from a simple infantry warning order to an irregular-warfare campaign, begins with the Marine Corps Planning Process. The heart of the MCPP as applied to a squad-sized element is the five-paragraph patrol order. Much of the first week of this phase of instruction deals with the initial mission planning and this patrol order.

In addition to a written exam on basic tactics and planning, the students will be asked during this phase to:

> With the aid of references, given a special operations mission, a completed five-paragraph order, and a terrain model; issue a five-paragraph patrol order, ensuring the plan is understood and tasks are executed in accordance with the SOF Imperatives, Mission, Commander's Intent, unit SOPs, and guidelines outlined in the references. (MSOF-PLAN-1436)

"Welcome to the phase and the basic planning process," the lead instructor, a civilian, tells the seventy-five Marines of Class 1-13 on their first day of the new phase. "As we begin, I want you to keep a few things in mind. You're all good Marines, even excellent Marines. Okay, that's a starting point. Now we want to see you develop as a

professional Marine and to take your skill sets and craft to the next
level. It all begins with the planning—planning that must be done in
a timely manner, with careful consideration of the time you're given
between mission notification and mission execution. Keep in mind the
one-third, two-thirds rule. Devote no more than a third of the time
for studying the mission and leave two-thirds of your allotted time for
the actual development of the plan. And never, never forget the advice
of General George S. Patton, 'A good plan violently executed now is
better than a perfect plan next week.' "

A five-paragraph order speaks to the situation, mission, execution,
administration, and to the logistics, command, and signal information.
Each of these five is broken down by the numbers in significant detail
and keyed by a host of acronyms and checklists that give structure
and thoroughness to the planning process. In support of this process,
1-13 receives classes in map reading, route selection, intelligence support, techniques of memory, field sketching, and the construction of
a terrain model. Patrol orders are usually given with the use of a terrain
model, with the squad or team gathered around the model. The class
is given instruction and a practical application in the construction of
terrain models. This is perhaps, with the exception of occasionally
crawling around in the mud, the only holdover skill from playing in
the sandbox as a preschooler. Through all the acronyms and military-
speak, there's no substitute for a bird's-eye, three-dimensional display
model of the ground over which the mission is to be conducted. Terrain
models can be highly accurate scale models of the target and the
ground around the target. I've seen them prepared with great care and
attention to include toy soldiers, little vehicles, and small cardboard
houses. They can also be, for a time-sensitive mission, drawn up in
the dirt.

Over the course of the phase, each student will be asked to write
a five-paragraph order for a squad- or team-sized raid mission or an
ambush mission, complete with the supporting documentation that
covers each step of the mission. These details address the task organization, enemy forces, route selection, commander's intent, concept

of operation, fire support, and so on. The student planners will do this more than once, and it will become part of their grade for the phase. Past the writing of these orders, each Marine will be expected to brief the mission or a portion of the mission for grade. The expectations for this are the same for the infantrymen as for the admin clerks. Again, this planning process is familiar to those with an infantry background, especially the infantry officers, but they've never approached it in such detail.

"We had a little of this in the Corporal's Course," said Sergeant Brad Hansen, the cyber-network operator, "but compared to this, it was just an overview. I'm going to be studying this material hard—for the test and for when I have to brief my patrol order. I really want to do well." On Friday morning of the first week, the students are released from the classroom with a mission-tasking folder and an assignment. They are to develop and write out in longhand a warning order, a briefing overlay, and a five-paragraph patrol order. A warning order is a formatted notification from the team leader or team chief to his Marines about an upcoming mission. It is a brief summary of the mission statement, an approximate time line, and a list of what equipment each Marine needs to have prepared to conduct the mission. The briefing overlay is a single-sheet transparency that has information such as weather data, communications frequencies, call signs, code words, primary/alternative routes, and a target list. The five-paragraph or team patrol order is the who, what, where, when, and why of the mission.

"This is the first time many of you have done this in this detail," the senior planning instructor tells Class 1-13, "and it will not be the last. Do your own work, but talk it up among yourselves over the weekend. Trade warning and patrol orders; ask someone to read yours and you read his. Very soon you will have to brief these orally. If public speaking is an issue for you, now's a good time to stand up and give these as an oral presentation to each other. Since this is a written exercise, and I have to read and grade all seventy-five, keep them clear, concise, and neat. Hold on to these mission-tasking folders; we'll build on them for the next planning exercise. And remember, outside the gate is good, but here inside the gate, it's what?"

"PROFESSIONAL."

"Roger that and don't forget it. You have my cell number and the cell numbers of the other planning cadre. If you have questions, call us anytime—day or night, weekday or weekend."

This instructor is a Pittsburgh native and a no-nonsense, retired Marine infantry weapons officer, or gunner. The term "gunner," as opposed to "gunny" for a Marine gunnery sergeant, marks him as a warrant officer who specialized in the tactical employment of all Marine infantry weapons systems. This retired gunner was also a Marine sniper instructor. His passion for planning and attention to detail is not lost on the Marines of Class 1-13.

During the first week, a half day of class is devoted to the optics in the MARSOC inventory. In addition to field glasses, spotting scopes, and illumination devices, there are the all-important night-vision goggles or NVGs. For training, this class will be issued and use the AN/PVS-15 NVGs—the same NVGs they will use in their operational MSOTs. They are also introduced to the more advanced PVS-21s that they will see on future deployments. All in 1-13 have some familiarity with NVGs, and close to half have used them operationally. For most, this is their first experience with the more modern PVS-15s.

"A great deal of our work is built around being able to see in the dark and shoot in the dark," says the cadre staff sergeant conducting the class. "We do this routinely, and our enemies do not—at least not for now. Effectively using NVGs takes practice—lots of practice—and you'll get that here and when you get to your teams. When it gets dark, snap your NVGs down and keep them there. It'll be awkward at first, and yes, there are depth-perception issues and field-of-vision issues, but they get better with time on the gear. With the binocular PVS-15s, you will be able to move at night like you move during the day. It's how we fight a great deal of the time."

The instructor teaching this class is not only a very good instructor; he is the first of his kind. He graduated from the ITC with Class

1-09—the very first ITC class. After three tours with an operational MSOT in Afghanistan, he is the first ITC CSO graduate to return to the school as an instructor.

Friday afternoon, the class receives a rappel and fast-rope orientation at the MARSOC rappelling tower. Most of these Marines rappelled during basic training, but for one or two, this is their first time. About half have fast-roped with their operational units and half of those, in a combat situation. This is another of those baseline evolutions to ensure all ITC students have done this at least once and that it will not be entirely new to them when they get to their operational teams. Amid all the change that has come to modern special operations, it is nice to see these "ropers" from Class 1-13 take their sections of climbing rope and tie on their Swiss seats exactly as I was taught to do it back in my day.

TACTICS

Week two and three of the phase are all about tactics—basic infantry tactics and, in particular, those tactics used by small units. Prior to the morning's classroom work, the class musters at 0515 for a ten-mile timed ruck march. They are on the clock again, so it's as much of a run as it is a march. But not all of them complete the evolution. One man DORs before the ruck march and another after, leaving seventy-three Marines to begin their work in tactics.

Approximately half the tactics instruction is in the classroom and half in the field. Beginning in class and moving to the wooded areas around the MARSOC Academic Facility, the students receive instruction and practical work in the fundamentals of patrolling, patrolling formations, security patrols, and combat patrols. They cover building caches, field sketching, fire support plans, intelligence collection, raids, and ambushes. A full day is devoted to imagery capture and the use of the Canon 30D digital single-lens reflex camera. Along with this versatile camera are a number of wide-angle and telephoto lenses and attachments. They also get a full day with the FalconView digital mapping software. FalconView is a Windows-based system that marries conventional two-dimensional technologies with satellite imagery. This system, along with the trusty Google Earth, are used extensively in planning and executing small-unit ground operations.

During this first week of tactics, the student MSOTs begin patrolling drills as a team. In the open and under the supervision of their TACs, the teams practice basic patrol formations—single column file, the wedge, the vee, and the extended and closed-up variations of these formations. They review standard hand-and-arm signaling, designating rally points, and crossing danger areas. The teams also begin to develop their SOPs, or standard operating procedures. These are preplanned movements in response to a command or a situational development, or a reaction to enemy contact. Regarding the latter, "enemy contact" typically refers to unanticipated contact or contact that demands an immediate, instinctual response. These SOPs are called IA drills, or immediate action drills. Small units must react with purpose and in concert when attacked or threatened, so all small units, to include these student MSOTs, will drill and drill on just what to do when they receive unexpected enemy contact—from the front, rear, side, or from wherever.

The second week of tactics, following a comprehensive written exam and a FalconView graded practical, the student teams then leave the MARSOC compound for more extensive fieldwork. After drawing weapons and NVGs, the student MSOTs head for the operational ranges on Camp Lejeune, just north of the Stone Bay complex. Most instruction in tactics follows a practiced format: teach technique in the classroom, demonstrate proper technique through cadre-led drill, and then conduct continuous cadre-supervised student drills to perfect the technique. The cadres go to great lengths to show the students just what "right" looks like, and each skill set is carefully demonstrated. Tuesday afternoon in a field classroom setting, the phase officer in charge presents a five-paragraph patrol order, complete with terrain model and the accompanying detail of a full-on patrol order.

Captain Allen Jacobs is a Chicagoan with two deployments as an infantry officer and two as an MSOT commander. He is the phase OIC, or officer in charge. When he finishes his tour with the MAR-SOC, he will be going to the Captains Maneuver Course at Fort Benning and then back to the Marine Corps for duty in an infantry battalion. Captain Jacobs's presentation is carefully critiqued by the gunner, who is not above a critical review of his OIC's patrol order. Following the "school solution" patrol order, the class heads for their field training area, where each team will go into their individual patrol base. Before they do, the phase senior noncommissioned officer has a few words for them.

"Gentlemen, this is where we get after it—in the field. This is where we work hard and we don't get all that much sleep. Some of this is going to be new to many of you. Some of you haven't done this for a while. Jump right in; stay engaged; do the little things. Pay attention and don't be afraid to ask questions, and above all don't be afraid to make mistakes. We'll start slow, but the pace will accelerate, so you're going to want to lock down this information now. In the following weeks and especially during Exercise Raider Spirit, it will come fast and furious at you.

"It looks like we're in for a few cold and wet days. It's going to suck. But if you don't take to this and these conditions, and to being out here training hard, then you're in the wrong business. You have to love this stuff and want to be here. This is also where you and my instructor cadre earn their paychecks. Any questions for me? Okay, let's get to it."

The first thing that the four student MSOT teams do is push out into the woods a hundred meters or so and set up a patrol base. A great many of these students have not set up a patrol base in some time. At least half of Class 1-13 have never done it at all. So the cadres and TACs direct their students in some detail in setting up their first patrol base. A patrol base is a small unit's bivouac when they are in the field—a tactical home away from home. A patrol base has its own special conventions and rhythms that have to do with security, weapons maintenance, eating, sleeping, communicating, and awaiting the next mission tasking. I've spent time with SEAL, Green Beret, and Ranger candidates in their patrol bases. It was finally good to have the opportunity to be in a patrol base with these student Marine special operators. Along with patrol-base procedures and protocols, there is the professional skill or knack of living out of a rucksack. In that seventy-some-pound rucksack is everything a special operator needs to live, sleep, eat, and fight for an extended period of time. Every item in the ruck is valued for its utility and necessity, and subject to be discarded when measured against another item that is more useful or valuable. A good Marine, or good Marine special-operations student, will pack only what he needs and knows where it is and how to get to it. Checklists help; experience counts. A good rucker can get to his rations, find his ammunition, tend to his hygiene and personal needs, and set up his bed and shelter in total darkness without showing a light. The Marines of 1-13 are not yet that practiced. They struggle with their gear, and the weather is not helpful. Their first night in the patrol base the temperature drops to forty-two degrees and it begins to rain. The rain continues all night and into the next day.

A patrol base will always balance the team's need for rest, refit, and mission planning with the need for security. Once an out-of-the-way site is selected for the patrol base, one with good concealment, the team goes to ground. Security positions around the base are identified and set in to make best use of the team's M240G medium machine guns and the M249 squad assault weapons, or SAWs. The team chief and element leaders carefully set in these gun and security positions. For a few hours after dark and at least an hour before dawn, everyone is awake. In these first patrol bases, the teams are on 50 percent security. Half the team is on security detail and the other half is tending to gear and personal maintenance issues, as well as any operational tasks, like communications and preparation for the future operations. When the team goes into their rest period, they do this in a set rotation; half the team sleeps while the other half is on security. In addition to manning weapons to protect the patrol base, a roving security patrol of two to three Marines slowly move in close proximity to the base for additional patrol-base protection. This first night in their patrol bases, those in Class 1-13 are lucky to get four hours of sleep.

The final three days are devoted to the practical application of infantry skills and small-unit tactics. The first day is a round-robin rotation. The student MSOTs rotate through five stations, each two hours in duration. One is a planning review of the five-paragraph warning order, conducted by the gunner. He covers the mechanics of the order as delivered by the phase OIC the previous day and some of the common errors the students made in their weekend planning assignments. The second is a spotting exercise. The students camp behind their M49 spotting scopes and study a tree line a hundred meters in the distance. Hidden in the tree line are twenty objects ranging from an entrenched shovel to a brightly colored earplug. The students must spot fifteen of these objects to achieve a passing grade. Station three is a field sketching exercise made more challenging by the rain. Here the students must study, inventory, sketch, and properly annotate a tent-and-vehicle compound and hand the sketches in for a grade. The fourth station is more instruction on the Canon 5D digital camera along with an assortment of telephoto lenses. Here the student photographers are asked to capture distant images from well-concealed positions. And finally, there is the Vector 21 Bravo/AN/PS-13 Defense Advance GPS Receiver, or DAGR (pronounced dagger). Briefly, these systems combine a set of binoculars that have a laser range-finding capability with a GPS system so the user can "lase" a distant object and, immediately and precisely, plot its grid coordinates for operational attention. It's a challenging day of field craft, made more so by the steady rain and a noisy nearby hand-grenade range, but the learning gets done.

The next two nights in the patrol bases are colder but dry, and the students seem better for the conditions. The infantrymen settle back into their field rhythm, and those new to living in a patrol base are acquiring the knack of living out of a ruck.

"This is what I've been waiting for—the real meat and potatoes of this work," said Sergeant Brad Hansen after his second night out. "I'm learning a lot; this is great."

"Y'know," confessed Sergeant Kerry Irving, "I just eat this stuff up, and I have ever since I was in the Boy Scouts. It can suck, but this is what it's all about." I ask about sleep. "We go two hours on security and two hours off. You doze, but you don't really sleep. About the third night out, tonight probably, it starts to catch up with you, so when you doze, you go down deep. It's all good."

Thursday is all about mission planning and mission execution—by the numbers. Two of the teams plan and execute a road ambush and two plan and execute a raid. But the student MSOT team leaders are cadres. The thinking is that they want these future CSOs to see it done right in a field setting before they do it on their own. Just after dawn each team is tasked for their mission by a FRAGO, or fragmentation order—an order to execute a small-unit mission that comes to a team in the field by radio. Then a cadre sergeant takes the team carefully through the process to include mission tasking, mission analysis, and issuing a warning order. They follow with the mission-planning steps and all the supporting tasks, to include building a crude terrain model for the patrol order briefing. The teams then go into pre-mission inspections, pre-mission rehearsals, a test fire of weapons (with blank ammunition), patrolling to the objective, setting in an operational readiness position, executing a patrol leaders recon, movement to the release point, and the final mission execution on target. They conduct all the small steps and details essential to a small-unit raid or the conduct of an ambush by a small unit. It's a great deal of information, but it's presented in a methodical and highly formatted manner. While designated cadres serve as the patrol leaders, the TACs and other phase cadres are circling the student patrols like border collies, helping with a better way to carry a piece of gear or by demonstrating an individual movement technique.

After another night in yet another patrol base, the student teams receive another FRAGO. Teams that were on the ambush the previous night are tasked with a raid and vice versa. And the process begins again. The student captains take the reins and start the target analysis and mission planning process. The student team chiefs begin working on the patrol warning order. A quick word about the composition of a Marine Special Operations Team—an operational team or a student ITC team. An MSOT is headed by a team commander and assisted by his second in command, the team senior enlisted Marine, who is known as the team chief. Each team has two mirror-image squads or elements, each headed by an element leader. There are other detailed and important positions within the team, but the big four are the team commander, the team chief, and the two element leaders. Throughout the ITC, the CSO students will rotate through these key leadership positions and be graded on their performance in these roles.

All tactical targeting is based on the Republic of Abyssinia scenario. Late Friday afternoon, two Aksum patrol bases are attacked and overrun, and two Sword of the Right Hand patrols are ambushed. Following a lengthy AAR, or after-action review, the weary teams return to the MARSOC compound to clean and turn in their weapons and NVGs. Then it's gear maintenance and overhaul, a hot shower, and a good night's sleep. Actually two good nights, then the student MSOTs will be back out in the field.

For the tactics portion, and indeed this entire phase, I do what I can to stay with student MSOT Three and their new TAC. This is the team with Captain Andrew Fraker, Sergeant Kerry Irving, and Sergeant Brad Hansen. Their phase TAC is Staff Sergeant Jesse Garrison. SSGT Garrison is from Charleston and joined the Marine Corps right out of high school. He's a ten-year veteran, married, and came to MARSOC from the Foreign Military Training Unit. As an infantryman, he had two tours in Iraq and was in the Battle of Ramadi in 2006. Garrison came to the school from the 1st Marine Special Operations Battalion, where he made three MSOT deployments to the Philippines. He's a quiet teacher, very professional, and speaks nearly fluent Tagalog.

LIGHT WEAPONS

For most Individual Training Courses, the classes begin the amphibious portion of their training immediately following their two weeks of tactics. For Class 1-13, due to range availabilities on Camp Lejeune, they will first train in light and medium machine guns before they begin their amphib training. The light-weapons week is almost a misnomer as they will continue to set up and live in team patrol bases and continue with tactics instruction and patrolling drills. And a full day this week of light weapons will be devoted to planning and the oral delivery of a five-paragraph patrol order.

Before the class loads out from the Stone Bay complex for the nearby live-fire range, the teams are again treated to a hard physical training session and a timed five-mile run. And again, there are two from Class 1-13 who decide that this is not for them and DOR. Usually those who drop on request are among those performing poorly—Marines who are having trouble keeping up, professionally or physically. But this is not always the case. On this occasion, one of the students who hands in his rope is a captain who is doing all things well. Yet, for reasons he cites as personal, he has chosen to return to the regular Marine Corps. His leaving the class is a reminder to students and cadres alike that this brand of military service is not for everyone. Most of the students *think* they want to be special operators. As the training progresses, they're learning that there is a stiff price to be paid, both in physical endurance and professional skills. The withdrawal of this fine captain is a surprise to all.

"It just goes to show," reflected Gunny Patterson, 1-13's proctor, "that special operations and MARSOC duty is not the only way a Marine can serve his country. He's a good officer, and I wish him well."

There are three weapons systems the Marines will work with, in addition to practical drill with their M4 rifles. The first machine gun, which is technically an assault rifle, is the Kalashnikov AK-47. Perhaps the most universal and recognizable of all current battlefield weapons, the AK-47 is the most widely manufactured and common military rifle in the world. The weapon, with its long, curved banana magazine and gas piston tube atop the barrel, is, in many respects, a symbol of those who oppose America on the battlefield and those who practice terror. Yet because it's also used by so many allied nations and friendly military forces, it's a weapon that all Marine special operators must learn. Manufactured by more than twenty countries and in various models, refinements, and configurations, the weapon has remained largely unchanged since it was first adapted by the Russian Army in 1947. The variant used by Marines in the ITC is the Romanian-made PM-90, but it's still an AK-47.

The second weapons system is the M249 light machine gun. The 249, often referred to simply as "the SAW," or squad automatic weapon, is a staple among Marine Special Operations Teams and, indeed, all U.S. military small combat units. The Belgian-designed, U.S.-manufactured weapon first came into the Marine inventory in 1985. The M249 is a fully automatic, area-fire weapon with a cyclic rate of fire of 775 rounds per minute. It uses the same standard 5.56 NATO cartridge as the M4 and is fed by a disintegrating-link ammunition belt that snakes out of a two-hundred-round magazine slung under the weapon.

The third machine gun is the M240G medium machine gun. Often referred to simply as "the gun," the M240G provides a small unit with the punch of the heavier NATO 7.62 ammunition. The 240 is another Belgian-designed, U.S.-made weapons system. Adapted by the Marine Corps in the 1980s to replace the M60 medium machine gun, it is a versatile gun that is used in a number of vehicle-mounted configurations or carried by an infantry squad. When deployed from a fixed position on its bipod, it provides a stable, accurate platform for delivering supporting fire for infantry support-by-fire movements.

"This gun," said one of the class infantry captains as he demonstrated its use to one of the non-infantry Marines in his squad, "is the finest weapon we own. If you take care of this gun and use it properly, it can do a lot of good things for you. I love it. Over the years it's covered a lot of Marines and saved the lives of a lot of Marines. In my infantry platoon, we called it the 'martyr maker.'"

The infantrymen in Class 1-13 are very familiar with the M249 and the M240G, and most have fired an AK-47. The non-infantrymen trained on the 249 and 240 during their one-month Marine Combat Training. Marine Combat Training is a brief weapons and tactics course for those Marines assigned to non-infantry specialties and immediately follows their basic Marine Corps training. Few of these Marines have ever fired an AK-47. All in Class 1-13 are tested on the disassembly, assembly, maintenance, nomenclature, operation, malfunction, and clearing of all three weapons systems. On the firing range, they sight-in and fire the weapons under the watchful eye of the cadre. Yet when it comes to weapons and range work in a class where half of them are experienced Marine infantrymen, there are, in practice, as many instructors as students.

In addition to the machine guns, the class spends an afternoon with their course-issued M4 rifles. All in 1-13 are familiar to one degree or another with this SOF assault rifle or a variant of the rifle. And all are familiar with the standard ACOG(advanced combat optical gunsight)-type sight (also know as the M150 RCO) that is a standard scope-type sight in the Marine Corps. This 4x ACOG scope is common to M16 and M4 rifles and is taught in Marine basic and combat-training venues. The special operations M4s used for this phase of the course are fitted with the ELCAN 1x4 sight, developed for special operations forces by Raytheon. The ELCAN features a long-range/close-in system that allows the shooter, with a flip of a lever, to shift from one power to four power. Only a very few in 1-13 have used this ELCAN gunsight, including the veteran infantrymen. One thing all these Marines have done is to BZO, or "battlefield zero," their weapons. Once on the range, with all the weapons systems, they go through this familiar drill of grouping their shots on the target, then adjusting the group to the center of the target.

After BZOing their M4s, the student teams are put through fire-and-maneuver drills. Basic fire-and-maneuver is a tactic used to assault a fixed position with half the team advancing while the other half lays down a base of fire. Then the advancing element halts and takes up firing positions, ahead and to the side of their teammates providing covering fire. Once in position, they take up the firing while the other element bounds forward with their advance. This leapfrog tactic is used by the student MSOTs to assault a target structure on the range and then to cover a redeployment or retreat from the target. This range, like many of the modern military firing ranges on Camp Lejeune, is automated so targets in the form of silhouettes pop up at various ranges and in the target-building structures and can be programmed to fall, or "pop down," after they are hit. They can be programmed to fall if hit once, twice, or after any set number of multiple hits. The number of hits can be tallied so an assaulting force can be graded on the number of hits per rounds fired. It's something of a participatory video game except for the reality of firing live rounds. The student teams take turns first assaulting a target and then recovering from the assault using fire-and-maneuver. The cadre sergeants run just behind the bounding student elements, carefully monitoring the fire-and-maneuver drills.

While three of the student MSOTs are on the shooting ranges, one is in a grassy area off the range giving five-paragraph patrol orders. Marines in groups of four or five gather around a hastily constructed terrain model along with a cadre staff sergeant. One student gives his brief while the others listen. Periodically, the instructor will step in with a correction, a teaching point, or an alternative methodology.

"A part of this is to give them practice and confidence in briefing a mission," the gunner said of the field-expedient patrol orders. "They'll all have to do this to an acceptable standard for grade. The other thing is that we want them to be thinking about planning and tactical execution all the time. This is to build muscle memory for Exercise Raider Spirit, when they will be in a continuous cycle of plan, patrol, execute, patrol, and sleep—with very little emphasis on the sleep part. They can't see this planning process enough or do it enough."

At the end of a shooting day, the learning day is only half-over.

The class moves from the range to the bivouac area, and the Marines immediately go into their patrol bases. That night, after a quick MRE meal, they ruck up and begin night patrols under the watchful eye of the cadre and their TACs. Yet they are not just out boring holes in the Carolina woodlands. They patrol to a set of coordinates and go into an operational readiness position, or ORP. An ORP is the first stage of setting up a patrol base—security positions are set in with the team's M240Gs and M249 SAWs. The ORP is a temporary position from which they will lay up in wait before moving on to the objective. In this particular case it's a commo ORP. After the security positions are established, the teams break out their radios. They make a communications shot with the AN/PRC-117, sending and receiving voice and data by satellite. They also send and receive high-frequency voice transmissions over the AN/PRC-150 and -148 MBITR radios.

Throughout the evening's patrolling, the teams work on their SOPs, to include hand and arm signals, security halts, danger crossings, immediate and hasty ambushes, and the all-important IAs, or immediate action drills, in response to unexpected contact. Earlier in the day, the teams walked through these drills without kit when they were not engaged on the shooting ranges. Now they do them at night, with kit and with NVGs. Moving tactically under a load in the flat green world of night optics takes a great deal of practice. They do this for four to five hours before making their way back to their patrol bases. For three successive evenings the teams patrol with their NVGs, drill on their SOPs, set up communications ORPs, and practice simulated raid and ambush positions. The cadres are there with them, periodically holding a critique session or executing a patrol halt to talk about how they could do the exercise a little differently or a little better.

Shortly after midnight of these night-patrol drills, they are back in their patrol bases, this time with a 25 percent security rotation. A quarter of the team is on watch in security positions while the rest of the team goes to ground for a sleep period. The next day, they are back on the shooting ranges, firing the light automatic weapons or, alternatively, drilling on their patrol SOPs and practicing their patrol-order deliveries.

"Our team is really starting to gel," Sergeant Irving says of his student MSOT Three. "The younger, non-infantry-MOS Marines are coming into their own, and they don't have to be reminded what to do. The officers and cadre sergeants are now starting to put these Marines in the role of team leader so they can see how it works from the front of the patrol. It just takes time, and we're all learning. Also this week, we're getting a little more sleep. Because we're on the live ranges, the cadre has to get us back into the patrol base for a proper amount of rest."

"Are you starting to think about next week along about this time?" I ask, knowing they will be in Key West. Sergeant Irving, as I'm learning, is one of the more senior and experienced of the ITC student sergeants. Like many of the captains and other senior sergeants, he quite often serves as teaching assistant to the cadre.

"Actually, we're trying not to think about Key West. There's a lot to be learned here and some good information to lock down this week before we move on to amphib." He smiles. "And I'm sure there will be a lot to learn down there. But a little sunshine and warm water will be nice. Very nice."

Thursday evening they remain on the ranges for night-firing drill. These drills center around the M240Gs and M249s and the use of the PVS-17B and -17C night-vision aiming scopes and the PAS-13D thermal aiming scope. The students rotate through firing the 13D on the 240 and the 17B/C on the 249. This night work is to familiarize all in the class with shooting at night with machine guns and these standard night-aiming scopes. While one team shoots, the other teams observe the target with their NVGs. Later, in Phase Three, they will work with their M4s and night-combat shooting techniques.

Friday of this first week with weapons is all about fire-and-maneuver and support-by-fire. Support-by-fire, like fire-and-maneuver, is a standard infantry tactic, but the execution of it with live rounds is a carefully executed standard. Support-by-fire is when a target is taken under fire by an element in a fixed position that is away from, and usually at forty-five to ninety degrees from, the assault element's projected line of advance. This supporting fire provides some measure of support and protection to those whose mission it is to assault the target. For Class 1-13, each team develops its plan for assaulting a range target under the covering fire from a support position. Once their plan is approved by the cadre, the team sets in their M240G medium machine guns, each with a gunner and an assistant gunner. The rest of the team moves to an assault position downrange and off to one side of the 240's gun-target line.

The drill begins as the M240s take the target under fire with a steady, rhythmic fire—knocking down silhouettes as they appear in and around the target building. The assault elements then begin bounding toward the target using good fire-and-maneuver discipline. As the assault elements close with the target, the support-by-fire 240s shift their fire away from the assaulters to targets in the distance. As the assault element moves onto and through the target, the support element ceases fire. Once the target is secured, other targets appear down range to simulate a counterattack. The assaulters then bound back in leapfrog fashion while the support-by-fire element carefully follows their retreat with supporting fire. Throughout the drills, there are cadre sergeants with the assault elements, supervising their movement. They are also hovering over the 240 gunners in the support-by-fire position. In the range tower overlooking the range, this live-fire ballet is carefully choreographed by the gunner. While he directs the pop-up targets, he is in constant radio contact with his cadre sergeants in the student support-by-fire and assault elements.

"Some of these guys have done this before," he says of the drill, "but a lot of them haven't. We just want them to see this under very controlled conditions, and to understand the process. When they get to their teams, they will do this again and again, with closer tolerances between the fire and the movement and the nearness of the supporting fires. They'll do this in the daytime and at night. Downrange they'll do this for real, and they'll be teaching it to partner-nation forces. In

Raider Spirit, they will do this again and again, usually at night, but with blank ammunition."

The class gets back to the barracks late afternoon for weapons cleaning and gear overhaul. Later in the evening, they draft and submit their mid-phase peer evaluations. The class now begins to break out a little differently in the eyes of their student MSOT teammates. During the initial phase of training, the basis of measurement was physical fitness—who were the strong and the not so strong, and who were the fast and the slow. There were also the issues of those who were or were not prompt and cheerful with the barracks duties and administrative chores. And, of course, who among them was most willing to help out a teammate. Now, in Phase One, there are military skills—who among them shoots well, moves well, leads well, follows well, and who does not. In a security halt, who is first up on his feet and then turns to help a teammate up. Some in 1-13 who perhaps initially peered low are seen in a different context now, both positively and negatively. But there's little time to dwell on it. Early the following morning, with a whole different set of training gear, they are on a C-130 transport headed for Key West.

AMPHIBIOUS TRAINING

The shift in focus in the training could not be more striking or more abrupt. On Friday afternoon, they were running across a combat range, assaulting a target building in an assault-by-fire exercise. The temperature was forty-five degrees. On Saturday afternoon, they are pushing their rucks through seventy-two-degree water in an estuary that opens into the Gulf of Mexico. Key West is a tourist destination and a cruise-ship port of call. The greater Key West area is also home to several Navy and Coast Guard installations and associated training facilities that lend themselves to the support of MARSOC amphibious training.

"It was a pretty dramatic transition," said Sergeant Brad Hansen. "We left Camp Lejeune early and landed at Boca Chica Key Naval

Air Station mid-morning. The busses were waiting, and by early afternoon we were moved into the barracks on the naval station. The cadre told us to be ready to get wet, so we had our gear set up for a fin. By mid-afternoon we were in the harbor pushing our rucks in front of us. It was exciting, but it was still a two-thousand-meter fin. That night we began sorting our gear out and getting ready for training in the boats.

"It's something we try to do with each class if we can get an airlift early enough," said the gunner. "We want them in the water the same day they leave Camp Lejeune. It sets the tone for our training down here. It's all about the boats, finning, and tactical amphibious operations. It's easy to get into a tropical mind-set down here after leaving the North Carolina winter. But these guys will work hard down here, and so will my cadre."

There are two main training areas used by MARSOC at Key West. The students are billeted in the Naval Air Station Truman Annex, which features a small-craft harbor that is protected by a man-made mole. The student barracks are located near a warehouse complex that doubles as a small-craft hangar and an open-bay classroom. This is where the Marines will conduct their navigation and small-craft instruction, followed by waterborne practical application in the adjacent harbor and seaway around Key West. A short bus ride away is the Trumbo Point Annex, an old seaplane base that houses the Coast Guard station, the Coast Guard chow hall, and the bridge access to Fleming Key. Fleming Key is a small, little-used, reclaimed piece of land that is also the site of the Army Special Forces Underwater Operations School. The two-thousand-meter fin course along the eastern shore of Fleming Key is one these MARSOC students will come to know well.

Sunday is given over to equipment overhaul and preparation and setting up the boats. The at-sea portion of this amphibious training will focus on navigation and the tactical use of small craft. For these students, their two weeks of amphib training will focus on the operation and maintenance of the fifteen-foot Zodiac combat rubber raiding crafts, or CRRCs. These fully inflatable, 325-pound craft are amazingly robust. They are powered by a fifty-five-horsepower Evenrude outboard that can move a load of eight marines across a choppy sea at close to eighteen knots. The outboard engines are of a special design with shrouded propellers for the safety of those in the water and can run on gasoline or diesel fuel. Fully loaded with outboard engine, fuel, and safety equipment, the craft weighs close to seven hundred pounds.

Days at Key West and amphib begin with reveille at 0500. The students are geared up and in the water by 0600, well before sunrise, for their daily two-thousand-meter fin. They must enter and exit the water tactically and in full utility uniform and a combat load that includes Rhodesian ammo vest, canteens, knife, life vest, and a fifty-pound floating rucksack. Most of the technique of this timed evolution has to do with the mechanics of transition—getting in and out of the water quickly. The finning itself has to do with simply moving through the water; if a student wants to improve his time, he simply has to fin harder. Those who are good swimmers are not necessarily good finners. Yet, for most, it's just a matter of conditioning and time in the water. The only thing a student can mechanically do is change his fins. I noticed that Captain Andrew Fraker's fin times were well below standard but that toward the end of the training he was some twenty minutes faster over the two-thousand-yard course.

"I was really down on myself," Fraker said of his early performance. "This was just not like me." In all other physical evolutions, Captain Fraker was among the class leaders. "But for some reason the standard-issue, rocket-type fins just didn't work for me. I managed to get some different fins, fins that were different in design from the rocket fins, and that made all the difference. I'm not up with the leaders, but I'm making the minimum times and then some. But then, I have some slow times to make up for."

The goal is for all the Class 1-13 finners to achieve an *average* two-thousand-meter time of one hour. On the last fin of the nine two-thousand-meter-fin evolutions, the class and Captain Fraker make the one-hour average. The fastest time at this distance was a swim pair who finned the course in thirty-four minutes, thirty seconds. During the fin evolutions, and indeed all in-water and on-the-water training operations, there is continuous cadre presence—in safety boats, on the radios, and conducting water-entry safety briefings and inspections and post-training accountability. Since this is considered high-risk training, a medical corpsman and first-aid equipment are staged afloat and ashore for all amphibious training. After each morning's fin, the students as a class ruck up with their wet gear and run back to the starting line. Then they get to go to breakfast. While the days are long and hard, the food at the Coast Guard chow hall is exceptional. And these MARSOC amphib students can put away chow by the tray-full, and then some.

One their second Saturday at Key West, the class does not have to do a two-thousand-meter fin. This day they will fin for five thousand meters. It's not a timed evolution, but a team competition. The student MSOTs are linked by a team buddy line and fin five thousand-meter circuits around the small-craft harbor at the Truman Annex. As with the two-thousand-meter fins, there are several instructors in the water with the students. These amphib students in Class 1-13 will push their rucks through the water for just under *fifteen miles* during their two weeks of amphib training. That afternoon, the class is given four hours off to walk out into historic Key West and buy souvenirs. That night, following evening chow at the Coast Guard mess hall, they are back in the classroom for a review prior to their written exam, which will take place on Sunday.

The daytime hours and many of the nights are taken up with small-boat navigation and small-boat operation. Classroom programs center around basic piloting skills, navigation, and the use of navigational charts. They work with nautical slide rules, dividers, parallel rulers, and marine compasses. The amphib students learn about speed-time-distance calculations over water and factors, like set, drift, tidal currents, and sea state, that can affect those calculations. Tactically, there is classroom training on conducting hydrographic and beach surveys and developing littoral survey charts.

In the harbor the students learn to operate and maneuver their outboard-powered Zodiacs. Each Zodiac carries one instructor and five or six students. The harbor is large enough for maneuvering drills and short high-speed runs to get the feel for the handling character-istics of these rugged inflatables in calm water. The crews practice docking drills and rigging of their craft for towing in case of an engine malfunction. This is in contrast to the activity on the seaward side of the mole or causeway where the Carnival Line cruise ships tie up on a daily basis. On the harbor side of the mole, the twelve MARSOC student crews conduct motorized and non-motorized drills during the day and simulate clandestine landing and withdrawal drills at night. On one afternoon, there is a soft-duck, helo-cast training scheduled. This is where the Zodiacs are slung under a Marine CH-53 helo, and boat and boat crew are deployed from an over-water hover. This training is conducted at the water landing zone just off nearby Flem-ing Key.

Past the finning, the classroom work, the bumper drills in the harbor, and a comprehensive amphibious-training written exam, the students, their boats, and their instructors spend hours and hours making open-water navigation runs in the waters around Key West. These evolutions begin with plotting the day's courses on their charts and calculating the estimated speed and time for each leg of the course. Then the students prep their boats and motors, conduct their pre-mission checklists, and head for the open water. Once each student has completed a daytime navigational practical exercise, they all go out and do the same thing at night. Often they are not back to the harbor and finished with their post-mission small-craft maintenance until well after midnight. Yet the next day, they are up at 0500 and in the water by 0600 for the morning's two-thousand-meter fin.

The days are long, and because the air and water temperatures average in the low seventies, it might seem that this training is not all that uncomfortable. This is not the case. The wind blows steadily from fifteen to twenty-five knots, so the nav runs are conducted in one- to three-foot seas. Running at speeds that average sixteen knots or better, the student crews have to cling to the sides of their boats and are pounded by the waves. The wet and wind combine to make for cold working conditions.

"I thought I was cold last week in North Carolina when we were out in the patrol base," said one of the students, "but it wasn't as cold as we've been in Florida. Here you're wet all the time, and except for a downwind leg, the wind just cuts through you. All you can do is hug the side tube and tough it out." He grins. "And it's just as hard on the instructor in the boat as it is on us. I almost can't wait to get back to Camp Lejeune and back out in the field."

Following each leg of the navigation runs, the student crews rotate positions in the boat. Each takes his turn at coxswain, assistant coxswain, navigator, assistant navigator, and bearing taker/timekeeper. Everyone has a job to do along with holding on and anticipating the next big wave. It's hard training, and along with the learning, there are the bumps and bruises that come with running a small boat in the chop at high speed. But this too is part of the learning process.

The final amphibious training problem is clandestine beach reconnaissance and beach survey of an enemy-held shoreline. The objective is a section of coastline on the southern coast of Abyssinia, one that is occupied by an Aksum guard force. Class 1-13 is tasked with conducting the survey/recon and then reporting to higher authority on their findings. The mission order comes to them in the morning, and the student MSOTs set to planning, just as they would for a land-based reconnaissance or for a direct-action mission. They are provided with a "local" fisherman whom the team leaders are allowed to question about the target beach and roving enemy patrols. Then they begin the now familiar process that starts with a warning order and time line and progresses through the collaborative planning process to a five-paragraph operations order. Then there are rehearsals, pre-mission inspections, and finally, mission execution.

After a night navigation run to a position off the target beach, the flotilla of Zodiacs gather at what is basically an offshore, operational readiness position—an ORP. Several boats motor quietly to a position just offshore—a maneuver that on land would be a patrol-leaders recon. Six scout swimmers slip over the side and make their way ashore. After the scouts determine there is no enemy activity, they signal the other boats that it is safe for them to come ashore. Some student crews take up security positions while others begin a detailed reconnaissance of the beach and back-shore area. Yet other crews form a line of swimmers from the shoreline out to seaward. They then sweep from one flank of the beach to the other, taking soundings with their lead lines and recording the depths on their slates. This is a technique pioneered by the Navy frogmen during World War II. With the survey and soundings complete, the recon force makes its way back seaward. This observer noticed that there were a great many similarities between an on-land reconnaissance and a seaborne reconnaissance, especially in the areas of security, hand-and-arm signals, and accountability. The steps in planning were essentially the same as those for a land-based ambush or raid mission.

This whole operation was not unlike what I did as a young UDT/SEAL trainee back in the late 1960s. And in the small-world department, I conducted day and night underwater swimmer operations on this very same beach when I attended the Navy Underwater Swimmers School, then located at Key West. Did we perform our reconnaissance training missions any better back then than these MARSOC amphib students do today? Of course we did!

"I was on one of the hydro-recon teams," Sergeant Brad Hansen said of his role in the final amphib problem. "We split the beach in half, my team taking from center beach to the west and another team taking the opposite section of the beach. We conducted surveys on four lanes starting center-beach and working our way out, with each lane separated by approximately twenty-five meters. My swim buddy and I were the closest team to the beach, only twenty-five to thirty meters offshore; the depth was relatively shallow for us. Part of the time we were wading, having only to fin from lane to lane to get our depth checks and bottom samples. The three sets of guys further out to sea were treading water the whole time and diving down to retrieve their bottom samples. We were all grateful to get into the water and conduct our surveys. We froze on the transit to the BLS [beach landing site] and froze again while we waited offshore for the scout swimmers to do their work. The wind had to be blowing twenty knots. The operations took about five hours start to finish, and we were cold the whole time. I couldn't wait to get to a hot shower."

"I was the lead coxswain for MSOT Three," said Captain Fraker of his role on the final problem. "From the IP [insertion point] to the ORP I simply followed Team Four's rearmost boat. Once we left the ORP and began our movement to the BLS, my job was to get our three boats on line and to the beach in the proper lane. Most of the team went into the water to conduct the hydrographic survey. The rest of us horsed the boats around and prepared them for a rapid withdrawal. Back at the base, I was in charge of collating the beach soundings and creating a hydrographic survey report. But I had a lot of help from my team."

When I asked about his overall impressions of the amphibious training, he had to think a moment. "I learned a lot about maritime operations and movement over the beach. I think what surprised me the most is just how physically hard this was. I come from a competitive triathlon/marathon background, and I know what it is to work hard and train hard. This was a rough two weeks. Clinging to the gunnels of those Zodiacs on the nav runs just beat the crap out of us. Except for those four hours we had to walk out in town, it seemed like we were working all the time. When we weren't working, we were sleeping, and we didn't seem to get enough of that. Now it's back to Lejeune for more weapons and Raider Spirit."

From my own viewpoint, I thought the class not only performed well but seemed to come together as a class. I know they were hard-pressed, but individually, each Marine seemed to be able to come up with a smile. More than once I got a "Hey, Mr. Couch, why don't you ride with us today?" And they were always ready to help each other, individually and as teams. It took two crews to move a single boat that was loaded with fuel, gear, and an outboard. Whenever a boat would come into the boat ramp and the crew splashed out to drag it ashore, it seemed that there was always another crew there to help them get their boat up the ramp and onto the hard stand. They seemed to be a tighter class leaving Key West than they were leaving Camp Lejeune for their amphib training. This again was from my perspective, but the hardworking phase cadre had the same observation.

HEAVY WEAPONS AND FIRES

Class 1-13 begins their second period of weapons now down four more Marines. Two DORed during amphib and two were sidelined with injuries. The injured students were able to complete their amphibious-training requirements but will be recycled with the next ITC to continue their training. They will join Class 2-13 at the beginning of their heavy weapons training. The initial heavy weapons week is not as intense as the previous week of light weapons, but it's no less important. The students work long days, but there is no night firing and no long nights out in the patrol bases. The class spends most of the week on the two defensive weapons they will use often and most likely be called upon to teach others to use.

The Browning M2 .50-caliber machine gun went into production after the First World War and is the longest-serving machine gun in the world. It is a simple, versatile gun, with cyclic rate of fire more than six hundred rounds per minute and an effective range out to two thousand yards. And it has tremendous stopping power. The fifty-cal, as it is universally called, is used on most armored vehicles as a turret-mounted weapon and is the preferred weapons system for the turret on an up-armored Humvee. It is also used on the newer armored vehicles using remote-control training and firing systems, which don't expose the gunner to small-arms fire. The second weapon is the Mk-19 grenade launcher. It's not as old as the fifty-cal, but the Mk-19 has been in the inventory for more than forty years. It fires 40mm grenades effectively out to fifteen hundred yards, at a cyclic rate of fire of 350 grenades per minute. The Mk-19, like the fifty-cal, can be sited on a tripod for defensive or area-fire operations or on a vehicle. Most of the Marines have used both these weapons, either on the range or in combat. Still they spend a full day on the operation, maintenance, and troubleshooting procedures with these systems.

On the Lejeune machine-gun ranges, the class operates the M2 and the Mk-19 from the tripod-mounted positions and with the weapons systems mounted on up-armored Humvees. For the infantrymen and many of the non-infantrymen, this is good range work but nothing new. In addition to proficiency with the two weapons systems, they drill on range procedures, misfires, and, with the fifty-cal, changing barrels.

The class spends three full days on direct and indirect fire support or, more simply, fires. The classroom work is split between presentations that cover the range of fire support that may be available to a deployed MSOT and a day with an indirect-fire simulator. At the Marine Special Operations School, there are state-of-the-art simulators for both indirect fire and close air support. The indirect-fire simulator has a flat-screen visual presentation where the student controllers can adjust the fall of shot from mortars or artillery. From their computer-generated "binocular-eye" view of the target, they can initiate call-for-fire missions, just as they would in field conditions. The terrain, targets, and explosions are all re-created on the color-graphic screen with the simulator technician taking adjustments from the student observers and putting them in the system. The commands are as they would be on a real fire mission. The close air support, or CAS, simulator is a large hemispherical apparatus where the student controller station is somewhat inside, with a surround-visual presentation. This simulator is capable of a range of joint terminal attack controller (JTAC) training. The ITC students train in the indirect-fire simulator. Later on, in their post-ITC training, many in Class 1-13 will receive JTAC training on the CAS simulator.

"I felt we got a great overview of fire support from the regimental fire support officer and his staff," said one of the class officers who was an infantry company deputy commander in Afghanistan and had served as a primary JTAC for company-level operations. "They covered it all, including the capabilities and limitations of indirect fires as well as of close air support using rotary and fixed-wing assets. The regimental FSO is a Marine pilot, and you could tell that he knew the game from the cockpit down to the mechanics of what we have to do on the ground to get the ordnance on target. It was very good."

In addition to an overview of the conventional fire support and the types of air-delivered ordnance, there is a presentation on the capabilities and call-for-fire procedures for the only Air Force special-operations airborne fires platform, the very capable and deadly AC-130 gunship. The AC-130H/U, the Specter and Spooky models, is essentially airborne artillery that can be effective against fixed targets or enemy armor. Also in support of SOF ground combatants are the helicopters flown by the 160th Special Operations Aviation Regiment (Airborne), specifically the MH-60L Direct Action Penetrators that carry a variety of rockets and heavy machine guns.

The only range work with indirect-fire weapons was a day on the multipurpose range with the M224 60mm mortar. This was very basic mortar work and a review for the infantrymen, but not for the non-infantry MOS students.

"This was my first experience with mortars, and I had no idea how accurate you could be with them," said Sergeant Brad Hansen of the training. "We understand the roles of the team manning the tubes and of the fire-direction center, but on the range we rotated through the spotter's role. Much of it had to do with proper procedure, but you could still walk rounds on target out to about a mile and a half. And if the bad guys are behind cover, you can still put the hurt on them."

If the mortar spotter's view downrange looked familiar, it was. It was the same view, same targets, and same trees and foliage as the graphic presentation from the indirect-fire simulator.

While two of the teams spotted mortar fall of shot, the other two teams were in the woods nearby, gathered around terrain models and giving five-paragraph patrol orders. This was similar to what the class had done during their off-range time in their light-weapons training, only this time the students are graded on their patrol orders. There are six terrain-model venues scattered over a half-acre section of a nearby wooded area, each with five or six students and a single cadre grader. The target is an enemy installation along a contested border area near the coast of Abyssinia. The enemy forces are Aksum militia and irregulars from the Sword of the Right Hand. The officer or officers in each group go first, followed by the enlisted Marines. But everyone, from infantry captain to communications sergeant, has to stand and deliver an acceptable patrol order. It's a lengthy process, with each patrol order and a short cadre critique taking about an hour and a half. The targets they are briefing are not just for this graded five-paragraph patrol order. This target will be their first assigned target for Exercise Raider Spirit.

The final days of the heavy weapons and fires portion of the phase are devoted to additional time in the indirect-fire simulator and classes on air operations. The air operations classes cover landing-zone management and marking procedures, hand-and-arm signals for bringing in helos, and radio-communication procedures.

"In addition to knowing the capabilities of your helos and how to communicate with them," the instructor tells 1-13, "you need to get to know these pilots and their flight crews. You may be working with Marine flight crews or the crews of the 160th Special Operations Aviation Regiment. The 160th, because they're a special-operation unit, will probably have more experience than Marine flight crews. But experience among all these crews can vary. You have to know what they can and cannot do, but you'll also want to get to know them personally. Take the time to go over to their facility and break bread with them. The better you know them and they know you, the better they'll be able to support you in the field."

RAIDER SPIRIT

Raider Spirit is the culmination exercise of Phase One. It's the exercise that the Marines of Class 1-13 have been looking forward to with mixed feelings. It marks the end of this phase of their training, but they also know it will be something of an ordeal. They know that as a student Marine Special Operations Team, they will be inserted into a contested area of the Republic of Abyssinia and that they will be tasked with an initial direct-action mission. From information they have gleaned from previous classes, they know there will be follow-on missions and that they will be in the field for an extended period of time. For just how long, they don't know for sure. But they know it will be more than just overnight or even two or three days—it will be at least a week. They also know that they will receive one mission tasking after another by fragmentation order, or FRAGO, that will keep them on the move and immersed in field operations.

Raider Spirit is similar in composition and duration as the final tactics-phase exercise in Army Special Forces training. The MARSOC cadre sergeants not only want to see their students perform, but they want to see them perform when they've been in the field for several days, on the move and with very little sleep. The exercise lasts from eight to twelve days. The exact duration can change from class to class. The daily missions are scripted and well choreographed, yet just how long the student MSOTs will be in the field is closely held by the instructors. The exercise begins midweek at 0600 with Captain Jacobs issuing the student teams a company operations order that will send them into the contested area in the Republic of Abyssinia. They are given an initial mission and told to prepare to remain in this contested area for future mission taskings. The teams immediately begin to plan for their first mission and prepare their kit and team radios for an extended period of operations. Just before dusk, the teams are inserted by V-22 Osprey aircraft and begin patrolling to their first objective. The exercise is conducted in a densely wooded training area just north of the Stone Bay complex. The teams are tasked with a series of raids and ambushes to disrupt the activity of the Sword of the Right Hand and elements of the Aksum militia inside Abyssinia. They may also be given reconnaissance and surveillance missions. The teams soon fall into a pattern of conducting a raid or an ambush just before dawn, moving from the target area into a security halt and then setting up a communications link to report their operational activity and to receive another mission tasking. From there they move to on to yet another patrol base. Then begins the now familiar process of rest, refit, and patrol-base security while planning for the next mission.

The targets themselves may be anywhere from four to nine thousand yards apart—as the crow flies. But since the routing from target to patrol base to new target is dictated by terrain and target location, the teams may move twice that distance. Most movement is at night with NVGs under simulated tactical conditions, which can be very slow going. The mechanics of patrol movement and the standard procedures that govern everything from patrol base activity to mission preparation to planning actions on the objective all take time and attention. The first full day out, the teams get no sleep. On subsequent days and missions, they will average about two hours' sleep per day. Several days into Raider Spirit, the teams will make their way to a central area for rest and refit. There they will get resupplied and go into their patrol bases for a rest period. Yet they are on contested ground, and the teams have to remain tactical with good security. This day the students will get between four and five hours' sleep. Then they are back on the move with a new mission tasking.

There are two cadre sergeants with each team at all times. After each mission, they hold a brief AAR, or after-action report, to critique the exercise mission. Then the cadres direct a change in team leadership and assign a new team commander, team chief, and two new element leaders. And the process begins again—patrol away from the old objective, receive new mission tasking, patrol to a new base, plan-rest-refit-hold security, and move on to the next target. With each new target there are the procedural requirements of setting up an operational readiness position, conducting a patrol leaders reconnaissance, getting the team set up on the target, actions on target, and a sensitive site exploitation of the target—by the numbers, each day and every day. As the days progress, the students become a little more tired and a little more sleep-deprived. But the fragmentation orders keep coming. Each new team of leaders has to motivate the Marines on their team and get the job done.

"During my turn as the team commander," Captain Andrew Fraker said of his turn at the helm of student MSOT Three, "we ambushed an SRH [Sword of the Right Hand] convoy and things were going pretty much as planned. Then we had a man down, a casualty, and that changed things. I tried to manage the fight and the casualty— big mistake. I should have kept my focus on the fight and let my team chief take care of the wounded man. This is something I have to work on: letting my subordinate leaders do their jobs while I stay with the big picture. As for the management of casualties, that was a big thing, and a part of almost every mission in one form or another."

"My leadership assignment was that of an element leader during a raid on an SRH meeting," Sergeant Brad Hansen told me. "From an informant, we knew the meeting was to take place on the bend in the road between 2400 and 0300. So we had to be in place by 2300 to wait for them. We had a support-by-fire element in place and an assault element positioned off the road where the meeting was to take place. I was leading the assault element. When the two vehicles met and the bad guys were chatting over the hoods of their vehicles, the support element opened up. Then we assaulted through the target area. We killed five SRH guys. They had chow and water in their vehicles so we appropriated those supplies for our own use. We made a few mistakes, like taking too much time on target to do our SSE [sensitive site exploitation] but overall it went well. I didn't have another leadership evolution."

During the progression of Raider Spirit, every student is graded on every evolution by the cadres walking with the student team, by cadres who are grading the target, and by input from the Sword of the Right Hand role players—the bad guys. Students who failed or did poorly while they were in a leadership position are often made to serve in a leadership position a second or even a third time. When I asked what was the hardest part of Raider Spirit, Sergeant Kerry Irving was quick to answer.

"For me it was that last day and night. We had been on our feet and moving for close to twenty-two hours. I like to think of myself as an experienced and proficient infantryman, but this final evolution took about everything I had. I know the other guys felt the same way. As we hurried to make our extraction time, we had to deal with simulated IED attacks, usually with flares and artillery simulators, that were surprisingly real, and as always, there's the management and care of casualties. At one point, three guys in the team were down, so we had to carry three Marines and three extra kits. That meant we were packing well over a hundred pounds per man, and if you were carrying a teammate, it was two hundred pounds. We carried the extra load for quite a while. I think we were all hallucinating a little during those final hours. Looking back on it, we call it the Zombie March."

Exercise Raider Spirit typically produces the most DORs in an Individual Training Class. For Class 1-13 and this Raider Spirit there were four. These Marines were all variously performing to standard, but the extended hardships of this exercise made them hand in their ropes and leave the class. From one who dropped, "I finally had a talk with myself, and I came to understand that I don't have the heart for this. I just don't want to ever be that uncomfortable for that long again." From another, "It's not just this exercise, which is the hardest thing I've ever done; it's more than that. I realized that this is not just a job, it's a lifestyle. And it's just not for me."

"These are fine Marines," Gunny Patterson said of the Raider Spirit DORs, "and had they been willing, they could have continued on and become special operators in an operational MSOT. But they chose not to. We see this take place during every Raider Spirit. There may be underlying factors, like a wife who wants her Marine home more often or the prospect of time away from home that makes taking a college course at night more difficult. Yet the bottom line is that you have to want to do this business. These four Marines all seemed to have the intelligence and professional skill set to get through the ITC, but for whatever reason, they hadn't the heart."

"Now what's in store for them?" I asked 1-13's proctor.

"Now we process them out and make them available for reassignment in the Marine Corps. These are good Marines, and we'll tell them that. We also feel they're better Marines for what they accomplished here. We'll tell them that as well. They can take what they've learned here and it will help them to excel at their next duty station. It's not easy to hand in your rope and admit this program is a little more than you'd bargained for. Or that this service is simply not for you. We'll thank them for coming here and giving this a try, and we do what we can to set them up for success in their next job."

There was only one actual casualty during this Raider Spirit. While patrolling at night, a sergeant from student MSOT Three fell over a log and onto the receiver of his M4. The collision of Marine and rifle knocked out two of his front teeth. The cadre sergeants immediately radioed for the phase corpsman to attend to him. He was able to push one tooth back into place, but the other was completely broken off.

"I'm all right, Instructor," he managed with blood drooling down his chin. "I want to keep going. You can't have my rope."

"We don't want your rope, Sergeant, but we've got to get you looked at and get this taken care of," the cadre sergeant told his student. "Then we'll get you back out here."

And they did. After some attention by the dentist the following morning, the sergeant was back with his team that afternoon, although he will be a candidate for some bridge work after the ITC.

"He's a good man," the cadre said of this sergeant. "He wants to be here and we don't want to lose a good Marine. He's a solid performer and he'll do well when he gets to the Regiment. It's always good to see a student who's performing well and who refuses to quit."

Like all special-operations units, MARSOC is a small fraternity and everyone knows everyone else. Reputation is everything. That reputation begins in training. During this phase, this particular Marine had established himself as an excellent student and a team player. The cadres will do all in their power to see a quality student like this succeeds in the ITC.

The end of Raider Spirit is the end of Phase One for Class 1-13. There is the TAC turnover that is much like that convened at the end of the basic skills phase. Lieutenant Colonel Dodd presides with Master Guns Denard seated alongside him. Present are the four outgoing TACs from Phase One and the new TACs from Phase Two. The performance history of each student is brought up on the big screen for all to see. His merits, deficiencies, scores, and evaluations are posted there and reviewed by the respective phase TACs. Unlike the previous TAC turnover, this time there are more evaluative metrics than just physical performance, tactical casualty care, radio procedure proficiency, and peer evaluations. Now there are tactics, planning, briefing, leadership, watermanship, and weapons handling in the mix. Most in 1-13 are performing to standard and their on-screen photos carry a green border. Close to a quarter of the class have deficiencies in one or more graded areas and are marked by a yellow border. Ten ITC students are marked with red borders signifying that they have failures that will have to be corrected if they are to remain in the class and graduate. Six of those Marines will be counseled by their new Phase Two TACs so they are made aware of their performance issues and how to correct them going forward. Four are individually brought before a Phase Board consisting of Lieutenant Colonel Dodd, Master Guns Denard, Captain Allen Jacobs, the Phase One OIC, the Phase One senior NCO, and Gunny Patterson. Three of these students are officially put on probation going into Phase Two. This board appearance also puts them on notice that if they fail to correct past shortcomings and improve their overall performance, they will be dropped from the course. The performance of a single Marine is considered too deficient in too many areas. He is dropped from the class.

At the end of Phase One there are sixty-one students—ten Marine captains and fifty-one enlisted Marines—in the class. A single sergeant joins the class from a previous ITC class. Sixty-two Marine CSO candidates begin Phase Two of the Individual Training Course.

CHAPTER SIX

PHASE TWO: SPECIAL RECONNAISSANCE

Their drills were bloodless battles and their battles, bloody drills.

FLAVIUS JOSEPHUS

Special reconnaissance, or SR, along with foreign internal defense, direct action, counterterrorism, and counterinsurgency, is a standing core activity for Marine Special Operations Forces. Special reconnaissance training, as a separate phase of the Individual Training Course for Marine Critical Skills Operators, is new to the ITC. For the previous nine Individual Training Courses, SR training was the last two weeks of Phase One and took place following the Raider Spirit exercise. For Class 1-13, it is a stand-alone phase and, for this class only, a shortened three-week phase.

Special reconnaissance is all about careful observation, detection avoidance, and imagery capture. These three disciplines are taught in this phase and then interwoven into the tactical flow of mission tasking, courses of action development, mission planning, and mission execution. The first week of the phase for 1-13, a shortened four-day week due to the long Easter weekend, has to do with "seeing it right." This is in keeping with much of MARSOC training that follows a crawl-walk-run format. This entails seeing it right, doing it under instruction, and then doing it under tactical training conditions. As a point of departure, special reconnaissance is different in concept from reconnaissance and surveillance as practiced throughout the Army and Marine Corps as a standard battle tactic. R&S is typically thought of as reconnaissance and intelligence gathering in preparation for, or to accompany, an immediate military action, such as a conventional ground assault. SR as practiced in special operations could well serve a conventional R&S mission role, but it is an enhanced capability for strategic, politically sensitive, intelligence-related, or evidentiary requirements. Week one of the SR Phase is all classroom work for Class 1-13 and a welcome change of pace for these weary students. Classroom work means that for this week, and this week alone, they will sleep in the barracks and in their beds. As with Raider Spirit, the balance of SR will be fieldwork. This means they will be in patrol bases, hide sites, or field mission-support sites much of the time. When they sleep, they will be curled up in sleeping bags with a weapon within arm's reach. And seldom will they sleep for more than two hours at a time.

Special-reconnaissance observation is usually done from a fixed location or what is called a hide site. Hide sites are generally classed as rural or urban, with many subclassifications and adaptations. A rural hide site could be a position just inside a densely wooded tree line or a stand of covering foliage. The site may be suitable in its natural condition for hiding the observer for a short period of observation time, or may be dug in to allow the SR observer to safely and clandestinely have "eyes-on" for an extended time. These rural hide sites are typically a shallow foxhole, large enough for two or three Marines and roofed with bow supports, a poncho ground-cloth covering, and finished with a covering of natural vegetation. They are basically shallowly arched igloos. Bows are cut from tree branches or, on a dedicated SR mission, collapsible backpack-tent bows are used. A well-set hide site, covered with leaves and pine needles, is virtually indistinguishable from the natural forest floor. When it's done properly, one has to literally walk over it to find it. During the first week of SR, the students see cadre-constructed hide sites on the MARSOC compound and then the student MSOTs begin building their own. A rural hide site can be used to observe a road, a road junction, a military installation, or any built-up area of interest.

Associated with the rural hide sites that serve as observation posts, or OPs, there is the field mission support site (MSS) where most of the image manipulation and communication takes place. In a rural SR mission, the mission support site is normally well back from one or more observation posts. Those in the OPs gather the observations and imagery capture and send it back to the MSS for processing and data transfer. The hide-site OPs are often small and Spartan, and designed for seeing while not being seen. The MSSs are farther back, away from the target and more secure. These are often hastily constructed, tented, and camouflaged structures with good light discipline and suited for radio and Toughbook computer operation.

An urban hide site is a position with a good field of vision from a doorway, window, or rooftop in an urban setting. From the urban hide site, the observer may want to view another building, a compound, a village approach, or some other rural or urban feature. An urban hide site is chosen for its vantage point to the target or target area and its ability to still conceal the observer. Typically, this means that the observer, who might be conducting his observations from a window, wants to be deep in the room and have some covering or screening on the window that creates some opaqueness when viewed from the outside. It could be as simple as the snout of a camera lens peeking between louvered blinds or a complex mini-darkroom constructed of PVC piping and black felt-like cloth. Such a box-type dark room could be built around the interior window casing of a hotel room and served by a smaller, secondary darkened box for interior-light management on entering the larger observation box.

"Deeper is better," one of the class captains told me, a Marine with multiple tours in Iraq and Afghanistan, and with an extensive Recon background, "both for observation and for sniping. And even better to be deep into another room or even a building away. We would set in our snipers so they were shooting from a window and through the opposing windows of the building across the street. The target has no idea where you are and may not even hear the shot. It works the same for an observation post. We did it this way and so did the Taliban."

The cadre constructed an urban hide site in one of the barracks computer bays as an example. Then the MSOTs set to building urban hide sites in their sleeping bays. An urban hide site usually serves as both an observation post and the mission support site. The MSS function may be just a few feet away, set up in another room in an urban site building or sited in a separate but nearby building.

The first week of SR is heavy on electronics and image capture. The students receive instruction on GPS mapping and navigation, and digital imagery processing. For the latter, they receive a crash course in the latest version of Photoshop, the same image management system that is commercially available. They also get time on the cameras, the main camera being the Canon 5D digital single-lens reflex (DSLR). This very capable and versatile camera forms the basis for a whole system of multidimensional imagery capture.

And finally, this first week of special reconnaissance serves as a recovery period from Raider Spirit. The Marines of ITC Class 1-13 slept hard and long over the weekend. Yet come Monday, it's a 0430 reveille and 0515 physical training. But on this particular Monday, the normally crushing Monday morning, team-centric PT competitions are replaced by a PERRES regenerative stretching and conditioning session. Later in the week there will be running and pool evolutions and strength-conditioning training, but this morning it's all about healing and recovery. Team PT is led by the phase TACs.

The TAC for student MSOT Three for Phase Two is a quiet, boyish-looking former Recon staff sergeant from Oklahoma. His name is Paul Brandies. He completed two combat rotations with the 2nd Reconnaissance Battalion in Iraq and another two with an operational MSOT in the 2nd Marine Special Operations Battalion. Like other Phase Two TACs, he is a teacher, and he's always nearby to offer assistance and guidance to his student MSOT. A great deal of the instruction on the cameras and the special adaptions of commercial imaging for SR application comes from subject-matter experts whose specialty is SR-related imagery. But the field craft, patrolling in a hostile environment, and hide-site construction are taught to the students by their TACs.

———

The second week of SR is the beginning of two weeks in the field, with the intervening weekend free. For Class 1-13, the frosty nights of Raider Spirit are behind them, and the second week in April is unseasonably warm, with daytime temperatures reaching the high seventies. Yet with the welcome warmer temperatures come the ticks and mosquitoes. Said one in the class, "I'll gladly trade the frost for the bugs." But the ticks are indiscriminate. They attack cadres, students, and writers alike.

The class is up early on Monday to draw weapons, NVGs, and radios for the week's training. This first increment of SR field training is conducted at the Homestation Lane Training Facility. This facility consists of two small village-like complexes made to replicate an Afghan village setting. It's operated by the Marine Corps Engineering School, Training and Education Command. The facility is a thirty-minute drive from Camp Lejeune proper and designed to train Marine engineers to counter and clear improvised explosive devices. Since the MARSOC students are doing nothing more than watching these compounds, or discreetly watching *from* the compounds, their activities do not conflict with the engineers' counter-IED training. Indeed, the engineers' training and vehicle traffic become reportable activity.

For this week, the mornings are taken with time on the camera equipment in a field setting. The students of 1-13 have seen most of the equipment in the classroom, yet some if it is new. It's the same that is issued to the operational MSOTs and packaged in specially designed kits for SR work on deployment. The basic camera is again the Canon 5D DSLR. There is a separate camcorder, but most of the work is done with the 5D. Associated with this basic camera is a daunting array of cords, cables, lenses, and attachments. There are nearly end-less combinations that mix and match the lenses and attachments. Without going too far into the mechanics, there are capabilities for low-light, infrared, and thermal imaging with telephoto lenses to 1000mm. That's a magnification of thirty times normal under some very marginal lighting conditions. With magnification and low levels of light come issues of stabilization. Even slight camera movement under these conditions can make for poor imagery. So there are devices that serve to make for stable camera/lens/attachment marriages and several different tripods for mounting camera arrays.

Afternoon periods are for patrolling to the target objectives, set-ting in hide sites, and getting observation posts and mission support sites functioning. There are four fixed training lanes associated with the two village complexes. Each team will set up two rural hides, one on each complex, and two urban hides, one on each complex. The patrolling is minimal and designed only to position the team at an observation location or an entry point to the village. The officers take turns serving as team commanders, with the senior sergeants rotating through the team chief and element leader positions. After a very short patrol order, the cadre instructors/TACs call their teams for final consultations.

"All right, this is the drill," Staff Sergeant Brandies says to Team Three. "I want you to be tactical throughout the day and throughout this exercise. It's a good time to shake off the dust from Raider Spirit and to get your TTPs [tactics, techniques, and procedures] back in order. This is a rural hide site, so I want to see two good observation posts set up and a well-camouflaged mission support site. Keep the movement between the OPs and the MSS to a minimum, but I want each of you to capture a good image, work it through the Photoshop software, and then transmit it back to the TOC [tactical operations center]. Get your image, go back to the MSS, work it up, and transmit it with the appropriate notation, okay? Now, each of you have a two-hour window to do this, but if you're done in an hour or less, swap out and get the next man on the camera. And while this is instructional, I still want you guys to be tactical. Team leader?"

"Right here, Sergeant."

"Let's get into the woods and on patrol."

"Roger that, Sergeant."

After a quick five-minute patrol order, the team is moving into a nearby tree line. The four-day second-week evolutions begin like this: on patrol early afternoon, into their hide sites mid to late afternoon, and observations early evening through the following morning. Then the teams come out, have an after-action review, refit, and prepare to begin the process again. During the course of these busy days, the TACs lead their student MSOTs in calisthenics and a five-mile run.

It's during this second week of special reconnaissance that the students begin to fall into the SR pattern of operational life in a hide site. The patrols to and from their hides, the commutes to the job site, are short and designed to get the team into the site from a patrol formation. And there are some tactical shortcuts and artificialities, as seldom would an SR element move into an urban hide site unless they could do so by blending in with their surroundings to remain unseen. The move into an urban hide could be made in civilian clothes with the SR team moving individually or in pairs over a period of time, so as not to call attention to themselves. Not always, but most SR movement to and from the objective area is done at night. In the hide sites, there is a pattern of life, a pattern that is built around security, observation, imagery capture, communications, and rest. When a team arrives at or in the vicinity of a hide, they put eyes on the target and never take eyes off. With eyes on, they then set in security and begin the constructions that make for a rural or urban observation post and a mission support site. Immediately, the team establishes their communication links to report the team in place and the target under observation. For this training the communications are redundant. The PRC-150s are used for a HF link and the PRC-117 for satellite comms. In an urban hide, getting the satellite antenna positioned to pick up a communications satellite and remain undetected from the outside is often a challenge. Once security is set, comms are established, OPs are set in and manned, and the MSS is up and running—the routine and patient work of an SR mission begins. Photos are taken, processed, annotated, and sent back to the forward operating base or the TOC. Team members are rotated through security, observation, imagery capture, and communications positions. And of course, the most welcome, a scheduled rest period. For this week the two-hour sleep periods, usually two of them per mission, are all the sleep the students get. These four hours are a luxury when compared to what they managed during Raider Spirit. Sleeping during nonscheduled rest can result in a negative spot report for the sleeper, and perhaps for the team and element leaders for not properly supervising their team. And the cadres always seem to appear just when someone on security dozes off.

During the hours in the hide sites, OPs, and MSSs, the student teams are visited by their TACs and photography instructors. During these visits, the teams "go admin" for training in low-light-level photo training and time-lapse photography. They also receive training on other selective pieces of equipment and techniques that are beyond the classification of this work.

"This was a big eye-opener for a lot of us," said one of the student MSOT Three sergeants with a Recon background. "At the basic reconnaissance course and in my battalion, we got good training in R&S—reconnaissance and surveillance. But this is totally different. I'm learning a lot this week, about camerawork and the computer. My computer skills were not all that good to start with, but when things get quiet in the early hours, I've been getting some extra instruction from one of my teammates. He has an information processing background. I help him with patrolling and weapons and he helps me on the computer."

The end of the second week's SR work comes to an end with the four student MSOTs patrolling back to the forward operating base at dawn. For almost all of the week the teams enjoyed warm days and comfortable nights. Early Friday a front moved through the area bringing high winds, cooler temperatures, and lots of rain. The breakdown and load-out of the FOB was a wet and miserable undertaking.

At 1300, the students are dried out and in the classroom at the Marine Special Operations School for their Sting Ray Fury warning order. Sting Ray Fury is a week-long SR exercise where the students will conduct four round-robin SR missions with different objectives and mission requirements. The previous week's work and mission sets put a premium on instruction. The Sting Ray Fury missions will expand to include the planning and tactical execution of an SR mission.

"All right, gentlemen, this will serve as your warning order for Exercise Sting Ray Fury." The briefing officer is Captain Mike Dougherty, the officer in charge of this shortened Special Reconnaissance Phase and for developing the phase into its intended six weeks of instruction. "You will deploy early this coming Monday to Forward Operating Base Lejeune. You are to be in place by 0730 and fully prepared to conduct special reconnaissance missions in Onslow County in the Republic of Abyssinia. From April 15 through April 19, as members of Marine Special Operations Company X-ray, you will conduct unilateral special reconnaissance missions in the vicinity of Charming Village, Crow Village, Mayan Village, and Jacksonville proper in order to confirm or deny the location and activities of members of the Sword of the Right Hand."

Dougherty is tall, thin, and fair. He looks a great deal younger than his thirty-one years. The captain grew up in Wisconsin and attended the University of Georgia. He came to the Marine Corps by way of Officer Candidate School. Dougherty saw action in Iraq as an infantry platoon leader and weapons company executive officer before receiving orders to MARSOC. After a tour as an MSOT team leader in Afghanistan, he was detailed to the Special Operations Training School as the Phase Three officer in charge, or OIC. When asked about his career plans after MARSOC duty, Dougherty explained, "I'll stay in the Marine Corps as long as they'll let me. This is what I want to do—what I've always wanted to do." He's married with two kids, both under three, and a third on the way. Mike Dougherty is one of the last of his kind, in that he completed a tour as an MSOT team commander but did not come through the ITC.

Following an overview of the exercise, Captain Dougherty gives each individual student MSOT their fragmentation order, a mission tasking that will guide their weekend planning for their first SR mission. While this FRAGO is delivered physically, future taskings or fragmentation orders will be transmitted by radio. Throughout the week of field SR training, the teams were fed intelligence information on the increasing tensions in the Republic of Abyssinia and the reported movements of certain key leaders of the insurgent organization known as the Sword of the Right Hand. Now the student MSOTs are being tasked with gathering timely and accurate intelligence on the movements of these leaders for possible follow-on, direct-action strikes. The notional movement of these student MSOTs in the country of Abyssinia is known only to their chain of command, the U.S. ambassador to Abyssinia, and senior members of the embassy staff. The teams are to be operating in a nonpermissive environment, which means they must accomplish their missions while avoiding detection and avoiding enemy contact.

The final week of Class 1-13's Phase Two begins just as the previous week ended—lots of wind, lots of rain, a very early reveille, and movement to the operational area. I asked Captain Andrew Fraker how his team was handling the work and the weather.

"Thank goodness for the weekends," he said. "Without a few days to dry out and overhaul our gear and to catch up on sleep, it would almost be unmanageable. But I guess if we had to stay in the field, that's what we'd do. With the exception of the week of SR classes, we've been out in the field for close to a month." When I pressed him on the phase material, he had this to say. "We're all a little overwhelmed by the incredible complexity and capability of the cameras and the associated equipment. There's so much to learn—with the equipment itself as well as the tactical employment of the equipment. Then there's the rhythm of being in a hide site. We're almost getting used to operating on four or five hours of sleep a night—and that's broken into two or three sleep periods. It's physically challenging, but much more of a mental challenge than I ever anticipated. It takes a lot of focus and self-motivation to be alert and make good decisions when you're operating on a short rest cycle. But again, it's a rhythm. You get used to it and it keeps you in a mentally tough frame of mind.

"What keeps me going are the Marines on my team. I've been blessed to lead some fine Marines in my previous tours, but these guys are the best. They're smart, capable, and motivated. And funny. You can't do what we do and not have a sense of humor. Most of the guys in the class who didn't want to be here have DORed. Those that are left are simply terrific. It's a privilege to have the opportunity to serve with these very special Marines. And yes, I could sure use a little more sleep, but there's always next weekend."

The phase cadre and the four student MSOTs set up in a compound near a MOUT-site complex on Camp Lejeune proper. MOUT stands for military operations in urban terrain. These built-up complexes are "combat towns" that have an Iraq/Afghanistan look and feel to them. They are complete with Arabic signage, narrow streets, abandoned cars, outdoor markets, and crude cinder-block and concrete buildings. There are facilities like this on all major stateside American Army and Marine installations, and Camp Lejeune is no exception. These MOUT sites are suitable for a range of urban military training, both inside the buildings as well as in the streets and courtyards around them.

The compound that houses Class 1-13—Marine Special Operations Company X-ray itself—looks like those I've seen in Iraq, with sandbagged emplacements guarding the access, concrete traffic-routing barricades, and generator power. The student MSOTs are billeted in a series of semi-trailer containers set in place as temporary, mobile housing. There is no bedding or furniture, just hard floors and wooden benches. Each team is assigned a single container for mission planning and conducting briefings. For sleep, they curl up on the floor for an hour or so when they can, or as scheduled while in their mission support sites.

The teams will conduct their special reconnaissance missions on four separate training lanes. Two of these training lanes involve carefully moving in close to one of the MOUT sites that, in the Abyssinian scenario, is an abandoned village. There they will observe the activities and suspected movements of Sword of the Right Hand leaders. A third scenario involves observing a transportation facility near a hotel in downtown Jacksonville, again tracking the movements of suspected leaders and members of the Sword. The fourth training lane is sited at a semi-rural resort area where Sword members have been known to congregate and conduct meetings. While the first two of these training lanes are on base and in a controlled paramilitary environment, the other two are not. Without getting too deeply into the mechanics of this training, the student team, dressed in appropriate civilian clothes and under close cadre supervision, take up positions for their observations. Key to this off-base training is that they must conduct and complete their mission while blending in with their surroundings. This means that they are not to call attention to themselves or their activities while coming, going, or in the conduct of their mission. All this requires some artificialities and oversight, but it gives the students a feel for what they may be asked to do overseas in a nonpermissive or semipermissive environment. It reminded me a great deal of some of my own training as a young CIA case officer—back in the day.

As this final week of training unfolded, I had a chance to speak with Captain Dougherty about this special reconnaissance training and what MARSOC has planned for future SR training at the ITC.

"The SR training we took from Phase One and the material we added for the three-week training for Class 1-13 will be further expanded to a six-week phase. So what will be different when we go to a full six weeks? Currently, 1-13 will leave here with some understanding and a pretty good overview of special reconnaissance and the image capture and image processing that we were able to teach them in the time allowed. When they get to their teams, those that really took an interest in photography and grasped this material and equipment will be able to move into the role of the team SR assistant or an assistant to the assistant. But they'll still need time with the equipment, and with that time comes proficiency. If we have another three weeks, then we can give them more instruction and more time on the gear. With this additional instruction, we hope to be able to develop a more extensive working capability. ITC graduates leave here with the shooting skills that allow them to seamlessly begin shooting training with their operational MSOTs. That's what we want from our SR package. We want a higher level of proficiency and to give them a more polished skill set to take to their teams."

"And it's not just the photography," Captain Dougherty continued. "We'll have the time to introduce them to some advanced SR techniques and equipment as well as what they may see in their operational units in the way of more advanced tactics and procedures—both of which carry higher security classifications. There's also the possibility of using our technology to help partner-nation forces to more effectively target extremist groups in their nations. We have to look past the Iraq-Afghan model that involved a great deal of direct action. There's sure to be a critical need for detailed and accurate information of what's going on in a region where we have interests and the ability to report this information in a timely manner."

But for Class 1-13, their final week of Phase Two is all about mission tasking, mission planning, and long periods of time in hide sites, monitoring the activities of members of the Sword of the Right Hand. As with Exercise Raider Spirit, there are four key leadership positions in each student MSOT: team commander, team chief, and the two element leaders. The designated team communicator is also a key role. However, the communicator in the MSS seemed, at least to me, to be as much a teacher as a communicator. Those who were more familiar with the team radios helped those who were not as proficient.

"I was an element leader during one of the SR missions at the MOUT site," Sergeant Brad Hansen said of his graded evolution during Sting Ray Fury. "We approached the compound wall from the woods to the south of the site, on the side away from where the bad guys were. We scaled the wall and moved into a building that had a good observation position over a large courtyard that was a bazaar. It was a little artificial in that we would never do that during the day. We got in place late morning and left about 2300. It was a long day. My element's job was to set up the OP and keep continuous eyes on the target. The other element set in security and ran the radios. Once in place, we rotated duty—some of us on watch, some on security, a couple of guys on the radios, and a few of us sleeping. Every two hours we rotated.

"Those in the bazaar, the SRH [Sword of the Right Hand] guys, were burying IEDs and parading around. We also saw and photographed the key HVI [high-value individual] we were looking for. We literally took hundreds of photos."

"My leadership evolution took place at a motel where we were to observe a clandestine meeting of senior SRH members," recalled Sergeant Irving. "I was the team chief, so my job was to see that everyone else was doing their job and the scheduled rotations got done quietly and on time. The hotel room had a good window on the bus stop where the SRH guys were said to congregate. We drifted into the motel dressed in civilian clothes and up to the room in twos and threes. Once inside, we set up our cameras and documented the comings and goings at the bus stop. The SRH guys lingered there awhile, probably for our benefit.

"I was an infantry leader and I've been in the Marine Corps for a while. But this was the first time I ever trained in civilian clothes. It gave us all a real feel for what it may be like on an operational MSOT in some foreign capital when we're there to watch and listen, and to gather intelligence. It's like we were hiding in plain sight and trying to blend in. It was very different. We got our photos of several HVIs and sent them back by radio. We had no sat comm [satellite communications] so we sent the information out by the PRC-150 from the room."

Friday afternoon, after returning from the Camp Lejeune compound to Stone Bay, the teams met in the large classroom where each team delivered a briefing on their SR missions to "higher" headquarters in the person of Lieutenant Colonel Dodd.

"I gave our team's briefing," said Captain Fraker of student MSOT Three's operations. "We began with the PIRs [priority intelligence requirements] that we were given and a synopsis of each mission. Then we selected a few photos of SRH HVIs and some of the buildings and equipment we were able to photograph throughout the week. After each team's briefing, the cadre followed with an after-action report. They pointed out our mistakes and ways we could have done it better or differently, and now and then," he added with a grin, "we got it just right."

I asked Captain Fraker about the special reconnaissance training in general. After a moment's thought, he said, "It was something new. The first-aid, the communications, and the infantry tactics were a review for me. With the exception of SERE, I've been trained in those skills and have done them for real on operational deployment. But this was a whole different mission. It was very technical and I can see where it will take a great deal of training and practice to do it properly. This was a real learning experience for all of us."

The Monday following Class 1-13's shortened SR Phase, the TAC turnover from Phase Two to Phase Three convenes. It's the same format as the previous turnover, from Phase One to Two. Yet there are subtle differences. There is a new formatting for the peer-review process and a new display for the character evaluation. On the visual displays for this TAC turnover, the results of a personality profiling instrument are listed along with time in service, time in grade, general testing score, and physical performance scores. These profiles come out as single-word descriptors—persuader, director, entrepreneur, prevailer, adaptor, administrator, and the like. And with another phase complete, ongoing performance scores were updated and the new scores, scores that relate to special reconnaissance testing, appear on each student's profile. I noted that there were a few additions to the human factors postings—notations like "financial issue at home," "mother undergoing cancer treatment," "wife pregnant; due during Phase Four," "youngest child has special needs."

"All right, gentlemen, we've had these Marines for three phases of training," Lieutenant Colonel Dodd says to open the proceedings, "and while we want to afford each Marine a chance to succeed, we have to start to identify those who can do this work and those who cannot. Going forward into Phase Three, we have to give our attention and training time to those who have the potential to serve on an operational MSOT. For those who clearly cannot, we have to make some hard calls. We can't waste any more of your time or theirs. Those Marines that really have no prospects of meeting standard here need to get back to the regular Marine Corps, where they can succeed. We clear on that?" There is a nodding of agreement around the table.

The Phase Two TACs then brief each member of their student MSOTs, again calling attention to his strengths and weaknesses. Again there are a majority of green-bordered students who are performing well. Close to a quarter of the class still show in the yellow zone. Eight, two from each of the four student MSOTs, are in the red category. Of the unlucky or deficient eight, four are counseled by their new TACs and four are brought before the performance board. Of these four red-tabbed students, only one is afforded the opportunity to continue. The other three are disenrolled from the ITC. Of those dropped from the course, the lead Phase Two instructor had this to say:

"Even though this is a onetime, shortened Special Reconnaissance Phase, the students were in the field for two of those three weeks. During the time in the field, dealing with the new material, as well as living out of a patrol base and the long hours in hide sites, we were able to get a pretty good look at them. Those on the bubble for poor performance in previous phases either showed us some change in attitude or execution or they didn't. Board decisions are always difficult but fair, or as fair as we can make them. Those who were let go clearly need to be someplace else. Those marginal students will have to pick up the pace or they will not be allowed to continue. At this stage, all of them seem to want to be here—and are showing the desire. It's just that some of them may not have the temperament or the intelligence to continue."

Following the TAC turnover I was able to spend a few minutes with Captain Dougherty. I had noticed that during the turnover between Phase One and this SR Phase there was an increase in the comments and discussion about the performance of the class officers. This trend continued in the TAC turnover from the SR Phase to Phase Three. I asked him about this.

"The training and performance evaluation of all our students is important, but the officers—the future team commanders—especially so. To one degree or another, many of these sergeants will grow into the job in the Regiment, but the officers have to be leading and performing to a very high standard when they leave here.

"Leadership training is a hallmark of Marine officer training and especially for Marine infantry officers. The twenty-six-week Basic School and the ten-week IOC [Infantry Officers Course] is some of the best combat-leader training in the world. So these officers have had excellent training, and most have a deployment history that makes them both well-qualified and experienced combat leaders. In many of their previous jobs, they had both training and experience that exceeded those of the Marines they were leading. But leadership in a conventional unit at the company and platoon level is different than what is needed here.

"When these captains get to their teams, with perhaps the exception of one or two of their classmates from their ITC class, they will be the *least* experienced of those on their team. Leadership in an MSOT is primarily one of establishing objectives. It's the team chief and his element leaders that do the work; they get the job done. So for these good captains, it may be the least hands-on command responsibility they've yet to experience." Dougherty paused to frame his words. "A team is like a group on a bus. The team commander determines the destination for the bus or the end state—the objective. The team chief is the bus driver. With input from his element leaders and other experienced members on the team, he chooses the route. He also makes sure the bus has gas, that the brakes work, and that the bus has been properly serviced. Now, the team commander owns the bus—it's his bus. And he has to answer to the owners of the bus company—let the owners know about the route and what the bus will do when it gets there, and how it will safely return. He also has to know what to do if there is an accident along the way, and a lot of other things. But the details of the bus operation he has to leave to his bus driver and the other passengers.

"Most of these officers get it quickly—some more quickly than others. Still others will not come to understand this until Phase Four and the Derna Bridge exercise. Yet some of them never do, and that's a real problem. The concept, the privilege actually, of how to lead these very capable and experienced Marines in the challenging world of special operations never quite reaches them. They're ineffective micromanagers. If they don't get it here and show us they get it, then they aren't going to graduate from this course. Of if they do, they will fail as an MSOT commander."

With Sting Ray Fury behind them, Class 1-13 is free to enjoy a delicious weekend off. Completing Phase Two are nine captains and forty-six enlisted Marine sergeants. When the class musters the following Monday at 0500 for team PT, there are ten officers and forty-seven sergeants. Their numbers now include one additional enlisted Marine and one captain—rollbacks from a previous ITC. For all in Class 1-13, this PT session is not nearly so gentle as the one that followed Raider Spirit and Phase One.

CHAPTER SEVEN

PHASE THREE: DIRECT ACTION

God is not on the side of the big battalions, but on
the side of those who shoot best.

VOLTAIRE

BASIC MARKSMANSHIP

"Attention on deck!" There is a massive scraping of chairs as the new Phase Three students from Class 1-13 come to their feet. They are uniformly dressed in their MARPAT combat utility uniforms of the green woodland pattern. Many are still red-faced following that morning's team PT. Yet something is different about them. All fifty-seven of these ITC students now have .45-caliber pistols strapped to their thighs. Around the chairs and under the tables are backpacks, body armor, and carefully laid M4 rifles. Behind the students are close to twenty-five Phase Three cadres. Most are shooting instructors. Half of them are active-duty Marines dressed in the brown desert MAR-PATs. The other half are civilians turned out in chinos and light jackets. A great many of them, Marines and civilians, wear ITC instructor sweatshirts. Except for their dress and an occasional neatly trimmed beard, it's difficult to tell them apart.

"Take your seats, men, and welcome to Phase Three." Colonel James Glynn, the school commanding officer, makes his way to the front of the room and begins to pace while he talks. "Good to see you all again. As you begin this important phase of instruction, I want you to take a moment to look back at what you've accomplished to date. You've had the basics; you've been trained in communications, combat medicine, amphibious operations, fires, and small unit tactics. You've all been to SERE school. You were the first class to attend our Special Reconnaissance Phase. So as you begin these next seven weeks of training, you're already more than halfway through the ITC. Most of this course is behind you. However, this is a very important phase. In this phase we're going to take your basic Marine riflemen's skills and adapt them to direct action and close-quarters shooting in stressful situations. It will be fun because we all like to shoot, but again, it will be stressful. That's by design. A fight to the death in close combat is also stressful. Here's where we lay the groundwork for you to succeed in that fight."

The colonel continues to pace, choosing his words carefully. "When you finish this phase, we expect you to be shooting to basic MSOT standards. We will expect you to be able to take your place in the stack on a direct-action mission with an MSOT assault team. The instructors in the back of the room are the finest combat shooting instructors in the world. Listen to them. And as much as this is a shooting course, it's also a thinking course. You'll have to think and think critically while you're moving and shooting. In the ITC we often ask you to think outside the box. Now we're going to ask you to continue to think and be flexible but remain disciplined and stay inside the box. You'll be shooting under some very different and demanding conditions, and you must do this safely. Yet while you think safety, you have to be aggressive and be comfortable behind the gun. You have to put rounds on target. This will come if you stay focused and listen to your shooting instructors. Remember, we're training you for proficiency in a close-quarters fight. You have to kill that other guy before he kills you." Colonel Glynn again welcomes them to Phase Three, then turns the floor over to the phase cadre.

A tall, affable gunnery sergeant with an easy smile makes his way to the front of the room. "Good morning, gentlemen. I'm Gunny Conway, the lead instructor for Phase Three. Let me also welcome you to the phase. We will be focusing on three areas of instruction: pistol, rifle, and the shoot house. We'll also take a few days with combat breaching. There will be some long days in front of you. We'll do PT early and work late. We're here to make combat shooters out of you. For us to do that, it will take a 100 percent effort on your part. This means there will be shooting skills you'll have to learn and be tested on. There will be timed drills and scored drills that will be stressful. You'll have to move, shoot, and exhibit situational awareness. This is all by design." Conway pauses to survey the class. "Many of you bring prior shooting experience with you. Some of you, a lot of experience. We ask you to leave it at the door. Listen to us and do it our way. When you get to your teams, you may do it differently, but while you're here, we want you to shoot the way we show you.

"Even though you're under instruction, I expect you officers and senior sergeants to step up and lead. Have the class where they're supposed to be, when they're supposed to be there, and with the proper equipment. And as the colonel said, think safety. Show us that you aren't able to safely handle a weapons system, and we'll see that you are out of here." Gunny Conway again pauses. "Negligent discharges. If you negligently break a round, then you are out of the phase. Depending on your performance to date, you may get another chance with the next class. You may not. Regarding attrition during this phase, it will happen. I'm not going to sugarcoat it. Historically it has been as low as 10 percent and as high as 25 percent. So pay attention, stay focused, and stay safe."

He turns to the large flat-screen monitor behind him and four bullets march onto the screen. "These are some words to live by during this phase. If you can be all of these things, you'll do fine while you're here."

Be professional
Be proactive

Be thick skinned
Be aggressive

"These will guide your interactions with the instructor cadre. Keep them in mind over the next seven weeks. Good luck and good shooting."

Most of Class 1-13 files out of the classroom to prepare for an afternoon of range work. The class officers and the senior sergeants assigned as team chiefs are asked to remain behind. They gather in the front of the room, where a solidly built captain with an easy smile moves quietly to the front of the classroom to address them. Captain Stan Keefer is an infantryman who grew up in Napa, California, and attended Sacramento State before joining the Marine Corps. He had two infantry tours in Iraq, including one in 2006 during the Battle of Ramadi. Since coming to MARSOC, he's made three deployments: one as a security platoon commander just after the formation of MAR-SOC, one as an MSOT commander, and one as a deputy company commander with a Marine Special Operations Company—all in Afghanistan.

"Let me add my welcome to this phase of the course," he tells the captains and senior sergeants. "As the class leaders, I expect you to work problems within your student teams and your class chain of command. You also have the phase TACs and your class proctor. That said, it's okay to come to me for personal or professional issues, and we can talk off the record. This phase is all about shooting, but it's also a leadership lab. Dive in. It's okay to make leadership mistakes. Make them here and learn from them so you don't make them on your operational team. If you're not in a leadership position, don't highjack the team leadership that's in place. Show good fellowship and lead by example. When you are in charge, it's a good chance to practice the leadership principles you will exercise when you get to your team. But don't micromanage your Marines. Make your intent known, give direction, and let them carry out their duties in their own fashion.

This is not an infantry platoon; let them do it their way. This is how it will be on your MSOT.

"This is also one of the few times in the ITC where you can occasionally step back from your leadership duties and focus totally on yourself—your individual shooting skills. You don't often get a chance to do that in this course, so enjoy it. Otherwise I will expect you to lead your teams and this class, okay? Now for your homework."

Periodically, the phase OICs, senior instructors, or the class proctor will assign homework to be completed individually or as a student MSOT. Captain Keefer asks that each student MSOT put together a list of collateral duties that might be assigned to an MSOT in Africa that is operating on its own from a remote village and has no support. Their duties involve training the local police in tactics and marksmanship. It's Wednesday, and he wants those lists by the following Friday, typed up and well organized. "A lot of these Marines have been on deployment where they are supported by an extensive logistics train," Keefer told me. "This will get them into the mind-set of operating unsupported in some remote village where they'll only have a weekly supply drop—if that. More immediately, it will get them in the frame of mind for the planning they'll be doing on their field exercises, both in this phase and in Phase Four."

After a class on ballistics and round placement, featuring a rather graphic presentation on the effects of a high-velocity round on the human body, the class moves to the shooting ranges. Shooting is deeply embedded in Marine culture. It's more than simply "Every Marine is a rifleman." It's something more like a religious state of grace, and those who shoot well are seen as more devout or holy than those who don't. In their basic training, all Marines receive two weeks of shooting instruction on the M16A2 rifle, and all Marines must qualify annually on the Know Distance Range, where they shoot for score at bull's-eyes from two hundred to five hundred yards. These are the minimums. Depending on MOS, duty assignment, and range availabilities, most Marines shoot a great deal more than this.

For MARSOC students in Phase Three, it's all about combat shooting and the shooting requirements from the perspective of small unit engagement, day or night. MARSOC Marines have to shoot well, both because of the particular demands of their battlespace and because they have to be able to teach these skills to others. The shooting phase of the ITC is designed to bring all the student shooters to a standard that will allow them to meld and train with an operational MSOT. CSO candidate experience varies. There are sergeants who come to the ITC from scout sniper platoons or from a Force Recon platoon who have a great deal of time behind an M4, both on the range and in combat. And a good many of the infantrymen have had multiple combat tours; they've all put rounds downrange for real. The non-infantry Marines may have only limited Marine Corps range time along with their annual rifle qualification, and no formal pistol training. Initially, all have to shoot a combat-qualifying standard with the M4 and the .45 before they move on to the close-quarter-battle training and the live-fire work in the shoot houses.

"All of these guys have time on the range with a rifle," one of the military shooting instructors told me, "and some of the infantrymen have time in the shoot house and MOUT training—military operations in urban terrain. And a good many of them have been in combat and/or shoot with their personal weapons on the weekends. But few of them shoot to the standards we ask of them here and few have shot at night under IR conditions. Initially, the 0300s do a little better, but it very quickly evens out. Those who pay attention, dry fire during their off time, and approach shooting with a focused aggression become the best shooters. We've had Marines with a supply MOS who have never fired a pistol in their life break out with top shooters in the class. Sometimes those with the least experience listen the best and work the hardest, and that kind of attitude pays big dividends when it comes to shooting."

The military shooting instructors are veteran Marines, nearly all staff sergeants. Most of them have a Force Reconnaissance background and several rotations with an MSOT in Afghanistan. The civilian instructors come from a variety of backgrounds—Marine scout/snipers, Recon Marines, Army Special Forces, and a few from the SOF special-missions units. The civilians also bring a "best practices" agenda from having worked with a number of civilian and military units, and many have attended some of the premier civilian shooting schools, such as the Tiger Swan Group, an innovator in combat shooting technique. Taking a quote from their shooting philosophy, "There is no such thing as 'advanced tactical skills.' There is only the perfect execution of the fundamentals under stress." This statement captures a great deal of what I saw on the ranges and in the shoot houses during Phase Three of the Individual Training Course.

Shooting instruction during this phase is a series of progressions. Dry firing, or operating the weapon without ammunition, precedes live fire. Daytime firing lays the foundation for nighttime firing. The standard or flat-range shooting drills lay the foundation for close-quarter battle and work in the shoot house. Simple drills become more complex. Class 1-13 will spend a total of eight full days on the open ranges and nineteen days with close-quarter battle and urban combat. Throughout their close-quarter combat training, they will often rotate back to the flat ranges to drill on the mechanics of shooting on the move. Five days are devoted to a final battle problem that will combine shooting instruction with operational scenarios. No other basic SOF training or SOF qualification course devotes as much time to shooting as does Phase Three of the ITC. On the open ranges, when the ammunition burn is at its highest, the class expends close to fifty thousand rounds each day. That's more than nine hundred rounds per student per day, with each shot under the close scrutiny of the shooting coaches. Yet there is no shooting the first day or two on the range.

"We've always known the value of dry firing," Gunnery Sergeant Conway said of this. "Even professional shooters dry fire a lot. A few classes back, we got out to the range and found that the range safety folks had shut us down. It was some kind of a base-wide safety-awareness hold. So we dry fired—and dry fired and dry fired. As it turned out, that class shot better than any of the previous classes.

After that, we ramped up the dry firing, and we have the students dry firing on their own time and on a daily basis out here. Each day, before we load magazines and go hot, everyone dry fires."

The ITC students will train on two weapons systems during Phase Three. Their primary weapon is the Special Operations Peculiar Modification of the M4 carbine. These SOPMOD M4 training weapons are all fitted with the SU231 EOTech holographic sight for this phase of training. The EOTech is a battery-powered intuitive sight that features an illuminated starburst reticle. It allows for easy target acquisition, day or night, and is specifically designed for combat shooting. The student rifles are set up with a rail system on the forestock that holds a post grip, a high-intensity white light, and the LA-5 visual laser/pointer system. Nearly all of the students have fired the M4, but not this particular modification. At their teams, Critical Skills Operators have their choice of a range of weapons, but at the ITC, they will train on this very capable SOF weapons system.

If their M4s are near state-of-the-art weapons, their secondary weapons system is not. The MARSOC secondary system is the .45-caliber 1911 pistol. It's an old design that's now more than a hundred years old. "I keep wondering when they're going to come out with the 1912 MOD," said one of the instructors jokingly. But the gun is popular, and many MSOT Marines carry it, preferring the 1911 .45 to more moden pistols. In the early days of the ITC, they were using older .45s—some of them much older than the Marines shooting them. Some of the pistol frames could be traced back to World War II. Now the newer .45s are making their way into the phase training. It's the same gun, but of newer manufacture, with some minor refinements and newer sights. The standard sidearm of the Army and the Marine Corps is the M9 Beretta pistol. It's a 9mm weapons system. The advantage of the Beretta is its fourteen-round magazine and that it is a double-action weapon—considered by many to be a safer gun. So why the .45?

"It has to do with our culture and that this gun is still carried by the Recon Marines," a cadre sergeant told me. "The .45 is our gun and it sets us apart. And it's still a very good gun."

Its primary advantage is that the .45 has a lot more stopping power than a 9mm. Yet it's a single-action weapon, which means that as a secondary combat weapon, it has to be carried with a round in the chamber and the hammer in the cocked position. And it's an eight-round weapon—seven in the magazine and one "in the pipe." But the students seem to like it a great deal.

"It's a lot better than the Beretta," one student told me—one whose MOS had allowed him to qualify on the M9. "It feels better in your hand. Because of the smaller magazine, it's easier to hold. It's like gripping your own wrist rather than your forearm. You can get your hand around it. I shoot better with it. And," he added with a grin, "it's a man's gun. As for the fewer rounds, that's no big deal. One hit with a .45 is all it takes."

"Because of the single action, it's a better first-shot gun," said another student with M9 experience, speaking of the .45's single action. "And that first shot may be the most important shot."

The shooting day begins with a safety briefing, and the safety briefing begins with a single-student recitation of the four MARSOC-modified Marine safety rules:

1. Treat every weapon as if it were loaded, even after you have insured it to be unloaded.

2. Keep your finger straight, off the trigger, and outside the trigger guard until you're up on target with intention to shoot.

3. Never cover anything with the muzzle of your weapon you are not willing to destroy.

4. Be sure of your target; consider its foreground and background.

Live fire begins with the .45s. There are four to five student shooters per shooting coach. They begin with the mechanics of loading, making safe, and holstering the .45. Then, by the numbers, drawing the pistol from the holster with a proper grip and pushing forward to the firing position. Then it's off safe, break the shot or shots, on safe, and reholster. Again and again, slowly and deliberately. Then gradually the student shooters, under the guidance of their shooting coaches, pick up speed—drawing, shooting, changing magazines, reholstering. And always the same—draw, off safe, break the shot, back on safe, properly return the weapon to the carry position in the holster, with the bail over the cocked hammer. The .45 has no adjustable sights; it's a point-and-shoot weapon. For a very few of the student shooters, it's the first time they have fired a handgun. Initial work with the .45 is familiarization shooting and getting used to using the pistol as a secondary weapon in support of the M4.

Live fire with the M4s begins with a brief semiauto familiarization shoot. All of these Marines have trained with the M4 or a preceding M16 variant of the M4. A few of them are familiar with the EOTech sight. The M4s are battlefield zeroed or "BZOed" individually for accuracy at 50 yards. Due to the arc of the 5.56mm high-velocity round and the height of the EOTech off the M4's barrel, the 50-yard zero will also zero the weapon in at 175 to 200 yards.

With the rifles sighted in, the shooting days are all about combat shooting drills. The students shoot from between fifty yards and three yards, stationary and moving, magazine after magazine. The targets are black-and-white human profiles—primarily of a bald, white, goateed male in a cutoff sweatshirt, holding a pistol—with the shooters registering center-of-mass or torso shots and shots to the head or brain. Scoring is dependent on the rounds that strike a target box on the chest, which is a kill shot, or those that fall in a triangle defined by the eyes and nose of the target, which is an instant kill shot. When a shooter has a malfunction with his primary weapon or expends a magazine, he immediately draws his .45 and continues the shooting drill. Drills are timed with the times reduced as the shooter moves closer to the target. There are shooting drills designed around changing magazines and drills that have the shooter moving from a standing to a kneeling to a prone position. One drill has them sprint from the fifty-yard line to the twenty-five, then engage the target, first from a standing position and then kneeling. All drills are conducted in full assault kit with body armor, Rhodesian-style ammunition vests, shooting glasses, and helmets. Cadres and students also wear Peltor ear protection or just "Peltors." These are Mickey Mouse–type ear protectors that fit under the helmet. They not only greatly reduce the crack of rounds with sound-canceling technology, but amplify other sounds around the shooter such as voice commands and other ambient noise. The Peltors are also fitted with earphones and can handle traffic from two radios, one in each ear. Peltors allow special operators to communicate, talk, and fight while protecting their hearing from the damage of gunfire and explosions. As an old warrior whose experience in combat and combat training was with little or no ear protection, I rate the Peltors at the top of the newer battlefield innovations.

The flat-range training with rifles and pistols is about combat shooting and getting rounds on target while moving or manipulating your weapon. It's also about safety while shooting in close proximity to others and the mechanics and conventions that accompany the shooting drills. These conventions and procedures allow for continuous training by multiple shooters to be done safely and effectively. The sequence begins with a shooter in the high ready position, looking over the top of his EOTech sight at the broad battlefield to his front. Seeing a target, the shooter comes off safe, sights in, presses the trigger, snaps his safety back on, and returns to the high ready—a proscribed and choreographed series of movements. When a shooter expends his M4 magazine, he swings his rifle smoothly from his shoulder position with the barrel down, draws his .45, comes off safe, engages the target, goes back on safe, and reholsters his weapon. He does this exactly the same way each and every time. When he changes rifle or pistol magazines, he does it the same way each time. He then reengages his target or makes his weapon safe and checks the area around him in the same manner as he did on the previous drill. When he drops to a knee to make a shot or to retrieve an expended magazine, he will call out "Standing!" as he comes to his feet. Again and again—the same way, every time. This builds procedural muscle memory that will be needed in the shoot house. Shooting on the flat ranges provides training wheels for the close-quarter shooting these student shooters will be doing in the following weeks.

For Class 1-13, the shooting is a welcome change from the sleepless nights of Exercise Raider Spirit in Phase One and living out of a rucksack for two of their three weeks in Phase Two. As Marines, they have a natural affinity for individual weapons. Yet the drills are all about accuracy and weapons manipulation, and the safety protocols that drive these drills are both precise and unforgiving. During work with the pistols, two students experience an ND, or negligent discharge. This is the unintentional discharge of a round. Both students are dropped from the class. The rest of the student shooters soberly observe this and press on with their shooting drills, ever mindful of what a misstep can cost them.

I've witnessed a good many SOF shooting venues, from basic range work to advanced close-quarters shooting. All are highly procedure-driven and designed to condition their shooters to execute the basic shooting mechanics in a safe, orderly, and expeditious manner, without conscious thought. It's the essence of combat shooting. When these basics are conditioned through repetition, they become automatic—executed at a subconscious level. The combat shooter is then free to look for enemy targets in the flow of the fight, and also retain the situational awareness to know where his teammates are in that flow. These SOF Marines in training execute these mechanics well, right down to the Marine-peculiar step of snapping closed the dustcover port of their M4s after making their weapon safe following a shot. For some reason, only Marines do this.

"Most of these guys come to us shooting pretty well," one of the range supervisors told me. He's a retired Special Forces master sergeant with a good many years as a contract shooting instructor. "After all, they've been in the Corps for four years or more. And at this stage of the training, most of the ones who shouldn't be in this course or don't want to be in this course have already left. These guys all want to be here, and for the most part, they pay attention and work hard. Each day they shoot with more confidence, and they become more proficient as they move through the drills. Time on the gun with the close, often one-on-one, attention we give them here can do a great deal in a short period of time. This builds muscle memory for when they get to the shoot house and into a real fight."

Throughout the drills, the shooting coaches are moving behind their four or five shooters like fussy British nannies, offering advice and encouragement. They always seem to find some extra time for the one who's having trouble, or a refinement for the one who's shooting well.

"Move fast, shoot slow—speed in the hands, slow in the shot."

"Focus on the target. Move your sights to your eyes, not your eyes to your sights."

"When that pistol comes up, it's all about front-sight focus. Sight picture and press."

"If you pull a shot off target, push that from your mind; get aggressive, get pissed, get focused, and get back on target."

By the end of the second week, most of the student shooters are grouping their rounds within the spread of an open hand from fifty and twenty-five yards and into the size of a fist at the closer distances. The shooting coaches stay with their same students for all of the range drills unless one of their shooters is having a serious problem. Then another or more senior instructor will step in to see if he can help that shooter with his issues. Friday of the second week of Phase Three is rifle qualification day. The students will first qualify with the rifle on the flat range. The qualifying shoot is a single graded pass that is an inventory of drills they've been doing the past week. It's a formatted combat stress-type course that has its roots in a rifle qualification course that certifies Recon Marines for deployment with an MEU Maritime Special Purpose Force.

The qualification shoot itself is a formatted move-and-shoot course with a top score of 100 points. This qual shoot parallels the students' shooting drills, but they're now on the clock and under pressure. The shooters will make two firing runs, both beginning at the fifty-yard line and closing to within three yards of the target. They must move and shoot in a proscribed way as they close with the target. There are a total of fifty rounds fired on the two runs, forty-four torso shots and six brain shots, each scoring two points. Both timed shooting runs begin at the low ready and have the shooter in full assault kit. Shooters on the course fire while standing, moving, kneeling, and from the prone position. Points are subtracted for misses and taking too much time. In something of a rarity, all of the student shooters in Class 1-13 score 80 or better and pass their flat-range rifle qualification on their first attempt. In this class two sergeants tied for the rifle honors with a high score of 98, with a third sergeant close behind at 97.

"We have very few students who can't pass this course," Gunnery Sergeant Conway said of the rifle qual. "The rifle qualification here and the pistol qualification next week are really just the preparation drills for the serious work in the shoot house and close-quarter battle. We have two students in this class who failed in the last class, one with the rifle qual and one with the pistol. Both were good students, but both had some serious problems with their shooting mechanics. We rolled them back to this class and allowed them time to work on their shooting during the interim. Now they're shooting with the class leaders. Some just get it faster than others. But all of them have to be shooting to standard before they move on to live fire in the shoot house and the shoot house qualification."

The night shooting evolutions are important, but they are not graded events. They begin with white-light shooting with the M4 using the rail-mounted high-intensity light. Then the students drill with pistols and handheld lights. These shooting drills, once again, are for familiarization, with close attention to procedure and safety. The serious nighttime shooting is with the LA-5.

The LA-5 is a cigarette pack–sized device mounted on the top rail of the M4 and houses two lasers that are factory aligned. One is a

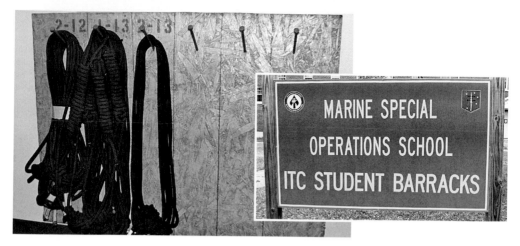

ABOVE RIGHT: A&S Goal. The goal of all Assessment and Selection students is to be selected for the ITC and move into the ITC barracks.

ABOVE LEFT: DOR Ropes. You hand in your rope and you're done. Outside the class proctor's office in the student barracks, the class pegs display the ropes of ITC students who have dropped on request.

TCCC Training. A tactical combat casualty care student prepares to treat a battlefield wounded while his teammate holds security.

Buddy Carry PT. Most physical training sessions involve a marine who has to carry another marine, often for several hundred yards.

Courtesy of the U.S. Marine Corps

Pool PT. At least once a week during most weeks of the ITC, students do their physical training session in the water.

Courtesy of the U.S. Marine Corps

Stone Bay Swim. Class 1-13 lines up for a "fin" in cold water of the New River. They have wet suits under their battle dress, weapons, and 75 pounds of gear.

A Proper Water Exit. After (yet another) 2000-yard fin, a student makes a proper tactical exit from the water with all his gear in place.

The Rappel Tower.
Most marines know
how to rappel, but
an afternoon is spent
at the tower for
rappel and fast-rope
training.

Eyes On. ITC
students in Phase
One conduct a
spotting-scope drill.
Various objects are
hidden in a treeline
that they must
identify.

See It, Draw It.
As a part of their
reconnaissance
training, Phase One
students make field
sketches of a target
complex.

Vehicle Ambush. Two students check a dead "tango," or terrorist, following the ambush of an enemy pickup truck. This tango is played by an ITC instructor.

Ma Deuce. Students train on the M2 .50 caliber heavy machine gun—the longest-serving machine gun in the U.S. arsenal.

Final Exam. An ITC student presents his patrol order around a terrain model while his cadre grader (seated) makes notes and his student teammates observe.

Course and Speed. A student crew conducts their route planning during small-craft drills. Calculations include course, speed, distance, and sea state.

Small Craft Launch. Amphib students launch a fully loaded Zodiac and 55-horsepower outboard at the Key West training facility.

Dump Boat Drill. Having flipped their Zodiac to empty it, ITC marines now turn their boat back over.

Courtesy of the U.S. Marine Corps

Surf Passage. Following a training mission ashore, a boat crew attempts to take their Zodiac back out through the surf without broaching.

Courtesy of the U.S. Marine Corps

Air to Sea. Amphib students insert into the water from a CH-47. They will continue the training mission by Zodiac.

Courtesy of the U.S. Marine Corps

SR Mission. An ITC student on a special reconnaissance mission keeps eyes on his target. Note the Cannon 5D camera on the ground, at the ready.

Commo in the MSS. A Phase Two student in special-reconnaissance mission support site makes a commo link back to the company headquarters.

TOP: At the Ready. Student shooters on the flat range look over their M4 rifles, ready to begin a timed shooting drill.

BOTTOM: And Engage. Sighting in with their EoTech sights, student shooters engage their targets, on the move. Note the holstered .45 pistols.

Secondary Weapons System. Much of the shooting is done by one-on-one instruction. An instructor works with a student on manipulating the .45 pistol.

ABOVE: Ready . . . Go! Phase Three students preparing to enter the shoot house. Note that there are no blank adapters on their M4s; this is a live-fire drill. *Courtesy of the U.S. Marine Corps*

RIGHT: Move and Shoot. A student team has just moved into the shoot house and is about to enter the first of the rooms they have to clear. This is live-fire training.

BELOW: Dig Your Corner! Two shoot-house students conduct a room-clearing drill. This is a walk-through, or they would have helmets, and eye and ear protection.

Engage the Threat. Who to shoot—the woman with the gun or the guy with the hand drill? *Courtesy of the U.S. Marine Corps*

Hooli Tool and Sledge. Two Phase Three students take down a training door with a hooligan tool and sledgehammer. *Courtesy of the U.S. Marine Corps*

RIGHT: Linear Breaching Charge. An instructor demonstrates the proper placement of a linear charge. Note the Nonel shock-tube firing leads.

BELOW: Another Entry Tactic. A student breacher practices with the Mossburg 590 breaching shotgun. For a few of the students, this was their first experience with a shotgun.

Stress Shoot Competition. A student shooter moves through the Stress Shoot while followed by two cadre instructors, one observing and one scoring.

Combat Town Patrolling. ITC students conduct drills in urban patrolling prior to Exercise Guide Strike.

Vehicle Search. A student team walks through the proper way to hold security and search a suspect vehicle.

MOUT Movement. During MOUT (military operations in urban terrain), the students conduct speed and security drills in a combat town.

G-Chief Meeting. Two student officers and their team chief meet with their guerrilla leaders during Exercise Durna Bridge.

Working with the G-Force. Phase Four students train marines who role-play as guerillas deep in the South Carolina woods.   *Courtesy of the U.S. Marine Corps*

Actions on Target. A Phase Four student briefs his team and Abyssinian guerillas on their attack on an enemy radio tower.

Under Fire. While his disabled Humvee is attacked, a TCC student officer calls for air support while his gun crew returns fire.

visible laser that puts a red dot on the target. The other is an infrared laser visible only through the shooter's night-vision goggles, and it becomes a green dot when viewed through the NVGs. The LA-5 also features intensity settings for both lasers and an infrared floodlight capability. It allows the shooter to see and to shoot accurately in the dark.

Prior to the first night's shooting, the students dial in their LA-5s so their visible laser is aligned with their EOTech sight. This creates a marriage between the impact of the rounds at fifty yards with the visible-red-dot laser. The green IR dot is aligned with the red dot. Now, when shooting in daylight or low-light-level conditions, the shooter has only to put the red dot on the target and press his trigger. His rounds go to the red dot. At night, when he's looking through his NVGs, these rounds go to the green dot. This adds something of a video-game element to the deadly business of getting rounds on target, but the basics are still the same. The only change to the shooting mechanics from day to night is that the shooter is looking over the top of his rifle, just over his EOTech sight rather than through it.

The student shooters first shoot from the fifty-yard line to recheck their sighting alignment and that their rounds are impacting on the green dot generated by the IR laser. Then they move on to the same combat-shooting exercises they just did during the day. Movement is a little slower and there is the same religious attention to safety—perhaps more so—but the shooting drills are much the same. The students spend three nights shooting under these low-light, no-light conditions. About half of the class have had at least some previous experience with nighttime shooting and IR-laser targeting. For a few of them, that experience has been in combat. The purpose of these nighttime live-fire drills at the ITC is to bring all the CSO student shooters to the same level of familiarity with the LA-5 and standard MARSOC night-shooting conventions. When these new ITC-trained CSOs reach their MSOTs, they will be ready to drill with the team veterans as they prepare for deployment rotation.

"I've done this before," one of the students told me, a former infantryman, "but it was with a different system. This is a little more high-speed, especially with the shooting drills. I think that transitioning right from the daytime drills into the IR nighttime drills allowed us to do this so well. I felt very comfortable behind this gun and the LA-5."

"This was all new to me," said another from a transportation MOS, "and I don't mind saying that I was a little nervous—I didn't want to make a mistake. But the instructor was right there. 'Just focus on the basics and take your time,' he told us, and he was right. It's a natural progression from shooting in the daylight. I've got a lot to learn, but I know I can get proficient at this. I feel good about it."

"I've used the LA-5 in training, but only in the daytime," reported Sergeant Brad Hansen. "For me it was getting used to handling the M4 with the NGVs *and* the IR laser. And the additional steps in the shooting sequence—see the target, turn on the laser, hold the laser on the target, off safe, shoot the target, on safe, turn off the laser, check the area around you and your shooting buddies, and look for other targets. That's a lot of steps. It took me a few nights to get comfortable and dialed in. But it's how we own the night."

CLOSE-QUARTER BATTLE

The fourteen days devoted to close-quarter-battle follow the two weeks of basic marksmanship. This training begins with a single hour of briefing from the lead shoot-house instructor. Fifty-five Marines from Class 1-13, all ITC-qualified on the M4, are in the room. They still must complete their pistol qualification, which will take place later this week, but these fifty-five will begin work in the shoot house.

"During this period of instruction we will teach you the basics of close-quarter combat," the lead cadre instructor tells them. "While this will be basic instruction, we have a number of goals here. The first, and it almost goes without saying, is safety. The second is to qualify you as a Level One combat shooter. Past that, we want to instill in you the mechanics and procedure common to close-quarters shooting so that when you get to your team, you can get in the stack and begin to train with them as you prepare to go downrange, okay?

"While these are only the basics, this is still high-risk training and we will always stress safety and situational awareness. But these are not precisely choreographed dance steps. These baseline drills and conventions will allow you to move into what we call initiative based tactics, or IBT. Every situation in close-quarter battle is just a little different. You will have to think and to make decisions based on the threat, and no two threats are the same. You must react to the threat with regard to your role as a member of a team in the house and in that room. We expect you to be aggressive and use initiative within the constraints of safety and basic procedure. In IBT, you have to actively engage threats and protect each other."

From the classroom they move a short distance to a training area and the school's primary shoot house. The shoot house is a single-story, partitioned building with catwalks that crisscross rooms defined by partitions and walls of rubberized, bullet-absorbent building blocks. No ceilings; those above can look right down into the room. This shoot house allows for single- and multiple-room clearing drills with movable bullet-trap targets that help prevent the erosion of the walls from high-velocity rounds. The first morning in the shoot house is all about dry fire and dry runs. The shooting instructors demonstrate proper entry and clearing techniques. Only then do the students begin walk-through after walk-through, first in pairs and then in three- to five-man teams—first single rooms, then multiple rooms. On the second day, the class goes hot with UTM rounds. UTMs (Ultimate Training Munitions—a brand name) are .556 rounds that fire a paint round through the students' M4 rifles. The only modification needed is a different bolt for the M4. These paint rounds are nonlethal and do less damage to the shoot house, while clearly marking the impact of a round. They are also cleared for force-on-force training, but that will come later. Perhaps the biggest advantage of UTMs is safety. The special bolts that will only fire a UTM round will neither seat nor fire a standard .556 cartridge.

After several days of drill, the students are moving a stack of five shooters through up to three rooms, clearing each as they go. Two student teams work a half day in the shoot house, while the other two continue to drill on a nearby flat range. Then they switch. "We keep drilling them on moving, shooting, and changing magazines," the lead flat-range instructor tells me. "This week we will focus on lateral move-ment and shooting in the three- to ten-yard range—indoor gunfight distances. Still, it's all about weapons manipulation. The more they do this, the better they will perform in the shoot house."

Midweek of their third week of shooting, the class shoots for score with the .45. All students must shoot a minimum score to continue in the shoot house and continue in the phase. The pistol qual, as was the rifle qual, is a Recon shooting derivative and one that puts a premium on shooting fast, shooting accurately, and shooting on the move. The qualification is timed start to finish. As with the rifle qual, fifty rounds are scored, with penalties for taking too much time on the course. There are ten stationary shooting stations and ten shoot-on-the-move stations. On finishing each station, the student shooter must holster his .45 and go to his primary or M4. At each station, the shooter begins with a new magazine in his M4, loaded with a single round. The round is a non-scoring round and serves to make the shooter's primary weapon "down." The shooter must then transition—release his M4, draw his .45, and shoot the station. The targets are a combi-nation of cartoon targets, steel, and steel poppers. The cartoon targets are the same paper-person targets the students have been shooting on the flat ranges—the same bald guy in a sweatshirt with a pistol. Steel targets register hits by making a ping sound. The poppers ping and then topple to register a hit.

"This does a couple of things for us," an instructor said of the pistol qual shoot. "It forces the shooter to initiate each shooting sta-tion from the holster. Secondly, it gets the students to feel when their primary weapon is dry. A combat shooter has to feel that last bullet go; he cannot wait to press the trigger to know he's dry."

Most in the class have little trouble on qual day, but two students fail to shoot a qualifying score. On the retest, which there is only one of, both qualify. For the first time in two years, there were no failures or rollbacks because a student failed to receive a passing score of the flat-range rifle or pistol qualification. Having lost another in the class for a non-shooting-performance-related issue, Class 1-13 stands at fifty-four as they focus on live-fire drills in the shoot house.

During the run-up to the pistol qualification, several students shot a perfect score of 100 on the qual course. One of them was one of the scout-snipers. But on qual day, the top scorer is a young sergeant with a former MOS as an aviation ordnanceman. He weighed in with a score of 99, the best on qual day.

"I had taken the M9 [Beretta 9mm] course a few years ago, and I've fired a .45 once before this, and that was just out with some of the guys plinking at tin cans." He shrugs at having broken out as the top pistol shot in the class on qual day. "I did just what they told me, and I did a lot of dry firing. My shooting coach was terrific—he gave me and the other guys in my group a lot of one-on-one attention. And," he adds with a grin, "I was probably a little lucky."

"How did you fare with the rifle?"

"Not as well. I shot a 96 on one of the practice days but only an 86 on qual day. I need to get some more time on gun and improve there."

This sergeant's experience with his M4 was not unlike the majority in the class. Most at one time or another had shot a better score than they did on the qualification day.

"It's the stress," Captain Keefer told a group of shooters on the range. "You have to manage stress and focus on getting rounds on the target. It's the same in combat. It's not necessarily the best shooter who wins the fight—it's the shooter who can best manage the stress of the fight while he's handling his weapon."

Class 1-13 ends their third week of shooting with more stress on yet another range. This time the name says it all; it's the stress shoot. The stress shoot brings all the flat-range shooting drills into play, both pistol and rifle, with a single competitive timed drill. One at a time, the student shoots begin with a 150-yard sprint to the first shooting station, where the shooter begins to work two fourteen-round magazines through his primary weapon and three seven-round mags in his secondary. The drill is about speed, accuracy, changing magazines, and transition from primary to secondary—all that the students have worked on for the past few weeks. They first shoot from the prone position, then kneeling and standing through two barricade stations, strong hand and off hand. All targets at the fixed shooting stations are steel silhouettes at one hundred yards. Scores are registered with pings on metal. After a speed reload, it's shooting on the move, left to right on the range, at cartoon targets at fifteen yards. Then the shooters advance through a series of cartoon and steel popper targets, going from M4 to .45 as they finish the stress shoot. Start to finish, it's a weapons-manipulation drill. The class shoots for score, but this graded event has no pass/fail criteria like the ones for the rifle, pistol, and shoot house qualifications. The scores do count for overall class performance average. And within an ITC class and for all shooting events, there's always the issue of bragging rights.

Because the student shooters run the stress gauntlet individually, it's something of a slow day and a fun day. But the TACs and shooting instructors are there with their students, talking with them about how to shoot the course a little better before they kit up for the competition. The TACs and instructors are also there to address lessons learned after the students have completed the course. At the end of the day, there is a great deal of speculation as to who shot well and who shot the best. But the cadre are keeping those scores to themselves for now. On this day and this stress shoot, three sergeants in Class 1-13 score a perfect 100. At graduation, there will be recognition for the class top shooter, which is a combination of all the graded shooting evolutions.

The progression through the shoot house continues, and this progression is on several levels. Now there are two shoot houses. While one of the student teams drills in one shoot house, the other is at a second house that features long hallways and stairwells and obstacles. Each new feature calls for a very formatted approach to the danger, and proscribed guidelines depending on where the student is in the file, or stack, of shooters. With each new feature it's a crawl, walk, walk-faster approach. There is no running in the shoot house with live rounds. First there are demonstrations, then talk-throughs and slow walk-throughs. Then the student shooters trade positions in the stack or move on to a different set of rooms or hallways. After multiple drills moving slowly and deliberately, they pick up the speed.

Each new venue brings a progression regarding the ammunition. All iterations begin with dry fire. Then they move on to the UTM rounds, and finally the frangible .556 rounds. These frangible rounds are designed to break apart on impact. While they are very lethal, they don't have the penetrating power of the standard green-tipped ball ammunition, so these frangible rounds may not carry into the next room of a house being operationally cleared.

Each day a new obstacle or wrinkle is added to the shoot-house training. Basic movements and safety considerations become more ingrained with practice. With practice, the student clearing teams become a little better with the free-flow of a room-clearing sequence and more comfortable with the situation-driven initiative based tactics. The targets also progress. At the beginning their old friend with shaved head, goatee, sweatshirt, and revolver is there with them in each room. Then he begins to turn up with a cup of coffee in his hand instead of the pistol. Then other cartoon targets appear, some men and some women—some holding weapons, others holding a package or a cell phone. Throughout all these progressions, the basics still rule. It's still all about the execution of the fundamental movements and procedures—again and again.

The close-quarters shooters of Class 1-13 also have video feedback on their movements through the shoot house. The shooting instructors have handheld or helmet-mounted video cameras and follow the student clearing teams from room to room. The feed from these video cams is downloaded to the student PCs in the barracks after each shooting day. There they can see what they did right and wrong during their movement through the shoot house, as well as again listen to the AAR from their shooting instructor. Quite often their TACs are there with them in the evenings to watch the shoot-house drills and again critique their performance.

Along with the procedure-driven shooting mechanics and safety requirements of these live-fire drills, there are the room-clearing protocols that accompany the shooting. After the student shooters become familiar with moving and shooting in a proscribed manner, they begin to use flash-bangs on entering a contested room. Flash-bangs are small grenades that are nonlethal and designed to expel no shrapnel, but they do give off a blinding flash and the bang is substantial. Basically, they are very large firecrackers with usually predictable second-and-a-half delays. But the concussion is jarring, even with helmets, Peltor ear protection, and body armor. As the students move through the house and engage threats, they must also quickly mark areas cleared and neutralized of threats. Areas that they have cleared or that have been inspected are marked with green ChemLights. Targeted individuals, referred to as "tangos," that have been shot are marked with red ChemLights. As they move past an engaged, dead tango, the student assaulters will rip the paper cartoon target from the bullet-trap target stand and drop an activated ChemLight on top of the downed tango. This simulates having checked that an enemy fighter is shot, down hard, and no longer a threat. Room clearing is a speed-driven, security-driven enterprise. The assault element wants to move quickly to clear the objective, but still has to ensure that they leave no viable threat behind them that might attack them from the rear. They also have to properly mark the area for teammates who may be close behind them. Each day in the shoot house, there is a new challenge to be incorporated into the room-clearing procedures or a new or different way to execute an existing procedure.

"You guys are doing well," one of the TACs tells his student MSOT during a midday break. "You're thinking and you're getting the natural flow of movement down as you progress through the house. The procedures are the same. That first man has to get in quickly and dig his corner, left or right. The second guy has to be just as quick to cover his back and to dominate the room as he moves along the opposite wall. Right now, all your attention is focused on the next movement and then the next. That's okay for now. Those of us that have been doing this for years can now do this without conscious thought, and it's this muscle memory that allows us to see a bigger picture. We can focus on the threat and think tactically without having to focus on the mechanics. It allows us to have greater situational awareness; we can look ahead and anticipate the unfolding tactical situation. It also allows us to mentally retain what just took place in the previous room or the room before that. This will come to all of you with time. Your OODA loop will get smaller and smaller—you'll see more and you'll know what you're seeing faster. The decisions will get made sooner and your actions will be reflexive. You'll get there—you're getting there. But for now it's all about the basics and knowing your role in the stack. And practice, practice, practice."

Except for the stress of moving and shooting in close quarters with live rounds, most in 1-13 master the dance steps of the shoot-house ballet. The ever-watchful shooting coaches and cadre are with them each step of the way, and there are consequences for minor procedural errors. Failure to properly engage a target can result in running a lap around the training area in full kit. "I failed to dig my corner when I entered a room," Sergeant Irving told me. "That night I was made to write a letter of condolence to the parents of the Marine who died because of my mistake." Some get it faster than others, and all know they must have it right for the upcoming shoot-house qualification.

———

Class 1-13 takes a few days from their close-quarters combat drill to spend some time on the breaching ranges. During these two days of breaching they will cover the basics of explosive and ballistic breaching—both methods of entering a compound, a building, or a room where their way is blocked by a locked door or gate. These breaching techniques are yet another set of skills where the level of experience varies widely. Most of the infantrymen have seen this in one form or another, and two of them have been to one of the Marine Corps formal breaching schools. Others have seen it or even worked as a breacher on one of their deployments. Close to half have had no previous experience whatsoever. Explosive breaching is basically using a small explosive charge to defeat a door lock or door hinge and blow open the door. Ballistic breaching has to do with using a twelve-gauge shotgun to defeat the lock or hinges of a door or gate.

The students are introduced to explosives and the safe handling of explosives. They work with TNT, C4, detonation cord, and blasting caps. They learn about the priming of explosives, firing trains, and explosive initiators. Similar to their introduction to the shoot house, the training is crawl and walk. There is very little running on the demo ranges.

"We just give them the basics here," one of the TACs says of the training, "so when they get to their teams they can adjust to the procedures and conventions of that team. At least they will have seen it once. They'll get a lot more of this during their work-ups for deployment."

For this short course in demolitions, the students get an introduction to time fuse and how to set up a non-electric time fuse–initiated charge. After a demonstration, the students cut lengths of time fuse and mate them with non-electric blasting caps on one end and a time-fuse initiator or fuse lighter on the other. After setting off charges of TNT and C4 explosives, they move on to the more modern, commercial-grade Nonel shock-tube firing assemblies. The Nonel systems are now the industry standard for commercial and military demolition-charge initiation. These firing trains come factory-assembled with dual blasting caps married to explosive "shock tubes" of various lengths to allow the blaster to command-detonate his charge from a standoff distance of his choosing. If handled properly, they are safe and reliable, and the current method for combat breaching. In their MSOTs, Marine special operators will have any number of preformed demolitions and breaching charges. The one they will build and use here in this short demo course is a linear det-cord charge.

Detonation cord is a clothesline-like plastic cord that is constructed with a core of explosive material. It is often used to tie in several explosive charges to go off at the same time. It can also be cut in lengths and bundled to form a linear explosive charge. Four to five lengths of standard det cord, when taped together, are sufficient to defeat the lock of a standard interior, hollow-core door.

"I'd never handled explosives before," Sergeant Brad Hansen said, "but we went through it step-by-step. First we cut the det-cord strips to the same length and taped them together with one-hundred-mile-per-hour tape [a military version of duct tape]. Then we taped a strip of hydrogel to the charge to tamp the explosives and make them more effective. And finally there were the calculations. We had to calculate the net effective weight of the charge and the minimum safe distance. The first is the weight of the explosives in the charge and the second is how close you can be to the charge when it's detonated. You write the NEW and MSD on the charge along with your name and date. And the charge is ready to be primed and used in a breach."

After each student builds a charge, the charge is set against a door, primed, and detonated per the safety requirements and procedures of the training range. In this training, the objective is to defeat a door lock, so the linear breaching charge is taped to the door vertically, between the door handle and the jamb. The student breachers are close to the minimum safe distance, but with full eye and ear protection, and helmet and body armor. If a charge fails to detonate, the name of the charge builder is noted for some good-natured remediation by the breaching instructors.

The other breaching method taught in this short breaching course is ballistic breaching. This is where the door lock or the door hinges are defeated with a shotgun. The shotgun is a Mossberg 590 pump-action model with a short barrel, a five-round magazine tube, and pistol grip in place of a traditional stock. The twelve-gauge rounds are of a frangible steel composition designed to have maximum short-range impact, yet with a minimum of shrapnel projection into the room behind the door. The technique is to attack the door lock or a hinge with two rounds and the barrel up against the face of the door. The shots are placed closely, one over the other, to form a figure-eight pattern. The students, in full kit, race to the door, double-tap it twice, reload, and return to the starting point. They run these speed drills again and again, all with great attention to procedure and safety.

"It took me a while to get used to it," one of the students told me, "as I had never fired a shotgun before. And it's the opposite of a rifle. The breaching shotgun is carried off safe, with no round in the chamber. You pump a round into the chamber just before you fire it, and you leave the expended round in the chamber, again with the safety off. That's the safe position and the carry position. We got a lot of practice with the weapon, and I now feel very comfortable with it." After all the charges are detonated and the shotgun breaching rounds fired, the lead breaching instructor calls the students in for a final AAR.

"These past few days are not designed to make breachers out of you but to give you some familiarity with explosive breaching and ballistic breaching. That shotgun is a good tool. It's reliable and it lets the clearing team in very quickly following the breach. Explosive breaching has its place, especially on a steel door and when you want to shake up those on the other side of the door. A couple of things. We've barely scratched the surface on the types of charges and the methods of explosive breaching. You'll get more of this when you get to your teams. There are refinements and ways to enhance your charge, and methods of charge placement you will pick up along the way. There are the little things, like keeping a few extra strips of tape on your helmet in case you need one to better secure the charge to the door. Or recoiling the shock tubes of your Nonel system so they deploy without tangles. Remember, you'll be doing much of this at night with gloves on. Buddy check each other; always have a buddy inspect your charge, and you inspect his. Even senior breachers inspect and want to be inspected. When you build these charges, be careful with each step and keep them neat. Be meticulous. Lives depend on it. Those of us who have been at this awhile have had charges misfire. Believe me, nothing is more frustrating to an assault element waiting to go in to get some scumbag than to have a breaching charge fail, let alone the danger of having to wait while a secondary charge is put in place. Okay?" The class nods as one.

"One more thing, guys," a senior instructor says. "Some of us have been in deployment rotation for quite a while. We've had literally hundreds of these charges go off in near proximity. Over time, it can affect you. I know guys who can still function, but they often find themselves standing in front of the refrigerator at home, wondering why the hell they opened the fridge door, know what I mean? So if you can get something between you and that charge, do it. Sometimes you're in a short hallway and you can't, so all you can do is put your head down and take some of the blast. But when you can, find a way to shield yourself. It'll pay off in the long run, good to go?" Again, the class nods their understanding.

At a later time during this phase, the class gets training on mechanical breaching and practical work using handheld rams, sledgehammers, and a combination pickaxe-crowbar called a Hooligan tool. In their teams, they will have gas-powered quickie saws that can cut into steel plating and expanded-metal barricades. They'll also have acetylene torches for thermal breaching.

———

Following their breaching training, the class is back in the classroom to learn about sensitive site exploitation or SSE. Nearly all of us have heard about the "rich treasure trove" of intelligence information that was taken from the compound of Osama bin Laden. Even though the value of what was taken is classified, the methodology of the taking is not. All special-operations assault elements have embedded search teams that go into action once the target or objective is secured. Designated members of the search team also serve as photographers and cataloguers. In the ITC, students are exposed to the basics of these SSE-team duties. In their MSOTs they will be trained to a SOF standard in sensitive site exploitation and how to methodically search for weapons, explosives, tunnels, hide sites, documents, and electronic data. Of immediate interest is the intelligence that a search team can gather that is actionable—information that can lead to an immediate follow-on target. And there are evidentiary considerations, even in times of war. During Exercise Guile Strike, the exercise portion conducted during the final week of Phase Three, and in subsequent field training exercises, SSE will be a part of their planning and their execution on target.

———————

The shoot-house qualification takes place during the third to last week of Phase Three. All the flat-range time, all the weapons manipulation, all the shooting-drill mechanics come down to a single graded, multi-room clearing exercise. Test day is a long day and a very tense one. Each ITC student must score at least 80 out of 100 points to qualify or he will not be allowed to continue in the course. He must perform to standard on this graded shooting drill to move on to Phase Four.

Team by student team, they kit up for this important graded exercise. They are attired as they have been for the last four weeks of shooting drill—helmets, Peltors, shooting glasses, body armor, spare .45 and .556 magazines, bundles of ChemLights, MBITR radios, and associated items of equipment normally worn on their Rhodesian vests, and of course, their body armor. They are placed in the stack with two shooting-coach instructors to form a three-man clearing element. Prior to the beginning of the graded exercise, each student shooter surrenders one of his primary magazines to the graders, who will ensure that at some point during the graded exercise, his M4 will experience a jam. The qualification-drill scenario may vary from class to class, but each student in a given class is graded on the same multiple-room clearing sequence. For the first time, they are in a live-shooting, multi-room clearing sequence with two experienced shooters; each of them is the only student. Several graders are on the catwalks overhead and one is following the clearing team from behind. All watch the student shooter carefully and grade his performance. The instructor-shooters are also graders. Following this graded event, those that pass go to the clean area, separate from those who are waiting to be tested. Those who have failed the graded evolution are also segregated, in yet another area. For the winners, it's all smiles and relief.

"It was a little intimidating," Captain Fraker told me, "but once that flash-bang went off it was game on. I didn't score as well as I would have liked, but it's behind me now and I'm glad that it is."

"I scored 95," Sergeant Irving said of his qual shoot, one of the better scores. "It was nothing we hadn't seen before, and it was pretty basic. Still, I was pretty amped up about it. But I got it done, and I'm ready to move on."

"It was everything we learned in the phase, jam-packed into five or six minutes of room clearing," Sergeant Brad Hansen said of the shoot-house qualification. "We cleared five rooms and a hallway, and I used both my primary and secondary weapons. And it seemed like it lasted half an hour."

On this critical live-fire qualification, six Marines failed to pass the exam—five enlisted Marines and one captain. One experienced a negligent discharge during a pre-qualification run through the shoot house—a major safety violation. Two failed for a violation of the one-meter rule. A shooter cannot bring his muzzle within a meter of another on his clearance team. These three students were immediately removed from training. The three other students in 1-13 failed for not performing to standard in the handling of their weapons systems during their graded evolution; their scores were below the 80-point cutoff for a satisfactory score. These three were taken to another shoot house to be drilled on what they'd done wrong. Yet, on the following day, all three failed their re-test. Of the unfortunate six in Class 1-13, only two will be rolled back to Phase Three with Class 2-13 and given a second chance. The others will not, and they were released from the ITC.

"They're all good Marines," one of the veteran shooting coaches said after the failures, "but this is serious business. The two who will be rolled back to the next class just need more time on the gun. They just have some mechanics problems, and we can work on those. My guess is that they'll come back here with the next class and crush this phase."

It was my observation that the deciding factor of who was to be recycled and who was not was their attitudes and their performance in other phases of the ITC to date. The two Marines who are to be re-cycled had performed well and were peered well by others on their team, so they will be retained and allowed the time to bring their shooting abilities up to standard. With the shoot-house qual behind them, forty-eight members of Class 1-13 move on to MOUT training, Guile Strike, their final field evolution of Phase Three. During the shoot-house qualification, a single Marine in 1-13 achieved a perfect score of 100.

MOUT AND GUILE STRIKE

Early Monday morning, with two weeks of Phase Three remaining, Class 1-13 is up early for a ten-mile timed ruck march. Following a round of stretching and an inspection, they are rucked up and on the stopwatch by 0530 in a light drizzle. While all in the class are making the minimum times, it's still an issue of pride to finish well and be among the top finishers. This day, the first across the line is Captain Andrew Fraker.

"I'm a good rucker, and today I just got out front and stayed there. It was good to come in first, but it seemed to take a great deal out of me—more so than usual. Later that day my vision became fuzzy and I went to see the medics. Long story short, they tested me and it seems

I've developed type one diabetes. My blood-sugar level is off the chart. I'll get some more tests, but it looks like this will take me out of the class. I couldn't believe it, and I'm devastated. But I guess you can't have diabetes and be a special operator. It's crushing to get this far and have to pack it in."

Captain Fraker is dropped from Class 1-13 and immediately begins treatment and further testing. He hopes to be allowed into 2-13 or a subsequent class, but that is, for now, out of his control. The class is down another Marine.

"On occasion, we get a good Marine who has something happen over which he has no control," Lieutenant Colonel Dodd said of this captain's plight, "nor, in many cases, do we. An injury or a condition like this can put a student beyond the medical constraints of operational duty in MARSOC and a Marine Special Operations Team. But sometimes, we can intervene and make an exception. We'll do what we can with Captain Fraker."

Class 1-13 packs out from the barracks and makes their way from Stone Bay onto Camp Lejeune proper, where they set up a base camp in four Quonset-type huts on Onslow Beach. The huts have electricity and concrete floors. Two serve as barracks and two serve as planning bays and TOCs (tactical operations centers), one for each of the two student-MSOT elements. The Onslow Beach complex also serves as a forward operating base, or FOB, for operations in the Republic of Abyssinia. Here, the student elements will be tasked with direct-action, special operations that will call into play most of the skills they have learned in the first three phases of the ITC. Collectively, this movement and training exercise is called Guile Strike. Before they get to the mission planning/mission execution of Guile Strike, 1-13 receives their MOUT training. This training takes place at a MOUT (military operations in urban terrain) training facility adjacent to the one that was used in the Sting Ray Fury exercise.

Generally speaking, MOUT training refers to combat training in that critical area between the edge of the village or built-up area and that first door that has to be breached or the first room that has to be cleared. Much as close-quarter battle is tactical movement from room to room in a house, MOUT training is the tactical movement from building to building, street to street, in an urban area. This urban complex features single huts, residential compounds, multifamily buildings, apartment flats, small commercial buildings, churches, mosques, and gas stations. This site, like most MOUT facilities used by the military, is more slanted to the built-up, cinder-block, urban terrain in Iraq than the rural, mud-hut village-like terrain in Afghanistan, as that was the site's initial utility. The site is a ten minute drive from their forward operating base at Onslow Beach.

Each student MSOT is taken by two instructors for his MOUT clinic. They first begin with vehicle takedowns and rehearse the proper way to stop a vehicle and to search both the vehicle occupants and the vehicle itself. It is a by-the-numbers, choreographed procedure done while the student teams maintain a rotating, L-shaped security cordon around the vehicle and driver. Scattered about this MOUT site are numerous abandoned vehicles. "If, for some reason, the driver does not want to open a door, or the glove box, or the trunk," the students are told, "then call the explosive ordnance disposal techs or the dogs in to investigate."

Under the direction of the phase cadre, the student teams patrol through the town in a loose, extended patrol formation. They hold on danger areas while their teammates cross them.

"Remember to look up," an instructor says to his team as it moves up a street with multiple-story buildings. "You cover the upper stories for your teammates on the other side of the street and they cover for you."

After a while, the teams begin to designate a single structure as the target and set up their practice patrols to converge on that building. "Moving through an urban setting is, in many ways," 1-13 is told, "like clearing a large building. You have to think on the move, hold down those danger areas or avenues of potential fire, and protect each other. Keep it fluid and keep it moving. Keep it tight and move aggressively. The bad guys can tell when an American unit is sloppy and when they have their shit together. If you move well and are tactically sound, they will probably leave you alone. Now, as you approach the target building, you'll want to compress your patrol, move into security positions, and get your initial stack set up on the door. Again, make this happen quickly but smoothly."

After a number of approach runs through the MOUT site to a target building, the teams begin to practice clearing the buildings. These are not the shoot houses with which they have some familiarity, but buildings they have never before been inside. Here they have to use their clearing techniques and initiative-based tactics in rooms, hallways, and stairs. But the basics are the basics—smooth is fast, dig your corner, hold on danger areas, protect your buddy. They do this in the daylight, without body armor, equipment, or any live rounds. As the training progresses, they will do these same drills at night with their NVGs, fully equipped and using UTM paint rounds in their M4s as these MOUT-site buildings are not ballistic shoot houses. Their .45 pistols have been modified to fire 9mm paint rounds called SESAMS (special effects small arms marking system) rounds. Both UTMs and SESAMS fall into a category of ammunition called simunitions. Simunitions allow for safe, unopposed close-quarter drill in just about any tactical training area. When the participants are wearing the proper protection, to include full face shields, they can be used for fully opposed force-on-force training.

Following four days of urban-combat training and drill at the MOUT site, the class is tasked with the first of their two Guile Strike direct-action missions. Over the past ten days, the phase cadre have ramped up the flow of intelligence reports that track developments in the Republic of Abyssinia and the increased activity on the part of the Sword of the Right Hand. These developments are centered in the border region along the Abyssinia-Aksum border, activity that has resulted in this mini-deployment of our two Class 1-13 Marine special-operations elements to that area. Each evening, following the previous week's shooting drills, the student MSOT leadership has been responsible for reading the message traffic and intelligence reports and briefing their teams on these developments. So the four student MSOTs, now two to an element, come to these final weeks of training well-read into the deteriorating security situation and elevated threat levels centered along the disputed Abyssinian-Aksum border region.

Early in this final week of Phase Three, the tasking messages are received, one to each of the two student MSOT elements. Two high-value individuals, or HVIs, that are key operational and operational-support operatives for the Sword of the Right Hand are thought to be hiding in two adjacent village complexes. Recent intelligence has isolated the buildings where the HVIs and their respective personal security detachments are hiding. With this information, the two MSOT elements are tasked with kill-or-capture missions for these HVIs.

In each of the two elements, one student MSOT is tasked with the assault while the other is given the role of security or that of a blocking force. Key team commander, team chief, and element leader assignments are made by the cadre. These are made in close consultation with the TACs and phase leadership. There are certain captains and sergeants they wish to see in leadership roles for this portion of the training. Once those assignments are made, the planning process goes forward, beginning with a warning order and team assignments for the planning of the operation. For the infantrymen, officers and sergeants alike, this is familiar territory, and all in the class are well grounded in the mission-planning process from Phase One. They know the drill—mission tasking, warning order, courses-of-action development, courses-of-action gaming, patrol-order rehearsals, the formal patrol order, operational rehearsals, and inspections. Last-minute intelligence on their target HVIs comes in by satellite link over the 117F radios. Throughout the process, the TACs and cadre are on hand to observe, grade, and serve as a resource.

Shortly before midnight at different locations on one of the Camp Lejeune MOUT complexes, two security elements move into place. This is a different facility from where the students received their MOUT training. The two assault elements move in quickly behind their respective security elements and converge on the target buildings. Yet these target areas and buildings are not unfamiliar, as they were the object of one of the students' special reconnaissance missions during Sting Ray Fury of Phase Two. Both assault elements are engaged by the HVI personal protection details, and both assault elements have to fight through this opposition, shooting and being shot at in a simunitions gunfight to get to their targets. After securing the area, the work of the sensitive site exploitation teams finds information that will lead to a follow-on target. After the extraction, they return to the FOB at Onslow Beach for their post-mission reporting, and the cadre weighs in with a detailed after-action review. Then it's two or three hours of sleep, and the two MSOT elements begin the planning cycle for the follow-on targets that surfaced from the site exploitation of the previous night's direct-action mission. The student MSOTs change roles, and the MSOTs who had security duty the previous night will now be in charge of the assault. This second mission differs slightly in that the target is in a different part of the MOUT site, and the students are operating on much less sleep. But it's the same planning, preparation, and execution-on-target drill. The teams again work through the post-operation requirements and sit in on the post-operation critiques. Finally, they get a few hours' sleep before a final Guile Strike review, the breakdown of the FOB before, and the return to Stone Bay.

During the direct-action missions against the Sword of the Right Hand, a single member of Class 1-13 was released for a twenty-four-hour hiatus from training. Sergeant Brad Hansen was allowed time to rush off to the hospital to be with his wife for the birth of their second child and first daughter.

———

The last evolution of Phase Three for Class 1-13 is just as it was at the end of Phase One and Phase Two, which is the TAC turnover and the phase cadre's final student evaluations. As with the previous phases, the meeting is chaired by Lieutenant Colonel Dodd with Master Guns Denard close by. Also there is Captain Stan Keefer, Gunnery Sergeant

Conway, and Gunny Patterson. In this familiar format, the Phase Three TACs line on one side of the table, with the Phase Four TACs on the other. Also attending are selected cadres from Phase Two and Phase Three. The student performance graphics now reflect rifle, pistol, and shoot-house qualification scores. Each student graphic is displayed on the big screen and briefed by the outgoing TAC. Aside from these scores and a new round of peer reviews, there are the TAC and cadre comments. Those performing well are addressed quickly.

"Staff Sergeant Smith is a solid performer. He moved well in the house and is always ready to help his classmates. He's good to go."

Or, "As you can see, Sergeant Smith got off to a slow start, but he's shown a steady improvement since the beginning of the phase. The two major spot reports were at the beginning of the phase." There may be comments from an instructor who worked with this student or a question from Lieutenant Colonel Dodd or Master Guns Denard, or perhaps not. From a shooting coach, "He came to us shooting very poorly, but he takes criticism well and he's a worker. He's still at best an average shooter, but he'll continue to work to improve himself when he gets to his team. I like his attitude."

Not all the comments relate to shooting. "Captain Smith did well throughout the phase. He can come across as arrogant, which is the reason for the low peering from Phase Two, but he's worked hard to correct that. His briefing skills are excellent and the commander's intent portion of Guile Strike was the best I've heard."

For those whose performance metrics were more scattered, which indicates a poor performer, the comments are direct and pointed. There are three who break out as having serious deficiencies. One is a young sergeant who was awarded a major spot report on the shooting range and whose performance in Phase Three and the previous phase was well below standard. His photo carries a red border on the performance graphic display. He is in serious trouble.

"Sergeant Smith seems to be doing just enough to get by," says his TAC. "As you can see, his peer evaluations are low. He managed to pass the qualifications shoots, but during Guile Strike, he seemed confused a great deal of the time. If he remains in the class, he needs to be monitored closely during the next phase and at Derna Bridge."

From a cadre sergeant, "Sergeant Smith just doesn't show the situational awareness to be an asset on an MSOT. I don't think he belongs here."

The other two student sergeants, whose deficiencies were of a lesser degree, are coded yellow on their performance graphics, their issues fully documented and discussed as well. It seemed to me that these three students performed poorly across the board. Two had performed to an acceptable level in Phase One because they were physically strong, but in the specific areas of tactics, fire support, special reconnaissance, operational briefing, and teamwork, they were universally deficient. At this stage of the ITC, the majority of the students are performing well within standard. Based on the recommendations from the TAC turnover meeting, the Phase Three Review Board meets to determine the fate of these three students. After some discussion, all three will be allowed to continue on to Phase Four. The one sergeant is put on formal probation; the other two are counseled on their deficiencies. All three are made aware that they must address these performance issues in the final phase of the ITC, or they will not graduate. Forty-seven members of Class 1-13 will move on to Phase Four.

———

One the final day of Phase Three, Captain Keefer calls in the eight remaining class captains. "Okay, guys, this is a free shot for you. What did you think of the phase?" After a pause, "Seriously," he prompts, "what can we do to make this phase better for Class 2-13?"

The captains have several suggestions for the phase OIC, and in the discussion, they uniformly have nothing but praise for the quality of the shooting instruction. Several admit, however, to sweating out the shoot-house qualification and say they were more than a little glad to have it behind them.

"That's it then," Keefer tells them. "Phase Four and Derna Bridge will challenge you in ways you never thought possible. My advice is to make the best decisions you can, and make them in a timely manner. You will be continually faced with the 75 percent solution. Many of us are used to the black-and-white and making the call when we have all the good information. That will not always be possible at Derna Bridge. But as I told you at the beginning of this phase, don't be afraid to fail. Make the best call you can and go with it. If it's wrong, fix it and move on. It's how we learn. And good luck to all of you."

CHAPTER EIGHT

PHASE FOUR: IRREGULAR WARFARE

The conventional army loses if it does not win.
The guerrilla army wins if it does not lose.

HENRY KISSINGER

Welcome to Phase Four and Derna Bridge, the culmination exercise of the ITC. During this phase you will be assessed on your abilities to operate as a member of a Marine Special Operations Team (MSOT) in an Irregular Warfare environment. You will receive instruction in Advanced Special Operations (ASO), Planning and Isolation Procedures, Defensive and Offensive Operations, Unconventional Warfare (UW), Foreign Internal Defense, and numerous other Special Operations skills. You will additionally receive a mid and final phase counseling. You may also receive negative or positive spot reports during the phase based on your performance. Throughout the duration of this phase you will be provided all the tools necessary to accomplish your assigned tasks. It will be up to you to utilize all the skills you have been taught throughout the ITC in order to be successful. Your overall evaluation will be based on your written test score, your peer evaluations, spot reports, and the instructors' assessment of your individual performance throughout Phase Four and the Derna Bridge Exercise. . . . You will conduct

*yourself with the highest level of professionalism that is expected
from a Special Operator and a United States Marine.*

This excerpt was taken from the phase initial counseling sheet that is read and signed by each student beginning Phase Four of the ITC. If Phase One was physically the most challenging, then Phase Four is the most mentally and professionally challenging. It is the phase where these Marine student special operators must demonstrate creativity, flexibility, and problem-solving skills in an ambiguous and unfamiliar environment. In previous phases, they used military skills to dominate the physical terrain and the human opposition in order to accomplish their mission. Now they must use interpersonal skills to navigate the human terrain to accomplish their mission. As Class 1-13 moves from a direct approach to special operations to an indirect one—from the regular to the irregular—a review of the defining terms may be helpful.

Regular warfare is that which is conducted by conventional means using guns, airplanes, tanks, and technology to impose one side's will on another through force of arms. Sometimes called modern conventional warfare, it is waged by a national force of divisions, fleets, and squadrons whose objective is to destroy the armed resistance of a similarly configured enemy. This usually involves taking and holding ground. *Irregular* warfare comes into play when the enemy does not present itself in the regular conventions of divisions, fleets, and squadrons. Or if the enemy does have army divisions and squadrons, they may be so embedded in the population as to make regular warfare not an option, or a much less attractive one. Irregular warfare is the process by which we take the fight to this decentralized, often low-tech enemy who, from his point of view, has the good sense not to directly confront our advanced conventional war-fighting capabilities. Irregular warfare is also used where it is in our interest to use a decentralized, irregular force to oppose an established military or political order. We may choose a direct-action approach in irregular warfare or an indirect one. Phase Four of the ITC will focus on the indirect approach.

Indirect action or indirect special operations have two major subsets—foreign internal defense and unconventional warfare. When the government of a friendly nation is opposed by an armed, irregular "insurgent" force, or even well-dispersed regular forces, and we step in to help them oppose this force, it's called foreign internal defense—FID. This enemy may possess no airplanes or tanks, his technology may be primitive, and his guns limited to small arms and crew-served weapons. But instead of hiding in fortifications or behind defensive lines, he hides among the local people or is dispersed in small, scattered bands of fighters. It's this tactic that makes this enemy so intractable, because unless we care nothing for the locals and the surrounding countryside, this enemy has rendered our divisions, fleets, and squadrons useless. It also presents a very difficult problem for local friendly forces and militias to contain. To oppose this insurgent force, we work to empower the friendly host-nation forces through a campaign using FID. We train them to defend themselves. When we succeed at this, they, the locals, can protect themselves and we are no longer needed.

Unconventional warfare or UW is generally the term reserved for dealing with an enemy, regular or irregular, who is in the seat of government, and our "side" or our interests seek to overthrow that existing order. It may be militarily or politically unwise to depose this government by conventional means—such as an invasion—or even by means of unilateral direct action. So we turn to the indirect and support those among the local population who share our goal of overturning the existing order. Of note, when we are engaged in UW and trying to overthrow an existing order, our local allies are in essence guerillas, yet we call them freedom fighters. When we are on the side of a friendly government in power and employ FID to counter those guerillas who oppose the established government, we call those guerillas insurgents. So when we speak of counterinsurgency, or COIN, we are usually addressing issues that relate to a FID campaign.

Counterterrorism relates to operations (direct or indirect) or assistance given to an ally who is a victim of terror. Terror is a tactic, one often used by insurgents but not always. We normally think of terror and terrorism in relation to insurgents in explosive vests, indiscriminately killing themselves and innocents in crowded marketplaces. So in this vein, we use COIN *and* counterterrorism to help a friendly government in combating insurgents who use the tactic of terror. Conversely, terror may be used as a weapon by an established, usually illegitimate, government to stay in power. It cuts both ways; terrorists can use indiscriminate violence to advance either cause—to gain power or to remain in power. The use of terror falls outside our democratic system of values, and we oppose the use of terror through counterterrorism measures. Terror is often the principal weapon by which a minority is able to exert or gain control over a majority. During the Cold War we sometimes found ourselves on the side of an anticommunist dictator who used terror to maintain his position. Let's hope those days are behind us, as the use of terror almost always puts those using it on the side opposite the people. Counterinsurgency and counterterrorism are both Core Activities of MARSOC.

Whether it's a FID environment or a UW environment, the irregular warfare contest is not for territory but for the people. Lose the people, lose the war, and vice versa, so again, the people are central to any irregular warfare campaign. A FID or a UW campaign often means we must deal with a local partner force on *their terms*. Using an indirect approach also means that it is through *their* actions, with our help, that the campaign is waged. That's why interpersonal skills are so important in any FID- or UW-related activity.

━━━━━

The work of our SOF direct-action teams in the killing of Osama bin Laden and the dramatic rescues of hostages notwithstanding, a great deal of the work of Army Special Forces, SEALs, and Marine Special Operations has to do with foreign internal defense. FID empowers the local people and their government to protect themselves so we can go home. We initially prevailed in Afghanistan in 2002 by way of a classic and superbly executed UW campaign. Our inability to follow up that victory with a FID campaign caused us to revisit that nation a decade later in force—when the Taliban reasserted themselves with a UW campaign of their own. FID and the important role of indirect SOF-centric skills will be a significant part of our future military deployment posture. We'll be addressing that future later in this book. So before we get to the training of Class 1-13, a real-world example might be helpful:

═════════

The routing of the Taliban in 2002 created a power vacuum in Kabul. The new interim central government meant little in the more remote areas of the country, especially those tribal areas along the Pakistani border in the province of Paktika. The thinking was that when, not if, the Taliban returned, our best defense against their resurgence would be to create relationships with tribes on the Afghan side of the border—tribes who could help us resist this return. These tribal enclaves have for centuries distrusted outsiders—Russians, Americans, whomever—back to the time of Alexander. Yet our special-operations forces in general, and Army Special Forces in particular, have been very successful in overcoming these misgivings. Following the expulsion of the Taliban and al-Qaeda, teams of Army Special Forces were scattered along the border regions to work with local Afghan tribes and to help win them to our side. These same Green Berets who helped to evict the Taliban a year earlier were now living with the tribes, gaining their trust, helping them to defend their villages and homes. Shifting from UW to FID required warriors who could understand other cultures and who were both disciplined and predisposed to live with and among the indigenous people of that culture.

One such team was ODA 361 (Operational Detachment Alpha, Charlie Company, 2nd Battalion, 3rd Special Forces Group). They were assigned a sector in Orgun-E Kalan and set up their team headquarters near the village of Orgun-E. This twelve-man A-Team was blessed with a very experienced and energetic team sergeant.

ODA 361 initially partnered with a local warlord and three

hundred of his Afghan fighters. Then they began to do what Special Forces do so well; they began to work with the Afghan fighters and convert them into a militia, under a program known as the Afghan Militia Fighters, or AMF. They also began to work to change the local population's perception of Americans. The plan was to win the trust of the people within the village of Orgun-E and the surrounding area. First there has to be security. Security in turn makes way for other accomplishments—government, health care, commerce, education, etc.—that are only possible if the locals are no longer fearful of an insurgent enemy. If successful, these accomplishments promote trust, stability, and information.

The team began to change the population's perception of the Afghan militia from one of their being undisciplined thugs to one in which they were seen as a professional militia with discipline and a code of conduct. The ODA built three companies of Afghan Militia Fighters. Through example and fair treatment of the Afghan fighters, the ODA was able to move control of these militia fighters from the warlord to the village elders. The locals began to see the AMF as protectors rather than a gang of gunmen.

"We had three companies of one hundred Afghan fighters per company," the team sergeant said of their organization in Orgun-E. "Two SF sergeants were assigned full-time to each company, but we all helped out as needed. The AMF weren't the most disciplined fighters, and each day we might see a new face or two, but they continued to train and learn basic infantry skills. In time they became very loyal and protective of their American advisers. Two companies were straight, by that I mean heterosexual, but one company had a homosexual Afghan company commander and a great many in that AMF company were also homosexual. Operationally, the three companies were about the same," he said with a smile, "but dealing with an openly gay company commander and Afghan fighters had its challenges—not so much for the Afghans, but for our guys. But when it came to getting the job done, the AMF companies all did well."

The team set about reestablishing a local *shura* (government), ensuring that all of the three tribes in the area were equally represented. The team leader and team sergeant sat through lengthy and laborious meetings with the elders and listened to *their* problems and *their* issues. The team leadership suggested courses of action, but it was the Orgun-E *shura* that would make the final decisions.

"It was important that the locals were empowered to carry out local governance," said the team sergeant. "The Afghans understood the nuances of tribal government, with its religious overtones, better than an American ever would. We were not seen as usurpers but as restorers of traditional tribal government."

As the situation in the Orgun-E and the surrounding area stabilized, the ODA and their Afghan allies began to enjoy operational success. They liberated supplies donated by humanitarian organizations that were being held by warlords, bandits, or powerful families and turned them over to civil affairs teams. The ODA and the militia saw that the supplies were distributed to needy families in the area.

"Our Afghans did several things for us that we alone could never have accomplished operating on our own," the team sergeant continued. "First of all, we had an instant intelligence network. The AMF was composed of all three tribes in the local area. They knew everyone in the valley and their affiliations. We made it clear in our numerous meetings with the tribes that we were not interested in prosecuting everyone that was part of the Taliban, as long as they did not conduct any activities against Americans or actively support Taliban insurgents. The remaining hard-core Taliban in our valley, and even in the valleys on either side of our village, were won over or removed; there was simply no place for them to hide—our irregulars would find them. We were able to apprehend several high-ranking Taliban due to the efforts of our Afghan forces. Through our Afghans, we knew immediately if a member of the Taliban or an al-Qaeda operative slipped into the village. The people would get word to the elders and our irregulars, and they would get word to us.

"One night, a Taliban fighter slipped into the village and planted a land mine under the music shop. By morning, the local Afghans had control of the land mine and the terrorist was in their custody. They brought the Taliban terrorist and the mine to our compound and turned both over to the team. We made a big deal of this and made sure all the credit for the capture went to the local Afghans. We put the terrorist in the system, and it turned out that he was a bad one; he ended up in Guantánamo Bay. That's FID when it really works.

"Through our fair treatment of the locals and the AMF, we became trusted members of the community and were allowed access to areas that would have been otherwise impossible. We were often granted the protection of the local tribes while moving through their tribal lands. The AMF were able to conduct detailed reconnaissance into areas where we were forbidden. Knowing the history of the area, our militia could alert us to an ongoing feud between two families that had nothing to do with the Taliban. This allowed the ODA to avoid local entanglements.

"Another task we were able to accomplish in Orgun-E was to get most of the bomb-making materials and weapons out of the hands of potential insurgents. Normally insurgents have to acquire weapons and ammunition through battlefield recovery—much of it left behind when the Russians pulled its forces out of Afghanistan. We put the word out to the elders, and through them to the outlying villagers, that we were looking for all explosive materials and heavy weapons—crew-served weapons, TNT, blasting caps, RPGs, mortars, heavy machine guns, and the like. We also discovered weapons and ammunition caches with the aid of our AMF; they would find things that we would have walked right over. Later on, when the locals came to trust us, they brought these materials in by the cartload. We had close to two football fields stacked three feet deep with explosives, ammunition, mines, and heavy weapons. Much of it was old and obsolete, but still usable. It was now out of the hands of those who might use it against us.

"A good FID program begins with understanding the locals and making their problems your problems—their concerns became our concerns. Sure, we had money and hired them to work for us. We paid them well, but not outlandishly. We lived off of their economy and we bargained in good faith for what we bought from them. But it was our understanding and respect of their culture that allowed for our success. Although we had our own compound for security, I made our team members go out in town to eat or buy what they needed. This also became our village, and the locals welcomed us."

In 2003, ODA 361's counterinsurgency program was going strong, and better results were on the horizon. Unfortunately the decision was made to disband the Afghan Military Forces in Orgun-E and to not replace ODA 361 when it was time for them to redeploy. A U.S. Army battalion was moved into the area to take over security. The AMF fighters were summarily released, and some three hundred trained Afghan fighters, now more skilled and more deadly than when ODA 361 arrived, were left unemployed. Each of these Afghan former militiamen had an extended tribal/family affiliation, knew the land, knew the language, knew the enemy, and had trusted the Americans in the ODA. That, and all the locals who had a vested interest in helping us to clear the remnants of the Taliban and al-Qaeda from their community, evaporated. The local militia was replaced with a large American footprint in the form of a battalion of paratroopers. Good soldiers, but without a clue about the culture in which they now found themselves, ignorant of the language, and looking at every Afghan as a potential target. They were operationally blind. It cost the U.S. taxpayers about ten thousand dollars a month to fund the local FID-trained militia in Orgun-E. It takes that and more to fund a deployed battalion for a day. Most importantly, hundreds of Americans were now in harm's way.

I asked this team sergeant what happened after the Special Forces team left. "What happened was terrible but predictable," he told me. "After we disbanded the AMF, the Army battalion moved into our camp. U.S. platoons began their own patrols out into the countryside. Now you had the worst of all worlds—a large armed American presence and three hundred unemployed Afghan fighters. Soon it was back to the Afghans against the outsiders. A hostile relationship with the tribal leaders developed and things fell apart. These were good American soldiers. It's just that foreign internal defense requires a very special skill set and a great deal of patience. Big Army often just doesn't have the knowledge, skills, or the patience to engage the locals within the framework of their culture."

In writing *Chosen Soldier* in 2005, I stated that the Special Forces soldier was the most important soldier on the current battlefield. My brother SEALs didn't care for that characterization, but I meant it then and I've stood by that assertion. I may have to amend that statement now that the MARSOC has FID as one of its Core Activities *and* has dedicated a full phase of their training to the application of indirect special operations and irregular warfare. And with this example in mind, let's see how Class 1-13 goes about this.

⸻

Phase Four of the ITC is broken down into two segments. The first is the classroom portion, which comes down to three weeks of classroom work and practical work in indirect warfare and the planning of indirect-warfare campaigns. Before we get into this curriculum, let me say that portions of this instruction include information that is either sensitive, classified, or both, especially when it comes to those tactics, techniques, and procedures SOF forces use to conduct targeting and the application of force in this environment. I will do my best to steer the reader through this portion of training with the unclassified version of this important warfare skill set. The second portion of this phase is a three-week practical application conducted in the field—an off-site, fully integrated irregular warfare scenario that emphasizes FID and UW skills, while also calling into play a great many skills learned in the previous phases.

It is again not my intention here to make comparisons between the basic SOF qualification venues, but this much may be helpful. Only the Army Special Forces Qualification Course and the MARSOC Individual Training Course feature irregular warfare–scenario training as a component of their basic-warfare qualification. Both do this with extensive classroom work and an elaborate, free-flowing field training exercise. The Green Berets do this in two phases. One phase of their training is exclusively for their officer candidates, and it's a very comprehensive, three-month, graduate-level cram course in irregular warfare. The enlisted soldiers then join their officers for the famous Robin Sage UW-based field training exercise that is a phase of training in and of itself. The Marine Special Operations School has elected to devote a single phase of their CSO training to irregular warfare and has made this training much the same for their officer and enlisted Marines. This would seem appropriate as the Special Forces Q-Course graduates are "branch qualified," which means their military career going forward will exclusively be in special operations. For the Marine Special Operations Officers, this is not the case. So to me, it makes total sense that the enlisted Marines, who will become career special operators, receive the full measure of this unique, valuable, and expensive training.

The application of indirect warfare skills to irregular warfare is not as simply taught as going to the shoot house or going to the pool. It is best taught through interactive, experiential training. This requires an extensive, complex venue that involves a credible real world–like scenario, a sweeping cast of role players, and a "setting" that is often difficult to replicate on a military base or at one of the combat-town complexes; it has to range over the countryside with a notional indigenous population in play. The conditions in which indirect-warfare students train and learn these skills has to be an interpersonal, free-flowing environment. Indirect-warfare training scenarios that begin at point A and end at point B may be navigated by any number of avenues. So this training is both nuanced and highly societal. On the shooting range, the student is trained and graded in terms of timely rounds on target, decisions made under stress, and safety. In an indirect-warfare environment, the student is graded on his critical thinking, complex decision making, interpersonal skills, and his ability to build and sustain relationships—all in an unfamiliar, cross-cultural setting. And he has to think ahead to the second- and third-order consequences of his decisions. There is no time or score. Accomplishing an indirect-warfare tasking has more to do with balancing a set of conflicting interests and making the best choice from a range of less-than-perfect alternatives—all while remaining within the moral and constitutional constraints of an American special operator.

The classroom portion of this phase of training features lecture-hall presentations and smaller, team-centric discussion groups. Both are free-flowing and interactive. The second segment is an extensive field exercise that is both subtle, challenging, and compared to any previous training these ITC students may have received in the Marine Corps, absolutely unique.

IRREGULAR WARFARE 101

Fully integrated, comprehensive irregular-warfare training presents challenges for the command sponsoring the training and the training cadres who conduct it. Certain aspects of irregular warfare, and by extension indirect special operations, are as much art as military science. They deal with shades of gray as much as the black-and-white. So the command sponsor is burdened with finding the right instructors and developing a curriculum that does not fall within normal military instructional guidelines. Finding experienced shooters who can teach shooting skills in the Marine Corps is not all that difficult. Finding someone who knows and understands the mechanics of standing up a partisan force in an unconventional warfare environment is another matter. Not only is there some art to this business, the art is often best conveyed by talking through a situation or learning through personal experience or reflection. Therefore, the cadre has more of a mentoring, discussion-leader, facilitator role than one of traditional lecture-hall instruction.

The first full week of the IW classroom work serves to transition Class 1-13 from the direct-action application of force in their Phase Three shooting to the indirect requirements of Phase Four. This shift from the kinetic to the interpersonal could not be more dramatic.

There are now forty-eight students in the class, eight officers and thirty-nine enlisted Marines. They begin the phase with brief comments by the phase officer in charge and the phase master sergeant.

"Okay, we know that you can move, shoot, communicate, render battlefield aid, and conduct mission planning, and that you've been physically toughened and sleep-deprived. You will do all of those things in this phase, and a great deal more. Now we're going to see if you can think outside the box, but not lose sight of that box. The phrase 'today will be different' applies to this phase, and then some. There's a written examination on the classroom portion of the phase, and it will take some study and focus on your part to pass that exam. In the field exercise, we will ask you recognize, analyze, and solve a continuous flow of problems while staying in character in a challenging and fast-moving scenario. You'll have to adapt to the conditions and navigate the human terrain. You'll also have to consider the consequence of your decisions down the line—those second- and third-order effects. Some of you may have some experience in this on deployment. That's good. We can build on that experience. For all of you, this is a training environment like no other and nothing you have seen before in your Marine Corps career."

Captain (major select) Shawn Daniels has an infantry and Recon background and has been at MARSOC since 2009. Prior to coming to the school, he had three rotations as an MSOT commander. He is five ten, a solid 180, and a very focused and intense Marine officer. He is passionate about training Marines, a dedicated family man, and the father of four. Following his remarks, he introduces his master sergeant. The phase cadre staff are not technically a company, but its size and talent base are in keeping with that of a company, and Daniels addresses his senior master sergeant as "Top."

Master Sergeant Adam Couture also comes from a Force Recon background, and he is a veteran of Marine Detachment One. His remarks are short and to the point. "There are three things you have to do to get through this phase; it's that simple. You have to have a good attitude, work hard, and set your goals for the phase. We'll talk more about these as the phase progresses, but think about those three, and good luck to all of you."

Shortly after the beginning of the phase, Captain Daniels meets quickly with the class captains. His remarks to them are similar to those of Captain Mike Dougherty from Phase Two and Captain Stan Keefer from Phase Three. "Gentlemen, you will get out of this phase what you put into it. The end is in sight, but it's not over. I want you to be fully engaged and proactive. Get into the mind-set of an operational MSOT. Make sure your Marines understand the desired end state of any given training scenario. Give them guidance, and let them do their jobs. In that way, they will learn and you will be training yourself for future duty as an MSOT commander."

The first few days of the class are a series of classified presentations that deal with the scope and reach of special operations within the definitions of irregular warfare, the role of SOF in past and current conflicts, and what may be the role of SOF in this area in the future. The classes also touch on what has been broadly termed advanced special operations. ASO is that area where the work of deployed special-operations elements begins to intersect or cross over into activities that might be more in keeping with the roles and missions of our intelligence services—areas where the terms "covert" and "clandestine" may apply. Some of the material might lend itself to what those of us with an intelligence background would call "tradecraft" rather than any military skill set.

The class then spends a day with briefings on other government agencies—the OGAs. Quite often in both regular and irregular warfare operations there are other agencies of the federal government involved. We normally and immediately think CIA and their operational Special Activities Division in the practice of irregular warfare. But there's an entire alphabet soup of entities that may come into play—the FBI, the DEA, the DOS (Department of State), and the DHS (Department of Homeland Security). Since irregular warfare may, on occasion, deal with drugs, personal security, psychological assessment, or evidentiary matters, there's almost no limit to just who in the federal government may be of assistance in an operational or liaison capacity in the Global War on Terror. So Class 1-13 receives an overview of these agencies and how they may assist them in an irregular-warfare/indirect-action environment. Depending on availability, representatives of these agencies make presentations to the class on the roles and capabilities of their agencies, which, again, tend to be beyond the security classification of this book.

A day of 1-13's classroom work is given over to a presentation by an FBI profiler and counterintelligence specialist. The program stresses the way we perceive others and the way they perceive us, and why. The students are introduced to the basics of nonverbal communication and how to quickly "read" others whom they may have to engage and enlist cooperation from. The class features a thumbnail individual assessment that is a highly predictable inventory of one's own personality traits. This assessment of just how *you* may come across to others, and your ability to quickly determine just how *others* may perceive you, is a strong basis for effectively dealing with people you need to influence on a by-with-and-through basis to accomplish a mission. This presentation could not be more different from what these same Marines were doing just a few days ago during Phase Three and Guile Strike. Yet to their credit, they are very engaged. Building rapport, carefully eliciting information, and skillfully influencing others are important tools in dealing with other cultures and for success in indirect special operations. It was seemingly appropriate that the students attended this day of classes in casual civilian attire—as they might be wearing when deployed with a partner-force nation or in a social situation with a counterpart overseas.

The second week of classroom work has the four student teams moving into individual classrooms where they will function as a team, a Marine Special Operations Team, for the balance of the phase. For this portion of instruction I again follow student MSOT Three, which now has two officers and ten enlisted Marines. All students have a thick binder containing the formatted course material they will study and be tested on. For this portion of the phase, the students are also the instructors. Each day two students come to class prepared to teach an assigned topic. Some use selected audio or video clips. All have a series of PowerPoint slides. A few deliver a lecture on their topic, but most elect to lead a guided discussion. It was clear to me that these student teachers spent a great deal of time in preparing their material. This students-teach-the-class approach is well bolstered by the cadre assigned to my team.

In this phase the cadre are called a field team as they will be with their student MSOTs now and during the field portion of Phase Four. This field team is led by an experienced staff sergeant from an infantry background and MSOT deployments to the Philippines, Southeast Asia, and Afghanistan. In addition to the field team leader there are two other staff sergeants who came to MARSOC from the Foreign Military Training Unit with FMTU/MARSOC deployment histories. They've spent time in Afghanistan, South America, Southeast Asia, and Africa. The civilian field team member is a retired Special Forces master sergeant from 7th Special Force Group with a great deal of time in indirect operations in Afghanistan and South and Central America. One of the staff sergeants serves as the TAC for the student MSOT.

"Each of you has important input to this process," Staff Sergeant Stan Sternbridge tells his students. He is their TAC. "You all have skills, perspective, and experience that bear directly on the application of indirect warfare. How many of you have experience working directly with the Afghan National Army?" Six hands go up. "The same problems, obstacles, communications, and cultural issues that you've had to work through with the Afghans will be the same wherever you go. In the future, you'll probably not have the conventional support structure around you that you've had in the past, but the challenges will be much the same."

Staff Sergeant Sternbridge is thirty-one years old. He is a solid six feet, blond and fair, and has the look of an academic more than a Marine special operator. In addition to his infantry and FMTU background, he has an MSOT deployment history in Afghanistan and

Africa. He has deployed to Kazakhstan in a FID-related assignment. Staff Sergeant Sternbridge is a Russian speaker and his wife is ethnic Russian. His two daughters speak both English and Russian.

"This format allows us to assess them on their subject-matter skills," Sergeant Sternbridge said of the student-teaching arrangement, "as well as their presentation skills. In a FID or UW environment, these Marines will have to be teachers of military skills. This approach also allows us to coach them on how they handle themselves in a teaching environment."

From my perspective, the student presentations and student-led discussions surface a great many real-world examples of FID issues in Afghanistan. The cadres are also able to bring real-world examples from Southeast Asia, Latin America, and Africa. There are, of course, the inevitable war stories to illustrate a point, but this is a very knowledgeable and skillful cadre. I hear a great deal of "Okay, that's one way. How else might we approach this problem . . . ?" or "Okay, give me another example of how our presence might alienate a host-nation force . . . ?" This field team has a great deal of experience. They use this experience judiciously in this interactive teaching arrangement, and they ask a good many open-ended questions.

The topics addressed during the academic, team-centric classroom portion of this phase include the basic principles of training foreign or partner-nation forces, working as an adviser, combating insurgency, and the collection and management of intelligence. There are also classes on the operationally supportive tasks of establishing a base of operations, logistics, and conducting offensive and defensive operations while working closely with a host nation or guerilla force. In nearly all these classes, the information begins within the known parameters of conventional operations and moves to the requirements of an irregular-warfare environment. "You have to do all the same things as an infantry battalion," the field team leader tells student MSOT Three. In the Regiment, he served as the operations/intelligence sergeant on his deployed MSOT. "But you'll have to do this without the battalion staff and logistics train. It's all on you. That's why detailed planning and advanced planning are so critical to your mission success."

Throughout this classroom phase, along with the classroom discussions, the PowerPoint presentations, and the real-world personal examples, there is the persistent theme of accomplishing all these things in a by-with-and-through environment. Again and again, the student MSOTs of 1-13 are reminded that they not only have to be able to execute a campaign in irregular-warfare defense (FID) and irregular-warfare offense (IW), but they must do this within the physical, geographical, cultural, and logistical constraints of a host-nation/partner-nation force or an irregular guerilla force. Staff Sergeant Sternbridge said it this way:

"In every step of the planning and execution of your mission, you have to consider how your goals and objectives translate into their goals and objectives. What's in it for them? Why are they willing to let you teach them what you know or advise them on what they should do? You must see all these things from their perspective. What does 'small unit' mean to them? Is that a squad- or a company-sized unit? What does 'fighting' mean to them? Is that killing the enemy or just a show of force—march and countermarch? How do they learn? Can they read? Does your partner force, or your partisans, speak the same language—are they from the same tribe? See what I mean? And what does winning mean to them? It may be that winning for them is for the insurgents to go back into the hills for a few months. That may not be a win within your commander's intent. Some of these things can be known in advance through research and careful planning. It could come from information you can only get after you're there, on the ground. But always, in your preparation and in your dealings with your partner- or host-nation counterparts, it's all about how they see things. It's all about the relationships. You get that right and the other things will fall into place."

During the classroom portion of the phase, Lieutenant Colonel Dodd calls the class captains in for a final officers' call of the ITC.

"Okay, gentlemen," he begins in his now familiar, polite Southern

tone, "you're about to go into a very important and intense field training exercise. This will be preceded by a collaborative planning effort.
This will be a chance for you to polish your planning skills and to
help the Marines on your team to become better acquainted with the
Marine Corps Planning Process as we apply it in an indirect-warfare
scenario. You should all know the planning process, but some of this
material is still fairly new to some of the Marines on your team."
Lieutenant Colonel Dodd pauses to frame his words. "As you're more
than aware, this is the final exercise before graduation. Above all, this
is the last time you may do an exercise like this in training. The next
time it will be for real, on deployment as a team commander with an
operational MSOT. Yet surprisingly, when you do this for real it will
be much like what you're about to do here. So take this seriously. You
will all graduate unless you show us in Derna Bridge that you're not
up to the challenges and demands of indirect warfare. Use this time
well and take nothing for granted.

"I expect each of you to step up to the task, polish your leadership
and interpersonal skills, and finish strong. Show us you have what it
takes to take command of an operational MSOT. I expect your best
effort, which will require that you continue to focus, work hard, and
to learn. Derna Bridge is an irregular-warfare exercise that keys on
the indirect special-operations disciplines of foreign internal defense
and unconventional warfare. As you all know, UW is a supported
Core Activity for us, where FID is a Core Activity. Yet they have a lot
in common. If you can plan for, process, and execute a UW campaign,
you will be able to conduct a FID operation and COIN campaign
within the scope of what is expected of a Marine Special Operations
Team. Keep in mind this is indirect and influential, and it's all about
relationships and your ability to interact with your partner-nation
counterparts. This means we will be grading you on your critical
thinking in an ambiguous, dynamic setting. Good luck to all of you."

The final classroom drill is a targeting-and-planning exercise that
involves some fieldwork. "We were given a large industrial target close
to Camp Lejeune," Sergeant Irving said of the exercise, "and asked to

look at it with an eye to what a small team could do to disable the facility—easily, quickly, and with a minimum measure of force to achieve maximum damage. We then conducted a nighttime reconnaissance of the facility. After the recon, we began planning how we were going to do this."

This exercise followed a classified presentation on target analysis and how to identify a critical node in order to disable a facility of this type. One of the goals of this exercise was to get the student MSOTs back into the collaborative planning process, and to get them into a by-with-and-through mind-set in the planning process.

"All right, you've all gone out and put eyes on a target," the lead targeting instructor tells the class—all four student MSOTs. He was also one of their Basic Skills Phase TACs. "You've gathered intelligence on the target, right? Now I want you to plan how you're going to do the mission and how you're going to brief the plan. Teams One and Two, you will take the information gathered by Teams Three and Four to plan your mission, and Teams Three and Four will plan their mission with the intelligence collected by One and Two. Each team will develop their plan on information gathered by another team.

"Some restrictions. You can send out a one- or two-man element to again put eyes on your target before you develop your final plan. There is no external support, there are no supporting elements to help you with this; you're on your own. You are to plan for this mission in a UW environment, one that is covert in nature. This means that no U.S. presence can be attributed to this action. And, for every American in your MSOT element, there has to be at least one foreign national, one guerilla if you will, on your team. This is not a full-mission commander's briefing, but team briefing. Still, I want to see a mission overview, team assignments, infil and exfil plans, actions on target, time on target, medical and comm plans, command and control, a QRF [quick reaction force], and a time line."

The student MSOTs set about planning while the cadre stands by to serve as a resource. "We let them deal with the problem," one of my field-team staff sergeants told me. "We're here to guide them and nudge them back on course if they get too far off track. They will do a rehearsal briefing for us here in the team room, and we'll critique that briefing. Then later this afternoon, all four teams will give their final briefing to the entire class. It's a good drill before they get handed their Derna Bridge mission order. This is the first time that they have to plan and brief a mission with notional non-Americans involved, so it has to be within their understanding of the mission and with their limitations in conducting this kind of raid. It's a good primer for what's ahead."

My team begins planning for this notional mission. The student MSOT Three team leader for this planning drill gave an excellent mission overview. Then in his final guidance to the team, "Guys, here's what I want—three things. One, keep it simple. Like all plans, it has to be easily adaptable to change once the mission is under way. Two, make it doable and easy to execute for our host nation partners. We have to make sure they understand each step of the plan. And finally, let's keep the risk low. This is a UW operation and we're not supposed to be there. Neither we nor our guerillas are in any position to take casualties. Questions? Okay, let's get it done."

This last planning exercise has to do with developing concepts of operations, or CONOPS, in a UW environment and with limited direct-action participation on the part of the Americans. Before the teams return to their planning bays to finish working the problem, there is a final presentation by Captain Daniels that addresses the exercise on this industrial-complex target and what will be expected of the students during Derna Bridge.

"Okay, let's get all this in perspective. You've all had classes in MCPP [Marine Corps Planning Process] and you've all used a collaborative planning process during your practical applications during Phase One and Two and during your Guile Strike exercise in Phase Three. You will take this same process into Derna Bridge, but with one key difference. Prior to this, you were given a mission tasking; you were told to assault this target or conduct surveillance on that compound, or to kill or capture a designated high-value individual at this location. You planned it, murder-boarded it [gamed it out], briefed it, and executed it. You will do the same thing here, but with one very important aspect. You will often not be tasked by higher headquarters to conduct a given mission. Different, right? You see, you are not a direct-action team sitting in the team house waiting for someone to hand you a target folder. You are the on-the-ground expert—you are ground truth. You will, however, have guidance from higher—the commander's intent and the end state of what your senior commander may desire. But, and hear me on this guys, you are the on-scene experts. You may be tasked with a mission, but a great deal of the time, you will task yourselves.

"As the team on the ground, you will know the lay of the land better than anyone. You will know the capabilities and limitations of those you are training. Those capabilities and limitations are military, political, and cultural. So you are best equipped to know what has to be done and how to get to the end state desired by the commander. Only you can influence our partner-nation forces in a way that's in keeping with the commander's intent. See where I'm coming from?

"So, when you're at Derna Bridge—or some location in Yemen or Africa or Southeast Asia—you may well be given guidance but not necessarily tasked with a specific mission. That mission will originate with you after you're on the ground and learn what needs to be done. Likely as not, you'll be working with a host-nation militia or an irregular force. You will assess their capabilities and train them. Your commander's intent may be that you help them to develop intelligence on a target or series of targets. Higher headquarters may look to you for guidance in which targets to prosecute and how. In essence, you will be operationally tasking yourselves. In doing so, you must balance the commander's intent with the resources at hand, the capabilities of your partner forces, and the political and cultural environment. You will push your concept of operations up the line, and you will be telling the commander, 'Here's what needs to be done and here's how we plan to go about it.' With this self-tasking, and the commander's approval of your plan—your concept of operation—you can then set about planning the details of your operation. And this, gentlemen, is why we go to all this time, trouble, and expense of the Derna Bridge exercise. There's only so much we can do in class. Then you have to get on the ground in a realistic irregular warfare situation, assess the conditions on the ground, and make it happen. You have to navigate the human terrain of your assigned area, decide what needs to be done, then tell higher what you want to do."

After developing a concept of operations for a joint American/host-nation operation to neutralize the industrial facility, the teams present their CONOPS to their field team cadre for a critique. Early Friday afternoon, each team formally presents its CONOPS to the entire class. Following that, Class 1-13 sits for their irregular warfare exam. That evening, they are back in the big classroom to receive their mission order for Derna Bridge.

IRREGULAR-WARFARE PLANNING

The Derna Bridge exercise begins with each team being issued a mission order. This order sends them into planning for a FID-related, joint combined exchange training (JCET) deployment. Excluding the wartime requirements associated with the decade-plus of SOF deployments to Iraq and Afghanistan, special-operations teams routinely deploy to friendly nations on JCET or CNT (counter-narcotics training) missions to conduct training in foreign internal defense. JCET is funded by State Department foreign-aid monies. CNT can be funded from a number of U.S. government sources and agencies. Both JCET and CNT deployments of SOF training teams are designed to bolster the military capability of a friendly nation with training conducted in that nation. Such training and the elements deployed to conduct this training can range from the overt to the clandestine—openly conducted or done very quietly away from media scrutiny—but always with host-nation approval and as a legitimate American military-force tasking. These deployments are finite and limited in nature to specific training objectives. The Department of Defense reports annually to

Congress on these overseas training activities. Prior to 9/11, a great deal of SOF overseas time was devoted to JCET and CNT activity, and as we reduce our footprint in Afghanistan, it will again become a core deployment component of our special operations forces.

The four student MSOT's deployment to Abyssinia is within the familiar framework of a joint combined exchange team mission. Previous planning exercises during the ITC have focused on timely, tactical execution, with at least notional support from traditional military infrastructure. In the Derna Bridge exercise, the students must plan for a FID deployment and a FID training curriculum where their support will be limited. In this exercise, they will be deploying from Camp Lejeune to the Republic of Abyssinia. They need to plan this deployment with careful consideration of what they can take with them, what the host nation can supply them (or what they hope the host nation can supply them), and what kind of logistical support, if any, they can expect from their own military. And what support and assistance can they count on from the U.S. embassy and the embassy staff, or country team, in the Abyssinian capital. These considerations range from weapons, to ammunition, to radios, to medical supplies, to proper civilian clothing, to training aids/materials, and much, much more. All has to be gamed out in advance, requested, inventoried, and staged for the deployment.

Within our special operations forces, there's a great deal of muscle memory and information about how to conduct JCET operations. Often, a team deploying to a nation to train host-nation forces will have been preceded by one or more SOF training teams. In today's climate, al-Qaeda-inspired insurgencies can spring up in just about any developing nation, at any given time. So there is the very real prospect of a SOF team, perhaps an operational MSOT, being deployed on short notice to any number of places around the globe to train a host-nation force in FID and COIN. They may be the first and/ or only American boots on the ground. The students of ITC Class 1-13 are provided with three files of information to begin the planning for their JCET deployment to the beleaguered Republic of Abyssinia.

The first of these documents is the mission order that provides the student MSOTs with their commander's guidance and intent. The second is a PDSS, or pre-deployment site survey. This PDSS is normally done by an advance element of the deploying MSOT a few months ahead of the team's actual deployment. A PDSS will answer a good many of the how, what, when, and where questions of the team's training mission to the host nation. Due to the constraints of time and worsening conditions in Abyssinia, which may, in some cases, be not unlike a real-world JCET deployment, the team will use a PDSS from a previous team's deployment to Abyssinia. The third document or file is a set of requests for information, or RFIs, that a team going forward would normally ask for as they prepared for such a deployment.

Over the weekend the teams, including my student MSOT Three, immerse themselves in a stack of exercise-related documents and again review the Abyssinia-Aksum-Sumal scenario. They also begin their homework on the Abyssinian 2nd Infantry Company, the host-nation element they will be training. The following Monday, they begin the team-centric, collaborative planning process. Prior to beginning the process, several of the student captains are shifted from one team to another. This is to simulate their very real-world duty of stepping into command of an operational MSOT and having to immediately begin a JCET planning process with Marines that are relatively new to them.

Perhaps the art of this kind of training, from this author's perspective, is the role of the cadre. They know from experience the mechanics of the exercise and where the probable friction points will develop that will cause the student teams to struggle. They've all done this for real overseas *and* within the artificialities of the Derna Bridge exercise play. There is a starting point and an ending point, and critical nodes along the way that are both teaching points and way points in the flow of the exercise play. The skill and experience of the cadre will dictate just when and for how long they will let a team or team element flounder as they learn from their mistakes—before nudging them back along the correct path.

"There is structure to this training," my team's civilian field-team member said of Derna Bridge, "but it's free-flowing. The role players react to the actions of the student team, and that will determine the direction and flow of the exercise play. If they get into trouble or charge off in an unproductive direction, we let that go on for a while as a teaching point. Then we, in various ways, help them back onto the correct path. Usually, the team will generate their own problems without any help from us. This is their first try at this and we expect mistakes—it's part of the learning process. On occasion, we get a team that's doing it all well and sailing through a portion of the exercise. Then we will throw them some curves or obstacles that result in dilemmas they have to resolve. They may have the military part of their mission pretty well nailed down. It's usually the relationships and interpersonal exchanges that trip them up, and from which they learn—about how to operate in this kind of an environment and about themselves. And this is real-world stuff—the kind of thing they will be asked to do not that many months in the future."

Our civilian field-team member, whose official title is subject matter expert, unconventional warfare, is a retired Army Special Forces master sergeant with most of his operational experience in the 7th Special Forces Group. Interestingly, all the civilian field team subject matter experts are retired Special Forces senior NCOs. They have spent their entire military careers engaged in FID and UW. Their deployment history includes literally dozens of JCETs and CNTs. Collectively, they bring more than a century of experience to MARSOC irregular-warfare training and the Derna Bridge exercise.

"It only makes sense that we are able to help with FID, UW, and the Derna Bridge exercise," my student team's UW expert said. "Special Forces has been conducting Robin Sage for fifty years. It's changed very little and stood the test of time. Robin Sage training proved its worth in El Salvador, Colombia, Equador, the Philippines, Iraq, and Afghanistan to name a few. Derna Bridge has proved useful in training MSOTs for stability operations in Afghanistan, and I think it too will stand the test of time. The principles don't change, whether it's the Pineland scenario in Robin Sage or the Abyssinian scenario in

Derna Bridge. Robin Sage is a purely UW exercise, but if a team can handle a UW campaign, they can manage an FID campaign. The MARSOC decision to include both FID and UW in Derna Bridge is a good one."

By Monday morning, the teams are seriously into the planning process. Their team rooms are now planning bays and become crowded workrooms, cluttered with computers, files, overlays, and maps. There are isolation protocols, with a security desk that monitors access to the room. Soon all four walls are covered with charts, itemized lists, time lines, mission-essential tasks, and information requests. It's ordered chaos that involves each member of the team. There is always at least one of the field-team cadre present with the students, day or night. The other field team members have already left for the exercise and their exercise-preparation chores. But the cadre sergeants don't say or do much. They are there to observe and, within the constraints of the exercise, serve as a resource or sounding board. On Thursday, the teams conduct their pre-deployment mission briefs.

My team delivers their brief to Captain Mike Dougherty, their Phase Two OIC. The briefing lasts ninety minutes, during which seven members of the team share the briefing chores. Captain Dougherty listens carefully, asking only a few questions during the course of the briefing. He then critiques the brief, but much of that has to do with refinements or alternative ways to present the material. After Captain Dougherty leaves, the cadre sergeants have their after-action review, but it too is short. I thought the team did a good job, and the cadre graders seem to agree. Now the team busies itself with cleaning and sanitizing the room, and begins their final equipment inspections and load-out for their deployment to Abyssinia.

THE REPUBLIC OF ABYSSINIA

Derna Bridge takes place within the notional Republic of Abyssinia and the real state of South Carolina. The MARSOC makes use of portions of the 370,000-acre Sumter National Forest and the 52,000 acres at Fort Jackson. Since the irregular warfare is a battle for the people, much of the exercise play takes place on private lands and involves civilian-volunteer role players.

"We've had superb support from the communities in and around Fort Jackson, Greenwood, and McCormick," says our retired Special Forces master sergeant on the field team, "just like the Special Forces in North Carolina are supported in Robin Sage. Perhaps only in the rural South do you find this blend of hospitality, willingness to volunteer, and patriotism."

In addition to the use of military property and federal land, there is a host of land-use agreements between MARSOC and the owners of private property here. These range from a building or a barn on a few acres to several thousand acres, all made possible by generous and patriotic Americans who want to do their part. I found this refreshing at Robin Sage and refreshing here at Derna Bridge. Derna Bridge is essentially four separate exercises, as each student MSOT follows a different exercise tract or lane, supported by both paid and unpaid role players. There are between fifteen and twenty active-duty Marines who will be attached to each team as members of the host-nation army or as partisan guerillas. Each team will have approximately eight paid contractors who serve as key individuals within the Abyssinian military or as partisan leaders. Additionally, there may be as many as fifty unpaid volunteers per lane who are scripted and act in character as citizens, partisans, or auxiliary-force Abyssinians. All this to train forty-seven Marines of ITC Class 1-13 in the nuances of foreign internal defense and unconventional warfare.

FID IN ABYSSINIA

On a very warm afternoon in mid-July, a C-130 and Class 1-13, with their gear, land at Fort Jackson, Abyssinia. There are two winter months when rural Abyssinia (western South Carolina) is nasty—January and February. In the summer, those nasty months are July and August. Class 2-12 had to contend with the cold and wet of February; for 1-13 it's the heat, humidity, and insects of July. After clearing customs, where the Abyssinian custom officers give their gear close scrutiny, the teams break off to their individual training lanes. Each team meets briefly with an embassy military attaché, who gives them a quick overview of the political situation in Abyssinia and of the growing tensions along the Abyssinian-Aksum border. Those teams that ask the right questions get good information that will help them with their JCET duties in training the Abyssinians. The teams then make their way to their respective training locations, each named for former Afghan or Iraqi areas of operations—Bora Bora, Hit, Al-Asad, and Kabul. My Team Three heads for Al-Asad. After a truck ride out to a forward-training base, the team leadership meets with the host-nation company commander and his first sergeant. The team is shown to their Spartan, non-air-conditioned quarters, and it's game on. They have their own barracks space but share meals with their Abyssinian counterparts.

"Our first meeting with Captain Chris Augustine went pretty well," one of the Team Three captains recalled, "but he clearly wanted more than we were prepared to provide. He immediately began talking about sniper training, close quarter battle, and advanced skills. He also wanted his Abyssinian soldiers to have M4s and NVGs. We initially were able to calm him down with a first-things-first approach. 'Let's start with the basics,' we told him, 'and then we can later move on to the more advanced stuff.' We were able to sidestep the sniper-training issue by saying that we were going to train all of his soldiers to be sharpshooters—that they all would be snipers."

As they would on a real JCET, the student MSOTs set up on existing training ranges and begin teaching safety and marksmanship to the Abyssinian soldiers—soldiers who just a few days ago were Marines serving in combat and combat-support billets at Camp Lejeune. When not on the ranges, the student MSOTs conduct classes in patrolling and small unit tactics, showing the Abyssinians how to conduct basic support-by-fire assaults. For me, this was very reminiscent of the cadre-led patrols and field-training evolutions during the tactics portion of Phase One.

During the range training there are challenges for the American military student-trainers. One comes in the form of a BBC television crew who wants to film some of the training and have to be met and contained by the team. Another involves a negligent discharge on the part of one of the Abyssinian soldiers. As a part of *their* training and culture, such negligence requires that one of the offender's fingers be cut off. The Americans must find a way to mitigate and defuse this situation, one that allows the Abyssinian officers and NCOs to save face and for the soldier to keep his finger. Both are training-scenario problems that have their basis in real-world JCET deployment history.

UW IN ABYSSINIA

Late one afternoon, one of the Team Three team sergeants goes to look for his squad of Abyssinian soldiers and finds they are gone—packed up and left. Through a series of intelligence reports, the situation becomes clearer. The Abyssinian Army is mobilizing to move in force to recover the portion of their territory along the Savannah River now occupied by Aksum irregulars. With their host-nation trainees headed for the front, the team is suddenly out of a job—but not for long. A fragmentation order arrives that re-tasks them to secretly enter the Aksum-controlled territory and meet with local partisans. There, per their commander's intent, they will marry-up with the partisan forces, or guerillas, train them, and conduct operations to disrupt and harass the Aksum security forces there. Later that day, the team is collected by an Osprey at Fort Jackson and flown to a regional airport southwest of Charlotte and not far from the Savannah River. From the airfield, they are met by a member of the guerilla auxiliary in two panel trucks and spirited away from the field. After a dizzying ride with many turns and double-backs, they arrive at the guerilla encampment. While the team sorts themselves out, the team leadership is taken to meet the guerilla commander—one of two they will be dealing with as they begin a covert UW campaign against the Aksum occupying force. The first guerilla chief they meet is Commander J.P. He is the head of a tribal group called the Bear Claw Clan, a clan renowned as proud and fierce warriors.

"He was very standoffish when we first met," the team commander said of his first meeting with J.P. "He had a lot of questions about why we were there and why his fight should be our fight. We had to work very hard to try to convince him we were there to help him—that his struggle was our struggle."

The first night, the team is not allowed into the guerilla base camp, and is made to set their shelters on the fringe of the "G-base." The following morning, they meet with their other guerilla leader, Commander Mike. This meeting seems to go better, and the Americans are invited into the camp.

These two guerilla leaders are very different. Commander J.P. wishes to return to his land and tribal enclave as soon as possible, as do his Bear Claw Clan fighters. They are very independent and will fight for the nation but wish to return home as soon as possible. Commander Mike has political ambitions in the new order and wants to run for public office. A good number of his followers want to be policemen in the area that is to be freed when the Aksum forces are evicted. There are twenty "freedom fighters" in camp, ten each loyal to their respective guerilla leaders.

Out of character, Commander J.P. is a retired Special Forces chief warrant officer who commanded an Operational Detachment, Alpha, for six years. His Bear Clan assistant leader is a Marine gunnery sergeant about to leave the Corps. Both are Hispanic and frequently, when they are upset, converse rapidly in Spanish. They are a formidable pair. Commander Mike is a retired Special Forces sergeant first class. His deputy is a former SF master sergeant, and in the small-world department, he was my cadre sergeant during Phase Two of the Special Forces Q-Course when I was writing *Chosen Soldier*, back in 2005. In his Derna Bridge role, he is rumored to be guilty of war crimes committed against captured Aksum soldiers. The previous week, this cast of guerillas and guerilla leaders were role playing as Abyssinian soldiers from the 2nd Infantry Company for another student MSOT. In this previous enactments these senior contract role players served as officers and senior NCOs in the Abyssinian Army. The Abyssinian soldiers, now serving as partisan guerillas with student MSOT Three, are junior enlisted Marines from the Camp Lejeune area assigned to support the exercise.

The team officers and team chief spend most of their time engaged with the guerilla leaders. "When we first met the Bear Claw Clan and their leader," said Sergeant Kerry Irving, now acting as the team chief, "things did not go well. He was suspicious of us from the start, and more so when we met the other G-chief. For a while, myself and team commander were trying to figure out what the deal was with them—who was the senior leader and how we should try to handle them. But there was always tension—between them and between them and us. And they kept us off balance. It seemed like one minute they would be very open and friendly, and the next, they would clam up and return to their tent without a word. We finally learned that we had to make small talk and exchange greetings before talking business. It was custom and we were slow to pick up on it."

"At first we tried to get these guys to work together as a unit, the Bear Claw Clan and Commander J.P.'s men," said one of the team's captains. "It just didn't work. Finally, one of the guys with a lot of time working with Afghans said, 'Let's keep them separate. They come from different tribes, so let's not try to force them into a single unit.' Once we got that down, things began to go a lot better. We set up two training lanes and worked with them as two squads. Most of our targets were squad-sized operations, so that worked out as well. But the leaders kept challenging us; there was always something. They wanted to know how much we were being paid and could we pay their men. They wanted M4s instead of their AK-47s. One day they wanted to attack an Aksum outpost manned by a company-sized garrison, the next they wanted the day off because it was one of their minor holidays. It was always something. We had to work through it."

"Dealing with the two G-chiefs was always challenging," said Sergeant Irving. "They were suspicious of each other and suspicious of us." He grins. "And they didn't understand my role as the senior enlisted sergeant. Their leadership model is different. Not so much for the Bear Clan G-chief, but the other one—he kept wondering why I was not an officer. And both kept asking us why we were here, why did we come to fight in the nation of Abyssinia? They kept challenging us; there were constant issues of trust. The guerillas themselves were reserved and aloof at first. Then we made an effort to spend time with them. I got together with their senior sergeant, and we set up a sharing of camp duties and security rotations. That helped a lot. After a while we fell into a patrol-base routine, and that routine worked for us. At first, we kind of had to work to remain in character, but then it became automatic. We started to believe these guys were guerillas, not just Marines on a detail."

I asked about training the G-force and about operations. "We began slowly and took some time to evaluate just what they could and could not do. We quickly got past basic patrolling and into actions on target. We set up classes on how we plan missions and the use of terrain models. Then when we began to work up the patrol order, we would assign one of them to brief a portion of the order." And the missions? "We began with easy ones, what we call confidence targets. The first was simply cutting a rail line. We showed them how to build a charge and how to set it on the rail to cut the track. Then we patrolled in, set up security, and pulled the fuse. They did it and we supervised. From there we moved on to an attack on a motor pool, a communications tower, and a supply depot. Gradually they became better with planning and with the operations."

In talking to one of the Marine role players I asked him about his experience, first as an Abyssinian soldier and then as a guerilla. "It's been a lot of fun and I learned a lot—I'm still learning a lot. I'd never shot an AK-47 before so it was a learning experience for me. I'm an admin specialist, and we shot more out on the range with our 'Americans' than I have during my last two years in the Corps. As for the guerilla operations, that's pretty much new to me as well, both the planning and the sneaking around at night. Except for the heat and the bugs, it's been great. But I'm looking forward to that shower, but that's still a few days away."

"Any chance of you putting in your paperwork for the ITC?" I ask.

He pauses for a moment. "Not me, but I know a few of the guys are. It's been fun, but these guys are in pretty good shape. I'm not sure I can handle the PT, and I'm probably going to be getting out."

"We work a lot closer with the guerillas here in the camp than we did with the Abyssinian soldiers back at Fort Jackson," said Sergeant Brad Hansen. "But then this is kind of a patrol base. Some of them volunteered for this duty and others were simply detailed to come out here. It was a good break for all of them from what they were doing. For the most part, they stay in character as guerillas and act the part as directed by their leaders. But I can see that some of them really try to help us and are pulling for us to succeed, just like real partisans. And we really are able to teach them something. It's all good—except for the bugs."

The final two problems are designed to draw the Derna Bridge exercise to a close. One is setting (fake) charges on a hydroelectric dam to take down the power grid for a period not to exceed four days. The students work through a trusted agent, someone who is notionally and in real life a maintenance worker on the dam. This agent stays in character, while the students learn a great deal about how to sabotage a hydroelectric facility.

The final UW mission is the seizure of a local regional airfield. The airfield is closed for nighttime operations and available for exercise play. This seizure is to secure an air hub for the landing of conventional Abyssinian forces for major combat operations that are to expel the invading Aksum forces from the disputed region. This is a coordinated attack with all four student MSOTs and their freedom fighters taking part. After the airfield is seized and the local, loyal Abyssinian police force arrives to take control of the facility, the work of the freedom fighters is done. Following this successful operation, and an extensive after-action review, the MSOTs and their allies return to their patrol bases to pack up and prepare to leave the area.

As a final engagement, the teams have to address issues of transition and what is to take place after the fighting is over and Abyssinia regains rightful control of its sovereign territory. The former Abyssinian freedom fighters present the Americans with tokens of appreciation, to include a plastic bear claw for each member of the team. The Americans present them with a miniature Marine globe-and-anchor pin. Then all hands go admin and begin a final camp breakdown and clean up.

―――――――

Phase Four ends with a debriefing and a final round of counseling. There is no final board per se as there is no transition to the next phase. Instead of being handed off to another set of phase TACs and cadre sergeants, the former students of Class 1-13 will be handed off to the Marine Special Operations Regiment. They will move on to their battalions, companies, and Marine Special Operations Teams. Each student/ITC graduate is individually counseled by the phase cadre and their TACs. All in Class 1-13 have met standard—some meeting these standards well and performing at a very acceptable standard throughout all phases of training; others, while meeting standard, just doing so to a lesser degree. Those thought to be marginal are called in by Lieutenant Colonel Dodd, Colonel Glynn, and their master gunnery sergeants for a candid discussion about their performance in the ITC, or lack thereof. Two of those who remain in Class 1-13 are evaluated, their performance found lacking, and are disenrolled from the course. Those graduating are made aware of their strengths and weaknesses, and cautioned that training is never over for a Marine special operator, that they are expected to continue to improve—

tactically, technically, physically, and professionally. The special-operations community is small, and the smallest component in this brotherhood is the Marine Special Operations Command. When they get to their operational MSOTs, these students will be expected to integrate into their new team and, while immediately taking up their new roles as Marine special operators, continue to learn.

=====

The graduation ceremony for Class 1-13 on August 5, 2013, is festive, formal, and as SOF graduations go, fairly short. The proceedings are accompanied by a superb five-piece Marine brass ensemble that plays the national anthem, "Anchors Aweigh," and the "Marine Corps Hymn" with exceptional skill. The ceremony is conducted at the base theater, with John Dailey presiding. In addition to honoring the thirty-five new Marine special operators, five of the graduates are singled out for recognition.

One receives the Colonel Peter Ortiz Honor Graduate Award for the Marine with the highest grade point average. The Major General Merritt Edson Leadership Award goes to the Marine with the highest combination of tactical and leadership marks. The Master Sergeant Eden Pearl Combat Marksmanship Award is for the class Marine with the combined highest rifle, pistol, stress-course, and shoot-house scores. This hard-shooting Marine is a sergeant who held a 96.25 average over the graded events. The top class scorer on a range of physical fitness testing receives the Sergeant William Woitowicz Iron-man Award. The Brigadier General Evans Carlson Gung-ho Award is for the class Marine judged by the cadre to have contributed the most to the spirit of the class. The names of the five honorees will be added to the award plaques displayed at the School Academic Facility. Following the presentation of the Class 1-13 plaque to the school, and a suitably inscribed and adorned paddle to their proctor, Gunnery Sergeant John Patterson, the featured speaker is invited to the podium.

Major General Mark A. Clark, commander, U.S. Marine Corps

Forces, Special Operations Command, briefly addressed Class 1-13 back in November of 2012. He is with them today as their MARSOC Commander and their graduation speaker. A Marine aviator, Major General Clark has a long Marine Corps résumé that includes more than a decade of service in special operations from tours in Afghanistan and Kuwait to being chief of staff, U.S. Special Operations Command.

"Let me first congratulate you and welcome you to the Marine Special Operations family. Your nation, your Corps, and your MARSOC need you, and we have plenty of work for you. You and your brother Critical Skills Operators will serve in critical roles in the War on Terror, and your contributions will far exceed what your numbers might suggest. Tomorrow will indeed be different. But just for today, let's take a look at just how far you've come. From a general population of some ten thousand Marines, you were one of the five hundred Marines we invited to attend the Assessment and Selection, Preparation and Orientation Course and the Assessment and Selection Course annually. You were then among the two hundred some Marines we asked to begin the Individual Training Course, and here you are as one of the approximately ninety ITC students who graduate to become Marine Critical Skills Operators this year. All Marines are special, but over the past eight months you have proven yourselves to be both special and professional. Again, congratulations and welcome aboard."

Following the graduation, the enlisted Marines will make their way to their battalions and from there to their operational MSOTs. The officers will have the weekend off before returning to the Marine Special Operations School for the Team Commanders Course.

CHAPTER NINE

TCC, THE ENABLERS, AND THE MARSOC

Humans are more important than hardware.

Quality is more important than quantity.

Special Operations Forces cannot be mass-produced.

Competent Special Operations Forces cannot be created after emergencies occur.

Most special operations require non–Special Operations Forces assistance.

THE FIVE SOF TRUTHS

THE TEAM COMMANDERS/TEAM CHIEFS COURSE

The Marine officers from Class 1-13, like their enlisted classmates, will also report to their assigned battalions. Before they do, they will attend the Team Commanders/Chiefs Course, or simply the TCC. This four-week course of instruction is designed to provide these prospective MSOT commanders and senior enlisted leaders with additional leadership, administrative, organizational, and professional tools as they take up their new responsibilities. The format for this course is one of open group discussion that's heavy on case study and situational learning—especially in the areas of leadership and personal interaction. There are also liberal doses of after-hours study to prepare for the following day's classroom work and early morning sessions over a light, in-class breakfast.

Leadership, both officer and enlisted leadership, has always been a priority in the Marine Corps, and the Marines are justifiably proud of the time and attention they invest in their leaders. This was no less the case in what I observed throughout the ITC and into the TCC. The TCC for the officer graduates of ITC Class 1-13 was only the third iteration of this course and included the second increment of senior noncommissioned officers, specifically those relatively new E-8 Marine master sergeants slotted for future MSOT team chief responsibilities. This mix of future team commanders and team chiefs in the same course is, in my opinion, a superb learning laboratory for these key leaders. The mutual support and chemistry of the team commander and team chief makes up what is among the most critical of relationships in all of MARSOC. It's the same for all special-operations small tactical units. While the Marine Special Operations School has crafted this course with the duties and responsibilities of these key MSOT leaders in mind, they took careful inventory of that training given to Army captains following the Special Forces Q-Course and the Navy SEAL Platoon Leader/Platoon Chief Petty Officer Course.

Within all our special-operations components, there is a great body of small unit leadership experience and anecdotes, both positive and negative, to serve as lessons learned. There are lessons that relate to internal leadership within the team, such as conduct in garrison or overseas—conduct that can run from the unauthorized to the inadvisable. Marine special operators are for the most part mature and responsible, but they are not warrior monks. Leaders need to understand and anticipate challenges to the good order and discipline of the Marines intrusted to their care. The MSOT commanders and team chiefs, like the parents of an extended family, have to work in concert regarding issues of duty, professional performance, and conduct.

A great deal of the leadership training in the TCC has to do with lessons learned from actual events and challenges that come directly from deployed operational MSOTs. Some eight of these vignettes have to do with off-duty conduct, operational security, accountability, operational funding, tactical performance, and rules of engagement. Invariably, these relate to those gray areas where it falls to the team commander and/or the team chief to step in and make clear what is appropriate and what is inappropriate. One afternoon of the course featured a panel discussion where the panel was comprised of team commanders from the 1st and 2nd Marine Special Operations Battalions. These team commanders talked about their challenges, pitfalls, and, very candidly, where they felt they had come up short or made a poor decision. The students, the future team commanders and team chiefs, had a great many questions for them. The next round of panelists were team chiefs, who, again, were candid about their challenges, duties, and responsibilities. What I took from these panel discussions and the questions asked of those empaneled was the level of trust that must exist between the team commander and team chief. Close behind this was the trust and confidence that the team commander and team chief have in their two MSOT element leaders. The humility and honesty of these proven leaders were not lost on those in the TCC who were about to assume those same duties.

Organizationally, there is a great deal these officers and senior NCOs have to understand about the various command organizations within which they will work. It might even be called a labyrinth of command relationships. Within the scope of their irregular warfare duties, they must work within the constraints imposed by host-nation and partner-nation forces, ever mindful of their commander's intent and the inherent obligations of being a Marine and a special operator. Additionally, while conducting JCET or CNT operations, they will have to work within the guidelines of the U.S. ambassador and his country team. Regarding their military chain of command, a deployed MSOT may work for the geographic combatant commander (often shortened to GCC or, often, the theater commander). This commander, along with his conventional command structure, has theater military responsibilities that extend to the deployed MSOT. The MSOT may also be under the direction and guidance of a *special operations* chain of command that involves task organizations streamlined for the conduct of special operations. These are the *theater* special operations commands, or T-SOCs. These relationships may change from deployment to deployment and theater to theater, or even change mid-deployment. The MSOT leadership has to know, understand, and navigate within these command relationships to accomplish their mission.

Past the command, control, and organizational issues there is the funding. Even prior to the drawdown in Afghanistan and the budgetary constraints imposed by the sequestration in 2013, there was a feeling in MARSOC that they would soon be asked to do more with less. They have always operated in a responsible and judicious manner; now they will operate in a more fiscally constricted environment. Lieutenant Colonel Dodd addresses this issue.

"Funding wise," he tells the TCC captains and the team chiefs, "we have two sources of funding. The Marine Corps has the responsibility to man, train, and equip our force within the constraints of a Marine infantry organization of our size. Our paychecks also come from the Marine Corps. Past that, the special training and special weapons that you all enjoy are funded by the U.S. Special Operations Command. Very soon you are all going to be fighting over school quotas for your CSOs and out-of-the-area training that is very specialized and very expensive. It's not all that cheap to send a team commander and a team chief on a predeployment site survey to some African capital. Here again is where the SOCOM dollars kick in. But like the other services, special operations is being made to budget their funds wisely. So we all have a responsibility to know who is paying for what and to use those dollars prudently and responsibly. We owe it to the Marine Corps, to SOCOM, and to the nation to be judicious."

When I asked about this Marine Corps/SOCOM balance of funding, I could find no precise answer. The overall SOCOM budget was 10.5 billion in 2012 and 10.4 billion for 2013. This included the relatively cheap costs of training and deploying the SOF ground combatants and the more expensive training of pilots and deploying military aviation assets. Using the 2012 numbers and a then Department of Defense budget of 750 billion, which is shrinking as I write, the direct costs in SOF dollars is about 1.4 percent of the total. When the costs to man, equip, and train personnel to a convention standard are factored in, the price rises to some 30 billion or about 4 percent of the defense budget. Special Operations still provides a great deal of bang for the buck, but 30 billion is no small line item for a nation struggling to pay its bills. In these times of heightened fiscal responsibility, both the Marine Corps and the U.S. Special Operations Command are closely watching their monies. In keeping with this multiple-source funding, there is the standard-issue equipment from the Marine Corps *and* the special equipment that is issued to Marine special operators. Both have to be maintained and scrupulously accounted for.

"Never forget," a former MSOT team commander told the TCC class, "that as the team commander, you own that equipment and you have to keep track of it—you, not some logistics clerk back in the rear. You'll have the gear you take with you on deployment, gear you may sign for and own while you are there, and gear that may have no written accountability but for which you may be held responsible. Keep your own spreadsheet and back it up, and hold those who have sub-custody of the equipment accountable. Remember, if something goes missing, it's on you."

In addition to these leadership, organizational, and funding issues, the prospective MSOT commanders and team chiefs are exposed to some of the real-world issues that will challenge them and their teams on future deployments. Heading this list of challenges is the changing face of the enemy. There was and is al-Qaeda Central under the post–bin Laden fractional leadership emanating from the Federal Tribal Lands in Pakistan. "Central" is a recent convention to distinguish the main faction of al-Qaeda from the many franchisees, most notably in northern Africa and the Middle East. As the operational MSOTs rotate away from the active and still-kinetic deployments in Afghanistan, they are sure to be needed across the vast expanse of Africa, where there are any number of non-state actors in play, many with al-Qaeda affiliations.

The class spent two days with Dr. Andrea Dew, codirector of the Center for Irregular Warfare and Armed Groups at the Naval War College. Under Dr. Dew's guidance, the TCC students wrestled with a mosaic of issues and dozens of groups that range across north and central Africa.

"Talk about an eye-opener," one of the class captains said of this portion of the training. "Before this I thought there were just an al-Qaeda offshoot here and there, but as we learned, it's a lot more complex than that. There are bandits, smugglers, tribes, clans, nomads, Muslims, hard-core Islamists, to name a few—some with al-Qaeda leanings and others not. Then there are the displaced militias and rival factions set in motion by the Arab Spring and the new central governments—some democratically elected and some not. As for the non-state players, many of them are mobile and heavily armed. How we respond to these challenges is going to take a lot of thought and careful planning on our part. When they told us tomorrow would be different, I guess, well, I'm just finding out how different."

As a practical application, Dr. Dew gave the future team commanders and team chiefs a tutorial on Mali, the embattled West African republic that's roughly twice the size of Texas. Since the early 1990s, Mali has enjoyed a stable, democratic government with peaceful transfers of power. In January of 2012, the Tuareg tribe was pushed out of Libya in the wake of the Arab Spring and returned to northern Mali. They were heavily armed from the looting of Libya's armories following the overthrow and death of Colonel Mu'ammar Gadhafi. The fierce Tuaregs proved to be more than a match for the much weaker Mali military. They were joined by al-Qaeda in the Maghreb (AQIM, one of the al-Qaeda franchises in Africa) and quickly took control of the northern two-thirds of the country. With this success, AQIM began to exert control and impose *sharia* law in Mali. The Malian military overthrew the democratically elected government in an effort to save the nation from a total Tuareg/AQIM takeover. In January of 2013, the French armed forces returned to Mali (Mali was a French colony until 1960) to join with the Mali Army in pushing

AQIM and their now-reluctant Tuareg allies back north. The reestablishment of democratic rule in the nation now makes U.S. military assistance possible.

"With this background," one of the TCC master sergeants said of this scenario-planning exercise, "we had to plan how we would go about getting information about the strength of AQIM and their current relationship with the Tuareg tribe. This was in the context of our being in Mali on a JCET. Our contact in Mali was a well-connected smuggler who dealt with both the Tuareg and al-Qaeda but also had ties to the Mali military. What information would we ask of this smuggler? How could he verify the truthfulness of what he was telling us? What was in it for him to work with us? It was the kind of 'ask the right questions and listen carefully' engagement that we'll be doing a lot more of in the future."

In another exercise, Dr. Dew had them examine the relationship/involvement of al-Qaeda in the 2008 attacks in Mumbai and whether it was in fact al-Qaeda or a splinter group of the Pakistani secret intelligence service, the ISI.

———

The following week began with classroom work on indirect fire support and close air support—collectively referred to as fires. For the captains from Class 1-13 it was a continuation of their training during Phase One. For the master sergeants, this was something most had done on deployment, but with a focus on the more senior-level planning and execution. In this portion of the TCC, prospective team commanders and team chiefs receive instruction on the planning and deconfliction of supporting arms. They also get some time in both the joint terminal attack controller (JTAC) simulator and the close air support (CAS) simulator. Over the course of our engagement in Iraq and Afghanistan, there have been significant advances in the technology and effectiveness of fire support. This support has become increasingly important, with the improvements in close air support platforms, new precision-guided ordnance, and the use of armed drones. Used properly, supporting fires can be devastating to the enemy as well as dangerous to the friendly troops. They can also be a contentious issue with civilians and civilian authority. So the mechanics of managing these fires is both formatted and procedurally driven. To me, these standard five- and nine-line call-for-fire requests seemed exceedingly complex, but these captains and master sergeants seemed to handle them with practiced ease.

Following the classroom drill, the TCC students adjourn to a nearby range and are put through what I can only describe as a live-fire, command-post/communications exercise. Each student takes his turn as the team commander of an eight-man patrol, seated in the trail vehicle of a two-Humvee convoy. Along with the student team commander there is his MSOT JTAC-qualified enabler and six host-nation soldiers—for this drill six cadre sergeants serving as Afghan commandos. The convoy is hit with a simulated IED that disables the lead Humvee, and is attacked by a lightly armed but professional enemy force. The team commander has two radio nets at his disposal. One is his MBITR radio on which he has to manage the fight. The other radio is a satellite link that puts him in touch with his task force headquarters to let them know he's in contact and to request close air support. Our embattled team leader has to internally manage his Afghan commandos, engage the advancing enemy through and with his JTAC air controller, and make sure that his higher at the task force understands his situation—enough so for the commander to release the fire support the team leader needs to protect his small force. Meanwhile, he's in a fight. The Afghanistan commandos in both Humvees are fully engaged with their M240s, and there are explosions (flash-bangs) going off nearby. The noise is both realistic and unnerving. Then one of the team leader's Afghans goes down, and the he has to execute a formatted call for medical extraction. Oh, yes, and there are civilians in the area—not between the disabled Humvee and the advancing enemy, but nearby. The proximity of noncombatants is always a serious complication in a call for fire support.

Just one training iteration takes close to thirty minutes, with periodic group AARs. Those awaiting their turn as the team commander are kept unaware of the scenario. Those who have taken their turn as the team leader under attack serve as the task force headquarters watch officers who have release authority for the MSOT's air support and medivac assets.

"I probably leaned more in those fifteen or twenty minutes than anything I've done here or in combat," said one of the captains. "I'm a logistics officer and I've called in air support to protect convoys in Afghanistan, but it was not like this. I was not in the middle of a firefight. For me, it was a matter of trying to keep situational awareness of what was going on around me, and to be very precise and methodical on the radio nets. And to stay calm."

"This was very, very real" said one of the class captains who was JTAC-qualified and spent a tour in Afghanistan as a fire control officer. "It was a well-constructed scenario and one that happens all the time downrange. The simulators help for getting down the procedures, but there's nothing like a lot of shooting, yelling, smoke, and noise to force you to step back, take a deep breath, focus, and do what you've been trained to do."

This day of training was ingenious, and well received by all the TCC students. "I only wish," said the logs captain, "that I could do it again, and apply all that I learned during that exercise. I didn't do badly, but now I know I can do a lot better."

Several of the more interesting days for the TCC students involved negotiations, mediations, and key-leader engagements built around real-world events from Afghanistan. Role players came into the classrooms to serve as "the other side" in these key-leader engagements. In each of these scenarios, there was a problem or issue that posed an obstacle or stood between an MSOT and their ability to carry out their mission. One had to do with a village elder's issue with the Kabul government's regional representative. The village elder, without the permission of the regional rep, asked the MSOT to intervene in an area not under the operational authority of the MSOT. Another had to do with an issue of Taliban activity directed at a nearby village and outpost that was within the operational area of responsibility of a nearby NATO conventional unit. And yet another dilemma involved a police chief whose local policemen were heavily outgunned by the Taliban. He was asking the MSOT commander and his team chief for heavy machine guns and rockets to deal with the issue—something that it was not in the power of the MSOT to authorize.

"These are vignettes taken from Afghanistan," said Captain Shawn Daniels. In addition to his duties as the Phase Four CIC, he also runs the TCC. "Yet, they can and will happen just about anywhere. These team leaders and team chiefs will have to plan ahead, be empathetic, and listen carefully. Then, within their commander's intent and mission objectives, they'll have to navigate the human terrain."

A great deal of time and attention went into these engagements, including the use of two Pasto speakers from the MARSOC language-training facility. One of them served as a village elder, a member of the *shura,* or governing council, and the other as his interpreter. Now the students had to work through an interpreter to conduct the engagement. Working through an interpreter requires skill, knowledge of the interpreter's skill, and the use of simple, direct language. Many of these students, captains and master sergeants alike, had had similar dealings during their previous deployments. And the captains had the additional experience from their key-leader engagements during Derna Bridge.

"You will do this often," Captain Daniels told his TCC students. "There are major and minor power brokers in every area, along with the competing issues of religion, commerce, culture, you name it. You have to sort these out, determine what you can and cannot deconflict, and bring the situation, as best you can, in line with your mission objectives. Going into any meeting with these power brokers, you have to know what they want from the meeting and what you want from the meeting—your objectives for the meeting."

The final few days of the TCC are devoted to campaign planning for MSOT deployments, what these future team commanders and team chiefs will be doing in a very short time. The officers are again reminded of the Principles of a Special Operations Officer, yet they apply to the future team chiefs as well:

1. Own the institution.

2. Provide leadership at the point of friction.

3. Be able to integrate and combine capabilities.

4. Lead planning, bridging top-down requirements with bottom-up solutions.

5. Influence higher, adjacent, supporting (commands) and (host-nation) partners to help achieve the desired end state.

THE ENABLERS

The Combat Support and the Combat Service Support Marines from the Marine Special Operations Support Branch are essential to the work of Marine Special Operations Forces downrange. In garrison, they are assigned to the Marine Special Operations Support Group. While these Marines often go by the moniker "enablers," they are more than that; they are a force multiplier. These supporting cadres are scalable and versatile, and can go forward in the support of individually deployed MSOTs or the operational requirements of a Marine Special Operations Company or Battalion. We'll get into the deployed packaging of Marine Special Operations Forces a little later, but for now let's focus on these Special Operations Combat Support and Special Operations Combat Service Support Marines. These Marines, along with their Critical Skills Operator brothers, are all considered MARSOC multi-dimensional operators. They work closely and seamlessly in preparation for overseas deployment and while on deployment.

The Special Operations Combat Service Support (SOCSS) Marines, or the more manageable CSSs, are the Marines who keep the forward operations base or bases habitable and functioning. While these Marines may be the least kinetic in their duties, they are essential to the smooth functioning of the deployed Marine Special Operations Companies and Teams. These are Marines whose MOSs have to do with supply, engineering support, motor transport, electronics, and the mechanical. Compared to the Combat Support Marines and the Critical Skills Operators, they are the smallest in number, with some ten to twelve per company, making two or three of them available to an MSOT operating independently.

"These are the guys that are fought over at the company and even battalion level," a support group master sergeant told me. "The Combat Support Marines, the intel guys, EOD techs, and so on, function within their specific MOS skill sets, and we use them almost exclusively in those designated rolls. The Combat Service Support guys are the 'utility infielders,' and the more versatile they are, the better. We all know who these guys are and what they can do, both within their MOS and their individual skills. Often, it's their non-MOS skills that are so valued. As we move into the deployment cycle, there's always a food fight for who gets what from this skills pool. I've had team chiefs and even company first sergeants come to me and say, 'I'll give up all my other draft picks, but I want Lance Corporal Jones or Corporal Smith for this deployment.' That's because Jones or Smith might be an electrician but he can also weld, coax a Humvee back to life, fix a radio, or serve as a ring-turret gunner. If he can game the supply system or is especially good in making friends with the in-theater contractors or Army supply types, then he takes on added value."

On occasion, one of these CSS Marines decides he wants to become a CSO, as was the case for Sergeant Todd Ewing with Class 1-13. Ewing had deployed twice as a CSS diesel mechanic with the 2nd Marine Special Operations Battalion. He knew very well what it was to deploy with an operational MSOT. Now he was back with the 2nd Battalion as a member of an operational MSOT.

"My team chief knows who I am and what I can do," he said with a grin. "And when a generator or one of the Humvees has a problem, he still comes looking for me. But I'm also the weapons sergeant for my element. No worries—I can do both."

The CSS Marines range from privates first class to corporals, with an occasional sergeant. Some 80 percent of them are first-tour Marines, so that makes for a great many PFCs and lance corporals. They move into the operational MARSOC components with the shortest training period of any Marine multidimensional operator. A new CSS Marine checking into MARSOC will first attend the three weeks of MARSOC special training called the MST course. At the MST they will receive training in tactics, marksmanship, first aid, and an introduction to PERRES physical training. This training is conducted by the Marine Special Operations Support Branch and is an orientation to the work of the MSOTs downrange and a SOF-centric approach to operational employment.

"In this short training period," the NCOIC for MST training said of this course, "we give them a look at the basics with a MARSOC flavor. We also tell them that they will go downrange—they will be a part of a Marine special-operations deployment package. This means that to the extent that they are willing and capable, we will give them duties and responsibilities that exceed their MOS or specific job description. When one of our young lance corporals shows he's willing and capable, the team chiefs will start requesting him by name. It's a great opportunity for a young Marine to excel and serve his country and, at a very junior level, make a contribution well above his pay grade."

So these CSS Marines are value-added enablers with a generalist portfolio. They support the MSOTs during pre-deployment training and on deployment, but they are typically looked at as a Marine Special Operations *Company* asset and assigned to the MSOTs as needed. This is in contrast to the Combat Support Marines that are assigned to and are closely aligned with the Marine Special Operations Teams.

The Combat Support Marines or CSs who deploy with the Marine Special Operations Forces are there primarily for their specific skill sets. Broadly speaking, they are the intelligence specialists, the communications specialists, the explosive ordnance disposal (EOD) technicians, the joint terminal attack controllers (JTACs), and the multipurpose canine (MPC) teams—Marine dog handlers and dogs. Each of these specialists can find themselves in harm's way with any number of regularly deploying Marine units. Yet the work of deployed MARSOC units is often more dangerous and in more austere conditions than that of conventional Marine units. Because of this, the Support Branch works closely with the Marine detailers to try to find and recruit the right Marines for combat-support duty in MARSOC. This does not imply that there are "wrong" Marines, just that it works best for all concerned if these Combat Support Marines understand that they will be supporting Marines that will likely be in continuous overseas rotation and often under challenging and hostile conditions. A good many Marines DOR from the Individual Training Course when they understand just how much time they will be away from home—in training and on overseas deployment. This duty is not for every Marine, and the same applies for those who serve in support roles at MARSOC.

The Combat Support Marines are typically more senior and more seasoned, and come to the MARSOC with a great deal of schooling and experience. Indeed, these veterans are among the most capable and highly skilled of all Marines. Unlike the CSS Marine enablers, these specialists are overwhelmingly veteran Marines—more than 80 percent are on their second-plus enlistment. When they arrive at MARSOC and the Marine Special Operations Branch, they will be processed through three phases of training. The first is the six-week Special Operations Training Course, or STC. This course parallels the three weeks of training afforded the CSSs, but with a much more robust shooting package and special operations tactical orientation. Then, like the CSSs, they attend SERE school. The STC is now conducted by the Marine Special Operations School and is mandatory for all CS Marines except for the explosive ordnance disposal technicians. After more than a decade of war, these brave and well-traveled Marine EOD techs are allowed to validate this course—for now. Past the STC, all CS Marines must complete MARSOC training in keeping with their MOS specialty. The design of this training is to allow for these Marines to bring their specific skills in line with the standard SOF tactics, techniques, and procedures. This MOS/MARSOC-related training goes by the bland title of Level One Training.

In further examination of these CS enablers, let's first take a look at the explosive ordnance disposal technicians—2326 MOS. Their calling was made popular by the Oscar-winning movie *The Hurt Locker*. These intrepid and talented Marines are the ones who deal with unexploded ordnance and improvised explosive devices— the dreaded IEDs. Between deployments they study and train on the latest IED developments used by our enemies, and then on deployment, they deal with them. If a situation looks wrong, like when the driver of a halted vehicle refuses to open the trunk of his car or the locals suddenly vacate a section of roadway that is normally crowded, the team or element leader invariably says, "We've got a possible IED; get the EOD tech up here." And if a team has to enter a building, and there's a suspicion that the door may be booby-trapped, then again, the call goes out for the EOD tech. He goes in first. The EOD Level One Training is a six-week curriculum. Over the course of the heavy deployments to Iraq and Afghanistan, these special Marines have often been in high demand and short supply. Since they are allowed to validate the STC, these EOD techs, after their Level One Training and three weeks of SERE school, immediately go into deployment rotation.

The MSOTs will have up to three intelligence Combat Support Marines with each team. Depending on the size and configuration of the MARSOC deployment package, a more robust intelligence support package may reside at the company level. An MSOT will typically be supported by what is termed as a direct support team—an element of three or even four of these intelligence specialists. The DST will usually have at least one Marine trained in signals intelligence, or SIGINT, one trained in human intelligence, or HUMINT, and a third who is an intelligence analyst. These Marines carry various intelligence MOSs in the 02XX/26XX series. They will often go into the field with their MSOTs, specifically for intelligence-related work or as part of the sensitive site exploitation (SSE) element within the team. Their Level One Training can last between four and six weeks. Along with six weeks of their STC and three weeks at SERE school, and the scheduling of these classes, it may take four months or more to prepare these Marine intelligence specialists for MARSOC deployment rotation.

All MSOT CSO Marines are trained in communications, but their focus is on tactical communications. An MSOT will normally have a dedicated communications specialist with a 06XX/28XX MOS. His job is primarily to handle the nontactical communications and the heavy lifting of data transmission from the MSOTs location back to the company or to higher headquarters. He also sees that the team's field and intra-team radios are functioning properly. If the team is tasked with a JCET mission, he will take the lead in communications training for host-nation forces. The Level One Training of a new communications CS can take between four and six months to prepare him for deployment rotation.

Another tactical enabler is the JTAC—joint terminal attack controller, 0861/8002 MOS. Prior to 2003, they were known as forward air controllers. They are the small unit offshoots of the Marine AN-GLICO (Army/Navy Gunfire Liaison Company) teams that control air, artillery, and naval gunfire support for a Marine Air-Ground Task Force. The JTACs are tasked with fire support. They are also responsible for training their MSOTs in operational supporting fires for special operations. Many of the CSOs in the MSOT are trained in CAS, or close air support, but for the JTACs, it's a specialty. They can manage several sections of aircraft at a time and ensure the proper delivery of precision-guided munitions. And as with the other enablers, they may be tasked with teaching this skill, within established parameters, to allied host-nation forces. The Level One Training for MARSOC JTACs is four weeks. Following SERE, STC, and their Level One Training, the JTACs will go into deployment rotation with the MSOTs.

And finally, there is the multipurpose canine (MPC) team, which consists of a dog and a Marine dog handler, 5811/5812 MOS (the Marine, not the dog). Depending on the type and kind of deployment, many MSOTs will have an MPC team. Dogs have become a staple in nearly all platoon-sized special-operations elements with a direct-action mission. Military working dogs are typically trained to a specialty such as guard duty or sniffing out explosives. As the name would imply, the MARSOC MPC teams have a multipurpose mission. What they are called on to do and how they do it is beyond the classification of this book, but they use their eyes, ears, and nose to good advantage in support of their Marine special operators. During operations in Iraq and Afghanistan, there were often times when a person of interest ran out the back door of a compound just as the Marines and their host-nation counterparts were coming in the front door. In cases like this, the fleeing individual feels he can duck down an alleyway and make good his escape on foot. But the escapee has forgotten about the dog. The heavily armed Marines may not be able to run him down, but the dog can, and often does. Following ten weeks of Level One Training, STC, and SERE, these dogs and their handlers go downrange with their MSOTs.

There is one other enabler that within the Regiment is usually deployed as a battalion asset and detailed out to the MSOTs on an as-needed basis. They are the cultural support teams. These are female Marines, usually an officer and an enlisted Marine working together. As appropriate, they are trained in cross-cultural disciplines and participate in key-leader engagements, village stabilization operations, and medical outreach programs. Quite often, these teams work with local women and will serve with the MSOTs where a woman-to-woman presence is useful in the conduct of special operations. In addition to their specific SOF CST training, these Marines, as with the other Special Operations Support Branch enablers, must complete the Marine Special Operations Training Course and SERE school. In this same vein, female Marines may be trained and serve in other combat support and combat service support roles. Yet the nature of Marine special operations often puts their combat support and combat service support Marines into direct ground-combat roles. There are new changes within the Department of Defense that seek to lift the restrictions on women in direct combat. These changes may or may not affect special operations. For now, MARSOC CS and CSS Marines, with the exception of the cultural support teams, are all male Marines.

Once the Combat Support enablers have completed their assigned MARSOC Level One Training, the STC, and SERE school, they are awarded the 8071 secondary military occupational specialty designation. While the CSS Marines will often serve only a single three-year tour with MARSOC, the CS Marines are on board for six years, with approximately five of those six in deployment rotation. Currently these enabling cadres join the deploying MSOTs and Marine Special Operations Battalions and Companies at various times during the deployment cycle. Within the Special Operations Branch, there are plans to further standardize and refine this essential support to the Marine Special Operations Regiment.

THE MARSOC SAILORS

Since the founding days of the United States Navy and the United States Marine Corps, the medical needs of both services have been served by Navy doctors and Navy corpsmen. This includes duties that are clinical or routine-care-related as well as the battlefield duties of field-trained combat medics. Perhaps the most iconic image of the Marine-Navy corpsman is Joe Rosenthal's photo of the flag raising on Iwo Jima. One of those "Marines" was Pharmacist's Mate John Bradley. Within the composition of an operational Marine Special Operations Team are two specially trained Navy corpsmen who are full members of that team. These "medical CSOs" arrive by a very different route than their Marine CSO brothers and are among the most extensively trained and qualified members of their team.

A young sailor's journey to become a CSO medic begins with seven weeks of Navy boot camp followed by approximately fourteen weeks of basic corpsman training at the tri-service Medical Education and Training Campus at Fort Sam Houston in San Antonio. This huge facility provides a variety of medical and technical training for soldiers, sailors, and airmen, of which nearly a third are sailors. Following three and a half months at Fort Sam Houston, the new corpsman begins his journey of medical and combat-centric training that will take him away from the Navy and his fellow corpsmen who serve primarily in fleet and clinical roles and bring him to MARSOC. This journey is essentially the same as that of the amphibious reconnaissance corpsmen, and upon finishing his training, he will carry the same 8427/8403 MOS as the Recon men.

The first stop is the seven-week Field Medical Service Technician Course, more popularly known as Field Med. The Field Med course is conducted at Camp Lejeune and Camp Pendleton by Navy corpsmen who are veteran medics. This course is designed to train these sailors in basic field medicine as well as give them the combat and small-arms training they will need to function in a Marine Corps unit. The course is also intended to immerse these Navymen in the Marine culture and the particulars of Marine Corps service. At the end of Field Med, they will still not be Marines, nor will they ever be, but they will understand a great deal more about the Marines with whom they will be serving and how a Marine unit conducts itself.

The next stop is the Basic Reconnaissance Course. This twelve-week course is difficult and demanding, and if there is a rite of passage in the pipeline of the MARSOC corpsmen, it is the BRC. Here they and their fellow Recon-Marine candidates will learn the basic skills of beach reconnaissance and amphibious operations, as well as surveillance tactics, techniques, and procedures. This makes these sailors Recon-trained corpsmen if not Recon Marines. From speaking with both MARSOC and Recon corpsmen, I learned that this is where they are accepted into the brotherhood that is the Recon/MARSOC community. After the BRC, the corpsmen have fully stepped into the role of apprentice warriors, and most from this point forward will readily identify more with the Marine Corps and their Recon/MARSOC teammates than they will with the Navy.

Following the BRC, our Marine-orientated, Recon-trained corpsman will head for three weeks of Basic Airborne School at Fort Benning, Georgia. From there he will travel farther south to the Navy Diving and Salvage Training Center in Panama City, Florida, for the eight-week Marine Combatant Diver Course. There he will train in open- and closed-circuit scubas, to include the Dräger LAR-V oxygen rebreather—the standard U.S. military tactical scuba. This is a Marine course that trains all Marine Recon and MARSOC combatant divers and where these special Navy corpsmen may first train alongside MARSOC Marines. After the Recon and MARSOC combatant divers leave, the corpsmen remain behind for the five-week Amphibious Reconnaissance Corpsman Course, a Navy diving-medicine course. Here they expand their medical knowledge and skills to learn about diver-related medical protocols and recompression-chamber operation. At this point in their training pipeline, these Navymen have been trained in field medicine, basic reconnaissance, and are fully jump- and dive-qualified. Now they turn themselves over to the Army to become combat medics and special operations independent-duty corpsmen.

The center for special operations medical training and the clinical soul of SOF medicine is the Joint Special Operations Medical Training Center at Fort Bragg, North Carolina. This Army school is the home for the Army Special Forces 18-Delta Medical Sergeants Training. In addition to the training of Special Forces, Marine Recon, and MARSOC medics, this medical center also provides training for SEAL corpsmen and the combat medics of the 75th Ranger Regiment. There is perhaps no finer military medical training in the world than what takes place at this Medical Training Center at Fort Bragg. The training comes to the future MSOT corpsmen in two iterations. The first is the thirty-two-week Special Operations Combat Medic Course that is the gold standard for combat casualty care and treatment. This is followed by the sixteen-week Special Operations Independent Duty Corpsman Course—training designed to give these combat medics and caregivers the ability to treat their Marine and foreign host-nation patients in the absence of local clinical support. When deployed and where there is no alternative, they practice medicine and, on occasion, veterinary medicine.

So it takes eighty-five weeks of training to create an amphibious reconnaissance corpsman—the same corpsman who serves on the Marine Special Operations Teams. Given time between duty stations, the Navy invests the better part of two years and some very expensive training to create these military medical practitioners. They are smart, talented, and trained to a rigorous standard. Their training and background allow them to set up clinics in remote areas in support of host-nation and stabilization operations. Bringing medical care and immunizations to a village that has none can create a great deal of goodwill. This can lead to cooperation and information from a local population that may be reluctant to work with outsiders. In addition to their tactical and irregular warfare-related expertise, they conduct the medical cross training within their MSOTs and supporting enablers. And if all this schooling were not enough, when our much-traveled corpsman arrives at MARSOC, he will attend the six-week Special Operations Training Course to bring some of his non-medical skills in line with MARSOC requirements. And, of course, SERE school.

The SEALs, Special Forces, and 75th Rangers take a slightly different approach to their medics. In these communities, they *first* train their prospective medics to become SEALs, Green Berets, or Rangers *and then* they are detailed to Fort Bragg for combat-medic, independent-duty corpsman, or special forces medical sergeant training as the case may be. Because of this Navy-provides-corpsmen relationship between the Navy and the Marine Corps, MARSOC will, for the foreseeable future, continue to draw their MSOT medics from the amphibious reconnaissance corpsman pipeline. I've heard it discussed that there may come a time when the MARSOC-bound corpsmen, or even future MARSOC medic designees, will attend the ITC. On completion of the ITC, they will then be sent to Fort Bragg for medical training before joining the Marine Special Operations Regiment. Until such time, the MSOTs will continue to call on these extensively trained Navy corpsmen to deploy with their operational MSOTs.

At the beginning of this chapter, I listed the Five SOF Truths, the fifth of which is *Most special operations require non–Special Operations Forces assistance*. Perhaps because of their expeditionary nature, MARSOC and the special-operations Marines have built a robust, integrated, and embedded support structure within their organization. They have made it flexible and scalable so it can be tailored to MARSOC deployment requirements, whether that's in support of a team, a company, or a full battalion. While non-SOF or general-purpose forces may still be required, they may not always be available in the constrained budgetary times ahead. So the independence and stand-alone capability MARSOC has created with enabling cadres may serve the Command well in future MARSOC and SOF deployments.

CHAPTER TEN

THE REGIMENT

*Here is courage, Mankind's finest possession, the noblest prize
that a young man can endeavor to win . . . when he plants
his feet and stands in the foremost spears . . . he has trained
his heart to be steadfast and endure and encourages
the man who is stationed beside him. Here is a man who
proves himself to be valiant in war.*

TYRTAEUS

NEW CSO ASSIGNMENT

When it comes down to what MARSOC is all about—who they are, what they do, and the seat of their culture—it's the Marine Special Operations Regiment. For the new Critical Skills Operators and Special Operations Officers from Class 1-13, the Regiment will be their home for the next several years, and for the enlisted Marines, for the rest of their Marine Corps career. These new Marine special operators will be assigned as needed to one of the three Marine Special Operations Battalions, and those assignments are made with regard to the manning levels and vacancies within the battalions. Where possible, assignments between the West Coast/Camp Pendleton–based 1st MSOB and the East Coast/Camp Lejeune–based 2nd and 3rd MSOBs are made with respect to the desires of the individual Marines. There is also the issue of the cost of a coast-to-coast move in the calculus, but where possible, the preferences of new ITC graduates are honored, although there may be less flexibility with the Special Operations Officers, depending on team commander vacancies.

Another factor that may enter the CSO-assignment calculus is language proficiency and language ability. With the drawdown in Afghanistan, the three Marine Special Operations Battalions are seeking to more formally "regionalize" their future deployment posture. The 1st MSOB will focus on the Pacific Rim and Southeast Asia; the 2nd, the Middle East and Southwest Asia; while the 3rd will concentrate on South/Central America and Africa. A fluent Spanish speaker may well find himself in the 3rd MSOB, while a Marine with capabilities in Farsi or Dari will most likely be assigned to the 2nd. All new CSOs and SOOs will have taken the Defense Language Aptitude Battery, which determines an individual's ability to learn a foreign language. Depending on ability, a new ITC graduate may attend between thirty-six and fifty-two weeks of language training en route to his assigned battalion. That language will determine his battalion assignment and vice versa.

When the enlisted CSOs arrive at their battalion, they are in-processed and make their administrative rounds. Ultimately, the Marine Special Operations Team will be their operational family, but the battalion is their administrative home. At battalion they will log into the travel system, have their security clearances updated, and check in with the battalion training cell. Their initial equipment draw will be at battalion. The new CSOs will all attend a family readiness brief and become a part of the battalion family support infrastructure. And finally, there will be a meeting with the battalion operations chief and/or battalion master gunnery sergeant for a welcome to the battalion and perhaps a "father-to-son" talk on battalion expectations, conventions, and maybe a few of the left and right boundaries imposed by their battalion.

Following a week or ten days at battalion, the new CSOs will check in with one of the battalion's four companies and from there go to one of that company's four MSOTs. Apart from language and former Marine Corps MOS considerations, they are assigned with regard to vacancies within the MSOTs. The specific requirements of the teams and the training records of the new CSOs are inventoried and matched, and the assignments are made by the company operations chief in close consultation of the MSOT team chiefs. Past the on-paper requirements, which will be covered later in this chapter, and the individual MOS skills the new men bring with them, there are personality factors.

"The new men come to us with a sanitized version of their ITC training jacket," a company operations chief told me, "so we have some idea where they are strong and have performed well, and where they may be weak. We also have their class proctor's comments. The team chiefs and myself have our sources at the school, so we may be aware of issues that are not in their records or training jackets. My job is to see that there is an equitable distribution of talent and that the needs of my MSOTs are best met with the new CSOs. When they first arrive here, myself and the company first sergeant have a chat with them. We welcome them and congratulate them on completing the ITC. We tell them that there's not only a place for them here, but that they are needed. Then we also tell them that the ITC is behind them, and their reputation in Regiment starts now. This may not be entirely true, but we've had Marines who were marginal performers in the ITC come here and do great things from the get-go. They are told that they will be judged here by their performance; if they're looking for a fresh start, then this is the place to begin. And finally, we tell them that the standards of a United States Marine apply in this regiment and this company.

"Each team chief handles his new men in his own way, but the team orientation is much like that at the battalion and company level. Only at the team level, the welcome-aboard and integration is a lot more personal. For a new man, the Marines in his MSOT are the brother Marines with whom he will live, deploy, and fight alongside for the next several years. Ultimately, the team chiefs will make the assignments within the team. On a team, experience trumps rank, so sometimes a CSO new to the team may find himself working for or under the direction of a Marine special operator junior in rank to himself. This seldom is a problem, and if it is, the team chief will fix it straightaway."

The assignment of the new Special Operations Officers, or SOOs, is handled by the regimental executive officer. His concerns are team-commander vacancies and matching the SOO's experience and ITC performance with battalion deployment responsibilities. Once the RXO has made his initial battalion allocations, the SOOs are detailed out to the battalions and the assignments are made by the battalion executive officer in consultation with his company commanders. The new officers are normally held at the battalion staff level until there's an MSOT vacancy, then moved through the company to the team. In a perfect world, team commanders are assigned toward the beginning of a battalion/company/team work-up, as they prepare for the next operational deployment. This preferred timing is true for the CSOs as well, but it's not always a perfect world.

"I'm headed for 2nd Battalion," a recent graduate of Class 2-12 told me. I knew him to be an infantry officer with an active deployment history and an excellent record in the ITC. "And I'll be deploying as a team commander with my MSOT in about two months." I also knew that a deploying MSOT from 2nd would be headed for Afghanistan—or in the case of this infantry officer, headed back to Afghanistan. "Fortunately I'm blessed with a very experienced team and a veteran team chief. It's happening more quickly than I thought and that's a little intimidating, but this will be my third rotation to Afghanistan. I know the area where we'll be assigned, but I know full well there will be a lot to learn on the job. But my team chief and element leaders have done this before, and they're all good teachers. We'll do fine."

From another officer from 2-12, "I'm over at 3rd Battalion and I'm out the door in six weeks. It's a JCET to Central Africa, and we'll be gone about two months." He's a logistics officer with a very solid record in the ITC. "This is the perfect situation for me. I will deploy as a second officer, so this deployment and this JCET will be a walk-through for me. When we return, I'll take over the team and make the next deployment." He too had nothing but good things to say about his team chief and the Marine special operators on his team, as well as the team commander who would mentor him on this first deployment.

These two officers were out the door and on deployment with atypical speed. Most SOOs, and CSOs as well, have the benefit of both individual training and team training before they deploy. Yet the fact that these SOOs were able to go downrange so quickly is a tribute to their Marine Corps leadership training and the training they received at the ITC and TCC. It's also a great tribute to the talent, experience, and leadership embedded in the standing MSOTs that allows for a new team commander to step in and immediately be effective.

MSOT SKILLS

Each of the three battalions of the Regiment has four companies, and each company has four Marine Special Operations Teams. The MSOT is the basic building block of the Marine Special Operating Forces, and within each MSOT there is a defined skill set—or a set of collective skills and a subset of individual skills. Some of these skills are required of all on the team and must be kept certified and current, such as tactical combat casualty care (TCCC), fast-rope insertion/extraction training, helicopter rope-suspension training, and parachuting. Other common/required skills are onetime qualifications, such as SERE training and the various vehicle training/licensing/operating certifications. Each team has to have a number of CSOs trained in specific operational skills, such as sniping, breaching, applied explosives, and antiterrorism force protection. There are CSO field-level skills that relate to communications, sensitive site exploitation (SSE), target analysis, technical surveillance, and field intelligence. The more senior CSOs are tasked with leadership and supervisory certifications, such as jump master, close-quarter battle (CQB) leader, and a range of classified, special-access programs that fall into the classification of advanced special operations. And there are the important, non-operational specialties/qualifications that relate to supply functions, contracting, and finance. There are also unique, highly specialized

MSOT skill requirements, such as martial arts instruction, PERRES coaching, and the operation of small portable tactical drones.

This diverse and comprehensive skill set is needed because an MSOT may be asked to operate independently or to conduct joint/combined partner-nation operations well away from any conventional support. So, in essence, they may have to attend to the duties and functions of a full battalion. This range of responsibility requires a great deal of training and advanced/special schools. When an MSOT returns from an overseas deployment, the team commander and team chief immediately begin to look at the next deployment, its specific or special requirements, and the pool of talent on the team to meet those requirements. When a new CSO reports to his new team, the team commander and team chief immediately take inventory of the new man's training and capabilities in light of the team's existing skill sets. Then he will be assigned duties and training to fill team and individual skill shortfalls. He could be assigned to fill any vacancy, but new CSOs will most often receive training/skill building in weapons, engineering, or communications.

The Marine Special Operations School provides training for a great many of these base-level and advanced skill sets, to include communications training for CSOs serving in the operational MSOTs. This training focuses on SOF-centric radios, tactical communications, and communications interoperability with other USSOCOM components. Other schooling is provided by sister-SOF training courses or contracted civilian training. New COSs assigned MSOT skills in weapons or engineering may attend the Army Special Forces 18-series training—18 Bravo for weapons and 18 Charlie for engineering. This training is approximately twelve weeks in duration and takes place at Fort Bragg, North Carolina. The 18-series training accomplishes several things. First of all, it provides comprehensive training in that discipline. For weapons, it's full-immersion training in all U.S. and foreign weapons systems. The 18 Bravo course is designed for "weapons sergeants" who will be teaching weapons skills to their teammates and to partner-nation forces. The same can be said for the 18 Charlie engineering training that provides instruction in construction disciplines ranging from drilling wells, to maintaining generators, to wiring buildings. The Fort Bragg 18-series also promotes "personal interoperability" between Marine MSOT CSOs and Army Special Forces A-Team sergeants.

MSOT TRAINING

When our new CSO gets to his team, his team chief will assign him his duties within the team and arrange for him to attend schools/ training as needed. Team chiefs continually work to balance the needs of the team with the availability of school quotas and training opportunities. A team chief will also consider the desires of his CSOs for a specific school or type of training. Sometimes he can satisfy all three and sometimes not. The needs of the team come first. Quite often, more CSOs want to be snipers than want to be field interrogators, and often it's the veteran CSOs who get the more personally desirable schools. The team chief will also do his best to see that his Marines get to those schools as soon after returning from an overseas deployment as possible. This will allow for team-centric training and the more integrated, MARSOC-centric training that takes place prior to deployment. As the veterans know, and the new CSOs will soon learn, the life of a special operations Marine is one of deployment and preparation for deployment—a seemingly unending cycle.

In the deployment work-up and deployment life of a Marine Special Operations Team, there are the individual training and individual skills that are mandatory for a team to rotate out on deployment. These required skill sets become a part of the team capability and makeup. There are also team-centric training and team-building exercises. Past this team training, there may be company-related and even battalion-centric training, but for the most part, collective training is built around the team and, in the latter part of the deployment work-up, possibly with the company. At some point, usually about 180 days from their deployment date, the team shifts from individual training to team or unit training. This unit-focused training is driven by the requirements of the prospective deployment and the "sizing" of the deploying force. It's at or about this 180-day point that the MSOT will acquire its enabling package—those combat support and combat service support Marines who will work with the CSOs on the upcoming deployment. With this in mind, the 180-day support-package lead time lends itself to a six-month deployment rotation. For the shorter, JCET/CNT-type rotations, the length of deployment and the associated enabler/MSOT integration may be adjusted and compressed.

At the MSOT level, the team and their assigned/designated enablers will schedule and conduct training to prepare for the upcoming deployment. This usually falls to the team chief, to schedule weapons, communications, tactical, cross-cultural, and team-building training. The MSOT will also be coordinating their preparation efforts with the company and battalion training cells who may be able to support this training. Toward the end of their unit-level predeployment training, they may be working more closely with the company and battalion staffs in command-post exercises/training. This training may be joint training with other SOF/conventional components who will be deploying to the same area with a similar or supporting mission. Training may be local in the Camp Lejeune or Camp Pendleton area or at some special training facility like the Army's National Training Center at Fort Irwin, Texas. Those responsible for unit-level training, at the team, company, and battalion level, will use all their resources and creativity to create meaningful and mission-specific pre-deployment training. They will also balance these training opportunities with the funds available in these budget-constricted times *and* the need to afford their Marines time at home with their families before they leave for yet another deployment.

For the better part a decade, beginning with the formation of MARSOC, deployment meant rotations to Iraq and Afghanistan. This meant that unit-level training was built around a model that prepared the MSOTs and their enablers for direct-action operations and, toward the end of engagement in those nations, the training of the local police and military units. So there was a shift from the direct to the indirect, and both team training and unit-level training reflected that. And along with that migration from the direct to the indirect, there was the size of MARSOC deployment package. During the force surge into Afghanistan in 2010–2011, when the troop strengths were at their highest, MARSOC deployments were close to battalion strength, with the battalion staffs serving in task-force, command-level positions and the company staffs in subordinate, task-unit-command roles. That has changed to a degree and will continue to change as the post-Afghanistan MARSOC role evolves. Yet this kind of change plays to a strength of MARSOC; it is a very versatile and scalable force.

Over the past decade, even during the force surge into Afghanistan prior to the phased drawdown that began in earnest in 2012, our special operations forces have maintained a presence in eighty-some nations around the world. While something on the order of half those forces were in Iraq or Afghanistan at any given point in time, there was still a global SOF deployment posture. MARSOC was no different. About half their MSOTs were sent to the active theaters and the balance scattered about Africa, Southern Thailand, and the Southern Philippines, to name a few. With the drawdown in Afghanistan and the reestablishment of a broader geographical focus for each battalion, the 1st Battalion and 3rd Battalion began to shift their focus away from Afghanistan. Not so for the 2nd. As one team chief told me, "We'll be in Afghanistan training Afghans for quite a while. We'll probably be the last ones there—whenever that is. I expect the last man out the door will be an MSOT team chief from the 2nd." So MARSOC moved from battalion-sized rotations to company-sized rotations in Afghanistan. There will come a time when MARSOC commitment in that nation will be a multiple-team or single MSOT presence. That's scalability.

I envision that the Marine Special Operations Forces will always retain the ability to deploy and conduct operations in a battalion/ task-force package. Yet, with a global focus moving to indirect special operations, their mission taskings will be met with smaller-scale deployments. This smaller deployment/smaller footprint lends itself to the more subtle and less conspicuous application of special operations forces. This means there will be more deployments in the joint combined exchange training (JCET) and counter-narcotics training (CNT) format than in the larger-force packages. And while there will be a great many single-MSOT taskings, the ideal or perhaps the most useful size may well prove to be the company or task-unit deployment package. So it may be instructive as well as useful to look at the future Marine SOF deployments from the perspective of a company deployment. First, let's take a closer look at the team.

Just behind the listing of a Marine Special Operations Team on the organization chart is the following notation: 1/11/2. This is military shorthand for a standard MSOT comprised of a team commander— a Special Operations Officer—eleven enlisted Marine Critical Skills Operators, and two Navy special operations–qualified corpsmen. The team CSOs are sergeants and staff sergeants, with two gunnery sergeants serving as element leaders. The team chief is an E-8 master sergeant. When operating independently, the MSOT will be assisted by enabling cadres of Combat Support and Combat Service Support Marines—enablers that can be mixed and matched depending on mission requirements. As discussed in the previous chapter, a deployed MSOT will typically be supported by six to eight CS Marines and two to three CSS Marines—once again configured per the needs of the deployment and the mission sets anticipated on the deployment. As the basic building block of the Marine Special Operations Forces, two teams may be married up and deployed together. In this configuration they form a task unit, with a task unit commander and enabling cadres tailored to support two MSOTs and their mission. Past this, there is the Marine Special Operations Company or MSOC, which MARSOC has crafted as a fully enabled and integrated deployment package.

The MARSOC company deployment package is built around four standard MSOTs and a headquarters element led by a company commander, a major, and a company first sergeant or master sergeant. The headquarters element is staffed with officers and senior NCOs to provide administrative, intelligence, planning, and communications support for the operational MSOTs. This basic MSOC manning is an 8/50/9 organization—eight officers, fifty enlisted Marines, and nine Navy medics. Lots of tooth and not much tail, but then this is the Marine Special Operations Company without their enablers— just the company staff and the MSOTs.

This company, the operational teams and the headquarters staff, is enabled by a MARSOC support package that's especially robust in the areas of intelligence and communications. When fully manned by its supporting CS and CSS enablers, this MSOC will roughly double in size to 135 Marines and Navy medics—10/116/9. Perhaps more than other service-component, company-sized deployed SOF elements, this MSOC is able to sustain itself under austere conditions with minimal outside support. This is because the enabling cadres are not specialists seconded from some general-forces component. They are all special-operations, multidimensional Marine special operators organic to MARSOC and trained for this mission. In addition to those CS and CSS enablers, there are company-level enablers, especially in the areas of intelligence and communications. Within this fully enabled company, one in four are specialists in communications or intelligence, with a sizable majority of those dedicated to intelligence. The operations-intelligence integration, often referred to as "ops-intel fusion," provides policy makers, geographic combatant commanders, and country teams (the ambassador and his staff) with a versatile and self-contained direct-action, special-reconnaissance, intelligence-collection, and host-nation training capability.

It might seem that a company of Marine special operators and their enabling cadres would be a duplication of the presence of a SEAL task unit or an Army Special Forces company. Yet, only a Marine Special Operations Company has the integrated intelligence capability hardwired into their organization. Only the SOF Marines come with the Marine Air-Ground Task Force (MAGTF) mind-set that embraces a scalable force whose capabilities and footprint in a host nation can be quickly tailored to mission requirements and the cultural and political dictates of that nation. If numbers are needed to create capacity, that can be done; if fewer are desirable due to local sensitivities—not an issue. The Marines' direct-action and maritime skill sets approach those of the SEALs; their foreign internal defense training is not unlike that found in the Special Forces. And their special reconnaissance training and focus are more advanced than either of those SOF components. Marines have been a presence at the gates and guard posts of American embassies around the world for the last hundred years. They are a familiar sight. Yet if the mission requires that a Marine SOF presence, a single team or a full company, be away from the capital city in some primitive region—not a problem. After all, both CSOs and their embedded enablers are Marines, and they can live in Spartan conditions for extended periods of time.

As the Regiment realigns its deployment posture with the battalion regionalization requirements and shift away from kinetic deployments, I see them moving forward in several areas. The first is a one-in-four deployment rotation instead of the one-in-three that has been the norm for all special operators during their combat rotations in Iraq and Afghanistan. Special-operations deployment preparation is lengthy and the special-operations training venues often require time away from home when not on deployment. This means our special operators, to include Marine special operators, have routinely been away from home half of the time. A one-in-four (three months in garrison for every month on actual deployment) rotation can go a long way in reconnecting these warriors with their families, lead to higher retention, and create more effective special operators.

The second area is language training. The needs of the battlespace in Iraq and then in Afghanistan meant that language training was often shelved or pushed ahead in favor of getting our special operators quickly into theater; they were needed in the fight. This has to change. If we are to be effective in indirect special operations and the mentoring of host-nation/partner-nation forces, then we simply have to be able to speak their language. As more time in garrison becomes available to the MSOTs, they will have to get more of their CSOs back to the Marine Special Operations School for language training. By the same token, with the MSOTs more fully manned than at any previous time, language training has to become an extension of the ITC. Marines with language aptitude and native-language skills need to be encouraged to volunteer for CSO training.

And finally, the Marine Special Operation Command has to be seen by the Marine Corps at large as a value-added, enabling force. Much of the expeditionary posture of the Marine Corps in the future will be the deployed Marine Expeditionary Forces. As touched on earlier, a MEU is a highly capable, battalion-sized force with a full range of supporting arms, to include tactical air and airmobile capacity. It's a very useful force. The Marines have perfected this at-sea, expeditionary, mobile-strike capability to a point that it can rightfully be called America's on-call, 911 force. An MEU will have its internal reconnaissance element and, in a purely tactical situation, one more that is able of serving as a forward presence for the MEU commander. The MEU will also have a direct-action, small-unit assault capability for personnel recovery or to bolster the security of an embattled embassy. But what if there's need for reconnaissance of the human terrain or for detailed intelligence on an insurgent threat? In the case of a natural disaster, what kind of humanitarian relief is needed and/or appropriate? Under just what conditions will the armed presence of a Marine Expeditionary Unit be made welcome—or best employed? It would seem that a Marine Special Operations Team, one well grounded in special reconnaissance and language capability, and versed in the local culture, should be the first boots on the ground. Then the capabilities of the MEU can be wisely and appropriately put to good use.

As this book goes to print, the Marine Special Operations Regiment is fully engaged around the globe. The 2nd Battalion is still making company-sized deployments to Afghanistan to train the Afghan National Police and the Afghan special-operations commando units. Marine Special Operations Teams from the 1st and 3rd Battalions have an ongoing presence in twenty some nations, from Africa to Indonesia.

EPILOGUE

The Marine Special Operations Command has come a long way in a very short period of time. It was born during a time of war and cut its deployment teeth in an asymmetrical and insurgent environment, with plenty of opportunity for direct-action missions—with and without accompanying host-nation forces. And these Marines have matured as a trained and capable foreign internal defense force. As the newest component of the U.S. Special Operations Command's force mix, they took the general requirements as levied on them by their new command and developed those requirements into SOF capabilities with their own unique Marine Corps imprinting. In the recruitment, assessment, selection, and training of special operators for their force, MARSOC built a Marine-like, task-organized, scalable, expeditionary special-operations capability that is complementary and interoperable with the other special operations ground-combat components. They also developed a very robust, stand-alone capability. Where possible, prudent, and expeditious, they copied other SOF training venues with a selective best-practices approach as to what would best serve in the training of Marine special operators and what would not. Finally, they took inventory of the heritage of the Marine Raiders of World War II, the Marine (SOF) Detachment One, the Marine Foreign Military Unit, and the Marine Reconnaissance community and used them as a springboard to reinvent themselves into a unique and valuable SOF component. And they've yet to celebrate the first decade of their founding.

The training of these MARSOC Marines is in many ways similar to that of their brother SOF components, but varying in emphasis. It is always difficult to compare training pipelines as there are basic, advanced, and specialized training in the collective formation of a special operator. Yet if we stick to the basic qualification standards (which in some cases include unit-level training), the Marines break out differently from the others, and in many cases, they break out favorably. For simplicity, let's again use the four primary SOF callings—direct action, special reconnaissance, foreign internal defense, and unconventional warfare. The subsets of counterterror, counterinsurgency, stability, and security force–assistance operations all flow from these four basic skills.

In the areas of marksmanship, combat shooting, and combat assault, the bread and butter of direct action, the Marine basic training and basic skill levels exceed the other components. A distant second might be the 75th Rangers, the premier SOF light-infantry and raiding force. In the area of basic infantry tactics, the Marines are on a par with Army Special Forces. Their amphibious and maritime skill sets are not nearly so robust as the SEALs but far exceed those of the Special Forces and the 75th Rangers. I found their scenario-based training for foreign internal defense and unconventional warfare second only to the Special Forces. Their special reconnaissance training has no equal in the other components. The additional attention given to Marine officer students compares favorably with the leadership training of the SEAL and Special Forces officers, although differing in design and purpose. SEAL officers are generally newly commissioned officers with only a few having had a single tour in the fleet. Officer candidates enter SEAL training with little or no ground-combat experience. Marine and Army officers are, for the most part, proven leaders and, after a decade of war, proven combat leaders.

Basic/qualifying SOF training venues vary from component to component, both in content and emphasis. All have ordered priorities that, if not stated, are a focus of their training. And they all are versatile. SEALs have very little training in UW or FID in their basic training courses, but they've been called on to do a great deal of FID in the recently active theaters. Some SOF units have core responsibilities that require recurring training and certification. SEALs spend a great deal of time between deployments in the water, but very little time in the water on recent deployments. A core Ranger tasking is airborne assault and airfield seizure in a company-, battalion-, or regimental-sized operation. But not since the invasion of Panama in 1989 have they seized an airfield. Yet they train annually for just such an undertaking. So, in practice, our special operations forces have their specialties within the stated range of their assigned or stated special-operations taskings. They train to these tasks, but when our nation is engaged in regional conflict, as it was in Iraq and Afghanistan for more than a decade, they deploy into the active theater and do what the geographic combatant commander needs them to do.

I'm often asked to compare the SOF components in the relatively unimportant metrics of who is the toughest or what program is the hardest. I'll not go there; it really has no place in how these components or these warriors serve their nation. At this stage of their post-9/11 professional development, the Army, Navy, and Marine SOF components know their mission sets and they know what they're looking for in a potential recruit for their force. They all have their selection methodology, and they all continually refine their selection processes and screens to find just the right men. They know the professional and physical requirements a young warrior must learn and demonstrate before he is qualified to move on to one of their operational units. Collectively, the case could be made that Rangers are the youngest, Special Forces are the smartest, SEALs are the fittest, and the new Marine special operators are the most mature. This said, any Army, Navy, or Marine special operator could prove to be an exception to that case. Each component trains their warriors in operational skill sets that are unique to the mission taskings of that component. There are professional skills that one component may do better than another or for which that component alone is solely responsibly. Yet all of these young warriors, and some not so young, leave their respective training commands with those five characteristics I spoke of earlier in this work: physical toughness, intelligence, mental toughness, ethical maturity, and patriotism.

So what is different in how MARSOC selects and trains their special operators in comparison to the SEALs, Rangers, and Special Forces? Is there a difference? I think there is. I have the unique perspective of having walked the basic training lanes with all our ground-combat special operators. And I do have a bias: It seems that I'm always partial to the guys I'm with at the time. As I've followed them over the years, in the field, on the shooting ranges, in or across the water, and even overseas, I have frequently said to myself, *These guys are the finest young men in America*. And each time I'm right. And so if they're all special, what makes the Marine special operators different—unique if not more special?

This is a complex question with more than one answer. In my opinion, much of it has to do with how the Marine Special Operations Command selects their prospective Critical Skills Operators. An important factor is that their selection is made from a pool of proven, serving Marines. Yet it goes well past some common background or training or experience in field craft, tactics, or military occupational specialty. And in some ways, it goes beyond the ingrained *esprit de corps* that is drilled into Marines from the time they step off the bus at boot camp. It's who these individual Marines are at this point in their service career and in the service of their nation. Among other SOF component trainees I speak with, a good many of them were there for the adventure and the experience. They knew little of the service and service life when they signed up for a program that assured them the opportunity to begin SOF training. As young men will do, they wanted to test themselves and had chosen special operations as their measuring stick. In some cases, after a single tour of duty they will get out and move on. This does not make them non-patriots, but it also does not elevate them to the status of a professional warrior. Most of them serve nobly and well. And a good many do decide that this is the life for them and they remain in uniform to become professional warriors. Four years in the Corps before a Marine can put in for special operations training and MARSOC duty eliminates most of those who really don't want to be in the military. It also eliminates most of those who might be tempted to stick around for a second tour to get that Been-There-Done-That T-shirt. The Marines I met in the ITC, almost to a man, wanted to stay in the Marine Corps for a career. In special operations if they could, in their previous MOS if they couldn't. Special operator was not just another bullet on their résumé; this was to be their professional calling—as a Marine *and* a Marine special operator. I have no statistics or basis for comparison, but I can only imagine that the Command's careful selection from a pool of career-minded warriors has to translate to a high number of ITC graduates staying in MARSOC for the duration. I would also bet that retention of CSOs in MARSOC is percentage-wise higher than that of those special operators from their brother SOF ground-force components.

Apart from this qualified Marine–first requirement that allows MARSOC to select from within the Corps, their assessment and selection process is as focused and discerning as any I've observed at other SOF training forums. Furthermore, this in-house/in-uniform recruitment and the careful screening process allow for a basic-training venue that does not have to continue the "weeding out" process. It can focus on professional training. I saw little or no shouting or harassment in the Individual Training Course. The MARSOC training/qualification program focuses on teaching and testing. A prospective Critical Skills Operator must meet standard—a very elevated standard—or return to the regular Marine Corps and continue to serve as before.

MARSOC has developed a corporate model, if you will, that finds, recruits, selects, assesses, and trains Marines to a Marine special-operations standard. Furthermore, I am constantly amazed at just how quickly they did all this. Other SOF recruiting/selection/training processes have been decades in their development. How those first MARSOC Marines were able to find the right Marines to form this brotherhood within a brotherhood, and then forward deploy effective Marine special operators in so short a time still has me in awe.

As for the Core Activities in their operational quiver and the emphasis they've placed on training to their Core Activities, these Marine special operators have managed that quite well. The U.S. Special Operations Command gave MARSOC great leeway developing their capabilities for SOF mission requirements. In addressing these requirements, MARSOC has created a versatile force, yet with an operational bias in favor of irregular warfare, that has served them well to date and may serve them even better in the future. It's hard to do it all well, so SOF components, out of necessity, must slight one skill set if they are to emphasize another. And all of the components, at one time or another, have found themselves being tasked with a special-operations mission set that forces them to use one or more of the skills they may have neglected. That's when the versatility and critical thinking *really* come into play. If your selection process seeks to find those individuals who are adaptable, innovative, and smart, then they will get the job done. If your culture is one that is expeditionary, task-organized, and self-reliant, they will get the job done in an austere, ambiguous environment where there is little support. It might seem intuitive that a Marine approach to special operations be overloaded in the areas of combat assault and tactical reconnaissance. But while not necessarily neglecting direct action and certainly not special reconnaissance, the thread that winds itself through the Individual Training Course, much like the asymmetrical training construct of Abyssinia, is indirect action. In keeping with their Marine "small wars" heritage and the legacy of the Military Training Teams (MTTs), these Marine special operators are very good at foreign internal defense.

Of all the SOF requirements, foreign internal defense, and by extension unconventional warfare, is perhaps the most time-intensive and expensive. It is also the most difficult to execute in operational conditions. FID is a calling that requires others, those partner-nation forces we train, to do the heavy lifting of countering insurgents, establishing security, and maintaining security. And this requires a balanced set of professional military, language, and cross-cultural skills. All this calls to mind the words that were attributed to T. E. Lawrence:

Just remember that it is their land and it is their fight and your time here is limited. Quite so.

———

If special operations is indeed both a set of operational taskings as well as the charter of our SOF component, what is to be the future of special operations and the role of U.S. Special Operations Command going forward? More specifically, what are we going to do with all this special operations talent and capability when both the direct and indirect operations of SOF are no longer focused in Afghanistan? Will those resources that were tied down in Iraq and then in Afghanistan for more than a decade be reallocated to Central Africa, Yemen, Colombia, the Philippines, or other nations where we are currently working with host-nation forces? In speaking with Admiral Bill McRaven, the current SOCOM commander, I know one of his priorities is to see his special operators and their supporting cadres spend more time at home. Since 9/11, many of our SOF operators have been away from home, deployed or training at a remote location, between a third and half the time. This has strained the force and needs to be addressed—perhaps with statutory limits on time away from home. The admiral also speaks to the future in terms of strengthening relationships with host-nation and partner-nation forces. He has as well gone on record as saying that direct special operations, when needed, only buy time for the application of indirect special operations. Therefore, if SOF is to move from the direct to the indirect, just what needs to take place? Again, I will defer to Admiral McRaven. In his words, if you want to know the plans for the future of SOF, "Ask Linda Robinson."

Ms. Robinson's *The Future of U.S. Special Operations Forces*, published by the Council on Foreign Relations (Report No. 66) in April 2013, is an excellent guide for what might be ahead for our special operators. In her forecast, she cites a shift from the direct to the indirect, with an emphasis on military training, civil affairs, and information operations, and a focus on building on partner-nation cooperation. She also makes the case for a more robust staffing of the Theater Special Operations Commands. She is an advocate of closer cooperation between the military and embassy staffs, and the host-nation government in the countries where they operate. Within the services, she surfaces two issues. One is the need for less bureaucratic wrangling between SOF and conventional forces *and* between the special operations components themselves. There needs to be better cooperation by all these stakeholders, which can lead to a more productive integration. The second is her call for SOCOM to be allowed a measure of authority associated with the management of the careers of officers serving in the special-operations components. Currently, the services are responsible for the careers of the officers serving in SOF components. This latter recommendation, she contends, will lead to a more professional cadre of SOF leaders and a fuller integration of SOF personnel in those agencies and bureaus responsible for shaping foreign policy. *The Future of U.S. Special Operations Forces* is a short (some sixty-five pages), concise guide to what may be ahead for SOF. It is available at amazon.com in hard copy or e-book. I highly recommend this report for anyone interested in the role of special operations in the future.

I don't ever foresee a time when we don't have a need for a conventional force that can, when and as needed, exert a global reach. Regional threats like North Korea, Iran, or even Syria may at some point require conventional military attention. And there are issues that may arise with the emergence of a more capable Chinese military and the resurgence of Russia. All these have to be closely watched and inventoried as they pose a threat to our vital national interests. Yet much of our time and attention going forward is going to be occupied by the persistent proponents of asymmetrical warfare—the same elements that led to the events of 9/11 and that have led us, rightly or wrongly, into the incursions into Iraq and Afghanistan. Hopefully there will be few of these regional wars ahead. Yet we will have to deal with those we classify as terrorists and the menace they pose to our homeland, as well how they threaten our partner nations around the world. Admiral James Stavridis, former NATO supreme commander and now the dean of the Tufts University Fletcher School of Law and Diplomacy, spoke to dealing with this and other threats. In an article for *National Security* magazine (June 2013) he surfaced a new national security triad: drones, special operations, and cyber warfare. While the focus of this triad is cyber warfare, the admiral did not overlook the increasingly important role of SOF in our national security considerations. He also suggested that while the limited work of targeted killing of enemy leaders may increasingly be assigned to drones, the indirect work of special operations forces training and mentoring partner-nation forces will be essential to our future security on the asymmetrical front. I fully agree.

—————

This brings us to the future of MARSOC and their role in the post-Iraq/Afghanistan evolution of SOF. As mentioned earlier, they did a terrific job of standing up their force in time of war. They have made significant contributions in both direct and indirect operations in the active theaters. Going forward, I believe they are well positioned to function in the collaborative, host-nation embed deployments that are likely to be the future of SOF deployments. The Individual Training Course that brings new Marines into the MARSOC force mix is forward-looking, adaptable, and balanced. More to the point, MARSOC has in place a refined, indirect-operations training phase and an emerging special reconnaissance training phase that are sure to stand them in good stead for future deployment taskings. The recent pace of operations has caused MARSOC to neglect language training, but that is being addressed even as I speak to this particular deficiency. MARSOC's integrated, scalable support structure is well positioned to serve future requirements. So, on balance, I believe the capabilities of Marine Special Operations Forces are just what Ms. Robinson and Admiral Stavridis had in mind when addressing the future of special operations. I believe Admiral McRaven as well will find them in keeping with his vision for the future of SOF.

As mentioned in the previous chapter, I think MARSOC can serve their Corps as well as the needs of SOF. In fact, per Ms. Robinson's call for a closer relationship between SOF and general-purpose forces, I see the role of MARSOC as a template for SOF/conventional cooperation. There will be parochial issues that need resolution, like the career path of Marine Special Operations Officers. This is sure to be a topic addressed by senior SOCOM and Marine Corps leaders. Given the need for professional staff officers and the requirements of partner-nation liaison, I recommend that the career path of Marine SOOs be "semi-closed." This means that when an SOO completes his initial tour at MARSOC, his preference, his performance, and the needs of both MARSOC and the Marine Corps should be inventoried. In the best of worlds, all can be satisfied. The officer can return to the Corps for future assignment, taking his SOF/MARSOC experience to his future Marine Corps assignment. Or he can be retained at MARSOC for future administrative, staff, or operational duty for the balance of his career as a Marine Special Operations Officer.

Given the timing of this work, I will be remiss if I don't address the future prospect of women in special operations and, specifically, the prospect of women serving as members of a Marine Special Operations Team. My position on this has been public and ongoing since January of 2013 when the Department of Defense directed the services to "proceed in a deliberate, measured, and responsible way to provide women the opportunity to qualify for currently closed [ground-combat] positions." Under more recent directives, the services and the Special Operations Command have been put on a timetable to admit women into their training pipelines, or provide a compelling reason why this should not happen.

MARSOC training, and indeed all SOF basic/qualification training, is long, difficult, physically demanding, and dangerous. Prior to 9/11, a DoD directive that would bring women into SOF training may have been viewed differently, and perhaps with a great deal more skepticism. Yet then as now, this is in part an issue of standards. The last decade-plus of continuous combat operations and the current train-like-you-fight/fight-like-you-train approach have greatly refined all SOF training. It has shaped MARSOC training as well as the recruitment, assessment, and selection of Marine special operators. The training and the standards have been well vetted, and furthermore, they've been codified in blood. Tactically, technically, physically, professionally, and morally, this is what it takes to be a Marine special operator. To become a Marine special operator, you have to meet this standard.

Yet there may be more to it as it would apply to women in this training. I'll not go into the particulars of upper body strength, hygiene, lack of privacy, sexual tensions, reproductive biology, and so on. The media has spun, and will continue to spin, this inclusion of women in ground-combat special operations as an issue of jobs, fairness, opportunity, or gender equality. A case can certainly be made for each of these. Yet there are three overriding considerations that must be addressed in a responsible, apolitical manner. The first, as mentioned, is that the standards in place are combat-proven standards—there can be no indexing. Run times, often with seventy pounds of equipment, have to be the same for all. The physical and strength-measurement criteria must be the same for all. The ten-mile MARSOC ruck march minimum times are the same for all. In combat, as on the combat fitness test, a Marine has to be able to put a fellow Marine over his/her shoulder and get that Marine out of the kill zone. Both their lives depend on this. There can be no compromise—no indexing of standards.

Secondly, those women who can meet this standard have to do so in more than ones or twos. MARSOC training, like all special-operations training, is lengthy and expensive. It now takes on the order of a year and a half to make a fully trained, combat-capable Marine special operator out of a fully trained, combat-capable Marine. About one in five Marines who report to the Marine Assessment, Preparation and Orientation Course will make it to the Marine Special Operations Regiment. This attrition is much the same for the Rangers,

SEALs, and Green Berets. It is unreasonable to open training to two hundred women to find the two who can meet standard.

And finally there are the ethical and cultural issues. Do we as a nation and an American culture want our mothers, sisters, and daughters in the business of sustained, direct, mortal combat? Taking human life, even with the moral authority of a warrior in uniform, is serious business. Are we sure that this is the role we wish for our mothers, sisters, and daughters, those who in our culture have traditionally been the caregivers? Is this *really* the will of the American people? If we, as a nation and a culture, do want this, then so be it. But it should be accompanied by a majority vote in Congress on this single issue, and not simply a DoD directive.

From this stated position, if it *is* the will of the people, then our military will comply and those with operational and training responsibilities in special operations will comply. This how we do things in America. And knowing what I do of all special-operations training venues, such a transition will be handled best by MARSOC. It may seem counterintuitive that the Marines, perhaps the most tradition-bound of the military services and SOF service components, would most readily handle the inclusion of women in their operational ranks. Some of this has to do with the corporate model of MARSOC and its policy of admitting only veteran Marines to the ranks. Along with their in-service requirements, MARSOC candidates are the oldest when compared to the other SOF component-training/qualification venues. With maturity comes understanding, adaptability, and compliance. A great deal of it also has to do with the fact that they are Marines, and Marines put great stock in simply getting the job done under whatever conditions they are afforded.

In closing, what may lie in the future for the Individual Training Course? ITC Class 1-13 is but the tenth class to graduate and move on to take their place in the Marine Special Operations Regiment. My perspective is that there will be very few major changes, but that there will always be continuous evaluation, reevaluation, and evolution. Unless there is a realignment of the Core Activities within MAR-SOC, the current curriculum seems to adequately prepare new Marine special operators for regimental duty. Based on feedback from the Regiment, the end user of the ITC, there will be continuous adjustments and refinements. Operational deployment experience in the form of lessons learned will find its way to the school and into the instruction, but I foresee no big changes.

Yet each class is just a little different from the one previous—a little more polished and a little more on point. As the role of our deployed SOF posture shifts from the direct to the indirect, this will surely be reflected in the ITC. As more ITC graduates come back through the Marine Special Operations School as cadres, this return of former grads can't help but bring focus and understanding to the process. There will undoubtedly be additions and changes in the advanced training offered by the Marine Special Operations School, but the basics that are the core of the ITC are just that. And for that reason, the basic content of ITC instruction will change little, but each class will be just a little bit different, and a little better than the last one—just as each MSOT going downrange will be a little different and a little better prepared than its predecessor. This kind of evolution and progression is endemic to our special operations forces. So while there may be little structural or formatted change to the ITC, no two ITCs will be the same.

If there is to be little change in the basic structure of the Individual Training Course, those Marines assessed and selected for CSO training will be different. The steady input of ground-combat veterans will begin to dry up. The candidate Marines will still bring valuable deployment history with them and an important blend of MOS talent, but they'll not have the kinetic combat experience found in previous ITC classes. And there will be a reorientation of the ITC to train younger enlisted Marines. As seen with the Assessment and Selection Preparation and Orientation Class 1-13 in Chapter Three, the formal assessment and selection for the ITC will focus on corporals and young sergeants. This is by design and necessity. As the Regiment approaches a fully manned complement of Critical Skills Operators, there will be only room for new Marine special operators at the bottom of the rank structure. This is all to the good. In this way, the Regiment can better grow their enlisted leaders in-house, from the bottom up. I would also think that at some point the ITC classes will become smaller. As the force shifts from a model of growth to one of sustainment, the ITC will become a source of replacements for career Marine special operators who are passing into retirement status. Yet the need for new Special Operations Officers may remain fixed, as the role of an MSOT commander is much more transient than that of his CSO brothers.

The Individual Training Course at this point is like a newly formed sculpture—the carefully crafted creation is in place and the clay is drying. But due to the adaptive nature of special operations and the versatile Marine approach to the warrior profession, there will remain a certain amount of flexibility in training Marine special operators—a workable balance between that which is traditional and the ability and willingness to change to meet new operational requirements.

———

In conclusion, I want to post a final note of thanks to the cadre sergeants, proctors, phase TACs, phase officers, instructors, and support personnel of the Individual Training Course, and a special note of thanks to the members of Individual Training Course Class 1-13. Each of you is represented in some way in the pages of this book. As for the three Marines whom I followed most closely in the ITC, perhaps some closure is due the reader. Sergeant Brad Hansen and Sergeant Kerry Irving completed the ITC and were assigned to the 2nd Marine Special Operations Battalion. Both subsequently attended and graduated from MARSOC communications training. Hansen is assigned to an MSOT in India Company, Irving to an MSOT in Fox Company. Sergeant Hansen will serve as the team's junior communicator but hopes, at some time in the future, to get to Fort Bragg to train as an 18-Bravo weapons sergeant or an 18-Charlie engineering sergeant.

Sergeant Irving, due to his infantry qualifications and experience, is assigned duties as an assistant element leader in his MSOT, as well as those of a junior communicator. The 2nd Battalion is scheduled to remain in Afghanistan to the end or our commitment there. So as this book goes to print, these two new Critical Skills Operators are either forward deployed or just back from deployment and preparing for the next one.

Captain Andrew Fraker did not fare so well. In fact, his journey to become a Special Operations Officer ended abruptly. In all my fourteen years of following special-operations candidates, I find his story as unique as it is both tragic and illustrative. Following the five-mile ruck march at the end of Phase Three, Captain Fraker finished first. Then he began to experience odd symptoms so he went to the MARSOC clinic for an evaluation. There he was diagnosed with type one diabetes. Even as Captain Fraker stood at the top of the class in physical fitness, it was ultimately decided that he could not be cleared for duty with the Marine Special Operations Regiment. So this fine captain was denied a recycle to join Class 2-13 and to continue with ITC. He was finished. His story is tragic in that he will not fulfill his dream of leading a Marine Special Operations Team, but illustrative of the dedicated and capable Marines who volunteer for duty in MARSOC. In Marine-like fashion, Captain Andrew Fraker put this setback behind him and returned to duty. He currently serves as a company commander with the 6th Marine Regiment, 2nd Marine Division.

Last, and by no means in the least, I want to thank my old friend Ollie North for his kind foreword. And I want again call attention to the lieutenant colonel's plea for support of the MARSOC Foundation, the 501(c)(3) charity (marsocfoundation.org) that does so much for our wounded MARSOC warriors and their families. I thank you for this as well.

Since the hardcover edition of this book was published, there have been two notable changes at MARSOC—one very important change that alters the career path of Marine Special Operations Officers and one seemingly cosmetic change that is, nonetheless, important.

Heretofore, newly qualified Marine Special Operations Officers, or SOOs, could expect to be assigned duties in MARSOC for five years, then be subject to orders back to the conventional Marine Corps in keeping with their Primary MOS. That has changed. Qualified SOOs will still be awarded the 0370 MOS but it is now a PMOS or *Primary* Military Occupational Specialty, allowing them to remain in special operations for the balance of their Marine Corps career. I suspect a few of these SOOs will elect to return to the regular Corps for future duty. But most of them will stay in special operations, and they will be most welcome in a wide range of SOF staff billets between their operational tours at MARSOC.

The other change has to do with the formal linkage of MARSOC with the Marine Raiders of World War II. In August of 2014, Commandant of the Marine Corps James F. Amos acknowledged the special relationship between MARSOC and the Raiders. While the official title of MARSOC will remain the U.S. Marine Corps Forces Special Operations Command, the subordinate commands will take on the Raider moniker. There will be the Marine Raider Regiment, with the 1st, 2nd, and 3rd Marine Raider Battalions, the Marine Raider Support Group, and so on. How important is this Raider heritage? In a word, very. The Marine Raiders of World War II, according to the Marine Raider Association and foundation, were awarded seven Medals of Honor, 136 Navy Crosses, and 330 Silver Stars. This Raider recognition honors both the Marine Raiders of World War II and today's Special Operations Marines.

INDEX